The Wages of Sickness

STUDIES IN SOCIAL MEDICINE

Allan M. Brandt and Larry R. Churchill, editors

Beatrix
Hoffman

The
Wages
of
Sickness

The Politics
of Health
Insurance in
Progressive
America

The University of North Carolina Press
Chapel Hill & London

Designed by Jackie Johnson
Set in Minion type
by Tseng Information Systems, Inc.

The paper in this book meets the guidelines for
permanence and durability of the Committee on
Production Guidelines for Book Longevity of the
Council on Library Resources.

Library of Congress Cataloging-in-Publication
Data
Hoffman, Beatrix Rebecca.
The wages of sickness : the politics of health
insurance in progressive America / Beatrix
Hoffman.
p.   cm. — (Studies in social medicine)
Includes bibliographical references and index.
ISBN 0-8078-2588-3 (cloth : alk. paper) —
ISBN 0-8078-4902-2 (pbk. : alk. paper)
1. Insurance, Health—United States—History—
20th century.   2. Progressivism (United States
politics)   I. Title.   II. Series.
HG9396 .H638   2001
368.38'2'00973—dc21   00-044735

05   04   03   02   01   5   4   3   2   1

CONTENTS

ILLUSTRATIONS

PREFACE

At the turn of the twentieth century, Americans attempted to confront the twin burdens of sickness and poverty in their midst. Responding in part to the rapid rise of urbanization, industrialization, and wage labor in this period, a group of inveterate reformers sought to mitigate the social impacts of this transformation. As part of a larger movement of Progressive reform that drew upon new forms of social engineering and expertise, activists, advocates, and legislators sought to fashion a program that would alleviate the disruptions of disease, especially as it affected workers. It was in this optimistic and tumultuous context that some reformers turned their attention to the possibilities of new forms of social insurance — sponsored by states — to guarantee wages during bouts of illness as well as to provide access to medical care. Model legislation to accomplish this particular task was devised and debated in New York State between 1915 and 1920. Beatrix Hoffman carefully and critically examines this legislative battle in *The Wages of Sickness.*

Investigation of such policies for sharing the considerable risks associated with sickness and disease make up a critical aspect of social medicine. Over the last century, almost all industrialized nations developed mechanisms for assuring their citizens access to necessary health care and welfare benefits when confronted by the vagaries of illness. These social insurance programs were typically justified on both economic and moral grounds. On the one hand, a healthy workforce assured continued productivity; on the other, citizens had a right to such protections from the state. Such arguments, however, did not effect legislation in this country. The United States has remained the only Western-developed nation not to implement a compulsory health insurance program. In this sense the United States truly is the exception that proves the rule. Beatrix Hoffman plumbs the social and political origins of this exceptionalism in *The Wages of Sickness.* As she demonstrates through a close examination of the ultimate failure of the New York legislation, there have periodically been historical moments of intensive public debate about fashioning health insurance programs in the United States. And these instances are greatly revealing of the economic forces and cultural beliefs that have proved to be obstacles to reform.

Hoffman's close reading of this particular episode in the history of unful-filled reforms offers the opportunity to investigate the wide array of interests on both sides of the battle for compulsory health insurance. Although previ-ous historical accounts have typically emphasized the role that the organized medical profession played in bringing down the legislation, Hoffman draws attention to other forces as well: employers and insurance companies eager to protect their economic interests from state intervention; labor unions con-cerned that the costs of such a program would reduce wages (an argument taken up by some women reformers as well). Together these interests came to constitute a formidable alliance against reform, utilizing in addition a power-ful cultural ideology that such state intervention was "un-American," a vio-lation of national notions of autonomy and responsibility. Soon compulsory insurance came to be branded as "socialized medicine." In the context of hos-tilities to Germany and its Bismarckian welfare apparatus (and later Bolshe-vik Russia), this label proved a devastating political stigma for the proposed legislation. Supporters found it difficult to achieve broad consensus around a proposal that, in its specifics, often divided reformers, be they labor activists or advocates of maternal and child health.

Those who followed closely the demise of the Clinton health care reform pro-posal will no doubt read Hoffman's account and experience déjà vu. But, of course, a central tenet of Hoffman's narrative is the historically specific nature of the debate about health insurance and the forces that led to its defeat. In this sense her book forces us to inquire about those specific economic and social forces that continue to block our capacity to assure access to health care. *The Wages of Sickness* is a powerful reminder that it is one thing to clearly identify needs and rights, and quite another to assure that they are met and protected. As Hoffman so clearly shows, in the past, we find the present.

Allan M. Brandt
Larry R. Churchill

ACKNOWLEDGMENTS

I am happy for an opportunity to thank the many people who helped me on the road to completing this book. At the University of Massachusetts, Joyce Berkman, Samuel Bowles, Bruce Laurie, and Bob Sutcliffe inspired me by example and encouragement. I was fortunate to be a graduate student in the Rutgers University History Department, which offered a rare combination of rigor, support, and community. This project first took shape in Rutgers research seminars led by Victoria deGrazia, Jackson Lears, Dee Garrison, and Jan Lewis, and I'm grateful to the students in those seminars for their careful readings and criticism. Paul Clemens not only read several drafts of this work but provided invaluable support and encouragement in his roles as graduate director and placement adviser. The members of my dissertation committee, Gerald Grob, Daniel T. Rodgers, and Deborah Gray White, helped me greatly with their comments, and I thank them for their hard work.

I cannot imagine a more wonderful adviser than Alice Kessler-Harris. Despite the extraordinary demands on her time she was always quick to read chapters, help put together a conference panel, or give yet another pep talk to a wilting graduate student. Our discussions of class, gender, and the state stimulated my thinking and continue to inspire me.

Alan Derickson, Linda Gordon, Carl Parrini, James Schmidt, and Kathryn Kish Sklar read the entire manuscript and offered crucial suggestions. I especially benefited from Kathryn Sklar's expertise as the biographer of Florence Kelley. Alan Derickson generously shared some of his research on the American Federation of Labor and health insurance. Thanks to many people who read and commented on various sections of the manuscript, including David Beito, Grace Hale, Alan Kraut, Allan Kulikoff, Molly Ladd-Taylor, April Masten, Robyn Muncy, Ronald Numbers, Jill Quadagno, Mary Ryan and members of her 1994–95 dissertation group at UC-Berkeley, and Scott Sandage. Mary Poole shared her important research on the racial ideology of the Wisconsin School. Kate Torrey of the University of North Carolina Press expressed interest in this project early on, and Sian Hunter has been an outstanding and supportive editor. Mary Caviness provided expert copyediting.

This project received financial assistance from the Schlesinger Library, the Rockefeller Archive Center, the American Historical Association's Beveridge Award, the Charlotte Newcombe Foundation, Rutgers Graduate School and History Department, and the Department of History at Northern Illinois University. My work would have been impossible without the help of librarians and archivists at the Wagner Labor Archives, Schlesinger Library, Rockefeller Archive Center, Hagley Museum and Library, Cornell University, Columbia University, New York Public Library, Metropolitan Life Insurance Company Archives, the New York Academy of Medicine, Salamanca Public Library, Syracuse University Archives, New York State Archives, SUNY-Albany Archives, the New York State Nurses' Association, the Nursing Archives at Boston University, Franklin D. Roosevelt Library, Meany Archive Center, Mount Holyoke College Library, Sophia Smith Archive, Rutgers University Libraries, the Schomburg Center, and the YIVO Institute. Patrizia Sione of the Kheel Center for Labor-Management Documentation and Archives (Cornell School of Labor and Industrial Relations) graciously tracked down some last-minute citations. In order to visit all these places, I depended on the hospitality of many friends and colleagues: Karen Balcom, Court Cline, Sue Frederickson, Mitch Gaslin and Karen Schweitzer, Becca Gershenson, Lisa Phillips, Christine Skwiot, James Sullivan, Andrea Volpe, and especially Lisamichelle Davis.

I am indebted to the friends whose support has sustained me: Amy and Andrew Forbes, Kari Frederickson, Carol Brierly Golin, Rebecca Hartman, Fiona Macaulay, Jennifer Nelson, Kathryn Pope, and Tammy Proctor. At Northern Illinois University, Eric Duskin, Allan Kulikoff, Simon Newman, Elaine and George Spencer, and Bruce and Kim Field offered welcome and hospitality. Thanks also to Elisabeth Bacher Hoffman, Monalise Hoffman, Richard Hoffman, and the Yarak family. Dana Yarak helped and inspired me immeasurably by reading every word of the manuscript with the eye of a true writer. His example of intellectual and political engagement, not to mention his warmth and his wicked sense of humor, helped me keep this project in perspective.

ABBREVIATIONS

The Wages of Sickness

INTRODUCTION

The absence of universal medical protection is a striking feature of American life. Despite a medical system known as the most technically and scientifically advanced in the world, Americans still struggle more than citizens of other developed nations to gain access to health care. Well over forty million people in the United States have no health insurance, while government and private insurers offer health plans that are limited, restrictive, or prohibitively expensive. Hospital emergency rooms have become the inefficient and costly providers of primary care for those who fall through the wide cracks in insurance coverage, and polls show that a majority of Americans are "frustrated and angry" with their health care system. The defeat of the Clinton administration's reform plan in 1994 ended hopes that the United States would adopt universal health coverage for all its citizens before the end of the century. Instead, the number of Americans without medical insurance continues to rise.[1]

This troubling picture would have come as a shock to reformers of the early twentieth century. When Progressives first proposed government-sponsored health insurance in 1915, their vision of protecting working people from the economic burden of sickness seemed well within reach. Inspired by the passage of Britain's National Insurance Act of 1911, New York reformers led a contentious, highly publicized campaign for compulsory health insurance in their state. Had they been successful, their plan might have planted the seeds of a full-fledged system of universal health coverage in the United States. Europe's national health programs sprang from similar compulsory plans established before the First World War.

But the reformers' vision was not realized. Instead, a coalition of doctors, employers, insurance companies, and politicians narrowly defeated the New York compulsory health insurance proposal in 1919. The Progressives' argument that sick pay and medical care would create a healthier, more contented workforce and benefit the nation as a whole was, in the end, no match for their opponents, who claimed that the proposal represented an assault on the independence of business, an attack on the sovereignty of the medical profession, and a subversion of American values.

The story of the New York health insurance campaign is more than an account of vanished possibilities or missed opportunities — a "lost reform," in the words of one historian.[2] This book argues that what did not happen shaped what did, that the failed crusade for health insurance was a formative moment in the creation of the American welfare state and medical system. The defeat of compulsory health insurance contributed to the making of a limited welfare state, a distinctive health care system, and a political culture and configuration of interest-group power that would resist universal health coverage for the rest of the century.

American Progressives had high hopes for the success of their health plan. In 1915, reform-minded Americans agreed that compulsory health insurance was, in the words of the surgeon general, the "next great step in social legislation."[3] During the Progressive Era (ca. 1890–1920), the term "compulsory health insurance" had a different meaning than it does today. At that time, it was intended to cover mainly industrial workers, not the very poor or the middle class. The term also described coverage for both medical care and for wage loss during illness, or "sick pay," while today sick pay and disability insurance are separated from health coverage.* In 1915, the American Association for Labor Legislation (AALL) published a "model bill" to create a health insurance system funded jointly by contributions from workers and their employers and state tax revenues. Covered workers would be eligible for free medical care, sick pay, and a small death benefit.

The campaign for health insurance was fought hardest in New York State. As with most Progressive Era legislation, reformers worked to establish health insurance systems in individual states rather than on the national level. After the AALL published its model bill, several states debated the need for health insurance, but only California and New York actually introduced health insurance legislation. The California battle was short-lived; in 1918 voters there defeated a referendum that would have amended the state constitution in favor of the adoption of health insurance.[4] In New York, the AALL introduced its health insurance bill in the state legislature four times between 1916 and 1919, and New York was the only state in which the proposal came anywhere close to success. On the final attempt, the New York Senate actually passed the bill, but it died in committee in the assembly. This defeat effectively ended the first

---

*For the sake of brevity, throughout this book the term "health insurance" always refers to *compulsory* health insurance. All other types of health insurance are referred to in full, such as "private health insurance," "commercial health insurance," or "union health insurance."

health insurance campaign and silenced public discussion of the subject until the New Deal.

Historians usually blame the repeated failure of health insurance proposals throughout the twentieth century on the intense resistance of the American medical profession. After the American Medical Association (AMA) and New York medical societies greeted the AALL's 1915 proposal with cautious support, physicians underwent a drastic change of heart. By 1920 most medical organizations, including the AMA, had condemned compulsory health insurance as a threat to their members' incomes and autonomy.[5] Physicians alone, however, did not deliver the definitive blow to the health insurance crusade. Groups that ostensibly had little in common with the medical profession — employers, commercial insurance companies, and the mainstream labor movement — joined together in an unprecedented and highly effective alliance against compulsory health insurance.

All of these groups opposed health insurance on economic grounds. Doctors feared that their incomes would drop if the AALL's bill became law. Employers denounced the burden of compulsory premium payments. Insurance companies rallied against the threat to their dominance of the life insurance market. The leaders of the American Federation of Labor (AFL) thought social insurance would undermine trade union benefits and forestall labor's demands for higher wages. But equally important to opponents was the perception that compulsory health insurance would erode their group's autonomy. For doctors to be free to set their own fees, for employers to limit their responsibility for the health of workers, for insurance companies to sell more policies, and for labor leaders to win the loyalty of workers, each group demanded the ability to operate independently, free from government (and reformer) interference. For these groups, protecting their economic interests was inseparable from defending their autonomy.

The opponents of health insurance were able to drive home this argument forcefully by defining their independence as central to true "Americanism," a notion that became especially potent during the patriotic fervor of World War I and the subsequent antisocialist Red Scare. Opponents of the welfare state have repeatedly used the concept of "Americanism" and the "foreignness" of reform proposals in order to camouflage their economic interests. But, just as profit and autonomy were linked in the minds of health insurance's antagonists, so too did their definition of Americanism embody and justify the economic self-interest of private groups. The medical profession's alliance with other private interests in defense of profit, autonomy, and Americanism would create a unified and powerful opposition against compulsory health insurance.

While New York employers, insurance companies, and physicians formed a near-unanimous bloc against health insurance, other groups, notably the labor movement and organized women, were bitterly divided on the question. The powerful AFL was relentlessly opposed, but many New York unionists, particularly members of the New York State Federation of Labor (NYSFL) and women-dominated trade unions, willfully defied the AFL's directives and threw their support behind the health insurance campaign. The dispute between the national AFL leadership and New York unions stemmed from their clashing views on questions of employer responsibility for worker health, the cost of health insurance to workers and employers, and the relationship of organized labor to the state. AFL opposition to health insurance was rooted in distrust of the state as a repressive force, while local and female trade unionists tended to see government action as a means for industrial workers and the unorganized to improve their working conditions and to gain rights as citizens.

Women's groups, too, divided over the question of health insurance. The story of the health insurance campaign is one of conflict and differences among women as much as one of solidarity and sisterhood.[6] The AALL expected women to unite behind its proposal because it included a provision specifically for mothers: maternity benefits that would have allowed insured women to take off several weeks from work for childbirth with sick pay. But this measure to protect women workers created furious controversy among New York's female reformers, with some arguing that the benefits would encourage men to exploit their wives by sending them out to work. Women played a major role in the New York Assembly battle over health insurance, as victorious suffragists adopted the AALL's proposal as part of their plan to use the new women's vote to promote sweeping social legislation. But when yet another group of women workers came forward to oppose them, the conflict weakened the reformers' campaign and made it still more vulnerable to attack.

The defeat of health insurance was a blow against gender equality in the U.S. welfare state. Health insurance was one of the few Progressive Era proposals that treated men and women equally and acknowledged the importance of women's earnings to the family, and it was the only one that offered maternity benefits. Its defeat coincided with the rise of social programs that ignored working women, shut down discussion of maternity pay, and institutionalized gender discrimination in welfare provision.[7] The United States today has the most miserly maternity policy of any developed nation, with no mandated paid leave at all for working mothers. The defeat of compulsory health insurance in 1919 insured that maternity pay, as well as universal health coverage, would be absent from the U.S. welfare state.

The New York health insurance campaign and its defeat reveal much about the nature of American politics in the Progressive Era. The state was not an autonomous entity separate from society; its actions were influenced and shaped by powerful interest groups.[8] But interests were not predetermined or automatic. All of the groups discussed in this book struggled among themselves to decide whether health insurance would help or hurt their incomes and independence. In the end, physicians, insurance companies, and employers were better able to agree on where their interests lay than were reformers, labor, and women's groups. The unity and economic power of the opponents of health insurance then allowed them to exercise a leverage over government that the plan's supporters could not hope to match.

Understanding the health insurance campaign requires attention to ideological and cultural forces. The ability of interest groups and politicians to defeat health insurance rested not just on their economic and organizational muscle but on their skillful deployment of the rhetoric of Americanism — rhetoric that would become an instrument of political and state power during the First World War and the Red Scare. The story of the Progressive Era health insurance campaign demonstrates that America's limited welfare state was born not simply of preexisting structural constraints but of political and ideological struggles and turbulent historical changes. American resistance to universal health care, then, has not been predetermined, inevitable, or insurmountable — and a different future is more than conceivable.

1

Patchwork Protection

THE SPECTER OF SICKNESS AND POVERTY

Ever since arriving in New York from Germany in 1882, Emil Bollhausen had followed his trade as a cabinetmaker. The skills he learned from his father in Berlin led to steady employment in New York City's furniture industry. Bollhausen married and had a son; with his wife's work as a janitress, the small family earned enough to survive. But in 1915, at the age of fifty-four, Bollhausen was doing fine handwork for an antiques dealer when he was stricken with pleurisy, pneumonia, and heart trouble. When he stopped work to enter the hospital, most of the family's income stopped as well. His son was tubercular and unable to work, and the family was forced to turn to the Charity Organization Society for help. A charity report described the Bollhausen family's rapid decline: "[H]ospital treatment, then a few day's work, illness again, no money to pay the doctor, the use of patent medicines suggested by neighbors, the hospital again with some improvement followed by four weeks in the country . . . work again too hard for him, another illness, dispensary treatment . . . eight months of sickness and treatment and still unable to undertake regular work."[1]

The story of the Bollhausen family was just one of hundreds of cases cited in a 1917 study of illness among New York City wage earners. The report, sponsored by the Russell Sage Foundation, surveyed 690 families on relief and found that sickness was a major factor leading to charity dependence for 452 of them.[2] These findings corroborated the experience of John Kingsbury, director of one of the largest New York City charities. In 1918 Kingsbury declared that the connection between ill health and economic dependence was "so direct and obvious to anyone who is in [charity] work that I have repeatedly said that good relief work tends more and more to be health work."[3]

The reformers who drafted the New York health insurance proposal drew on evidence like the Russell Sage study to argue that the poverty and insecu-

" 'The Three Fears.' The Greatest of These Will Be Banished by Universal Health Insurance" (*American Labor Legislation Review* [1919]; photograph courtesy of The University Library, University of Illinois at Chicago).

rity endemic among American workers were, to a great extent, the result of ill health. Since few employers offered sick pay, even a short illness could mean a devastating loss of income for a worker's family. In 1916, the U.S. Public Health Service estimated that each of the country's thirty million workers missed an average of nine days of work a year because of sickness, costing them over eight million dollars in lost wages.[4] Few workers could amass enough savings to tide themselves over in an emergency. One result of this was "the common custom of 'passing the hat' around the shop for the benefit of some sick worker"; one working woman told reformers that a collection was taken "practically every week, in her factory" in aid of fellow workers whose income had been cut off in time of illness.[5]

Forty-two states passed workmen's compensation laws between 1911 and 1920, so at least some wage earners could receive compensation for injuries received on the job.[6] Disease and sickness, however, even if directly caused by working conditions, were not covered by workmen's compensation. And many of the illnesses common among workers were indeed related to their jobs. Miners, stonecutters, and textile workers suffered from high rates of respiratory illness, especially tuberculosis.[7] A doctor in New York City, asked in 1916 about the most frequent ailments among the working populations he treated, said that hemorrhoids and chronic constipation were common among factory operatives, and that fur workers, cap makers, bakers, and hairdressers tended to suffer from tuberculosis, bronchitis, and asthma. The most prevalent illness he found among all workers was duodenal ulcer. Reformers attributed many such medical conditions not only to specific workplace hazards but also to the long hours that left workers exhausted and unable to fight disease.[8]

The stress and exhaustion of work could also lead to health problems after hours. Laborers had no time or desire to exercise or seek fresh air. A doctor who studied ailing clinic patients in New York City "found many men who had begun work when only nine or ten years old. They had no experience in recreation as we understand it." Often relaxation was found only in drink, and alcoholism ravaged bodies as well as families and communities.[9] Poor nutrition, overcrowding, inadequate sanitation, and lack of preventative health services and education added to the medical problems of the poorest city dwellers. Crowded tenement housing was a notorious breeding ground for tuberculosis and other respiratory ailments. Residents of Columbus Hill, an impoverished "colored" neighborhood in New York City, suffered from high incidences of nutritional disorders like rickets, as well as syphilis and bronchitis.[10]

Infant and maternal mortality, a significant threat for all classes, was devastating among populations with a large number of working mothers. African American women, especially, found themselves forced by economic necessity to work as long as possible during pregnancy and then to return to work quickly after childbirth, a practice that researchers said contributed to the shockingly high infant mortality rate in poor black neighborhoods.[11]

Wage workers feared illness doubly because it was inevitably accompanied by a loss of income. A bout with influenza or pneumonia led to both physical suffering and serious financial difficulties. Whether for skilled male workers earning twenty dollars a week or for women pieceworkers making only five, stopping work meant stopping wages. And lost income made it difficult to pay not only for life's basic necessities but for doctor bills as well. Lack of medical care commonly led to the vicious cycle of worsening health and continuing inability to return to work. It was this cycle that compulsory health insurance intended to break.

While reformers worked to find an overarching solution to these problems, a minority of American workers used a variety of methods that promised to protect them from sickness and economic insecurity. Progressive America had a patchwork of protection, ranging from free dispensaries, to immigrant fraternal societies, to private insurance policies. The existence of this "system" served both sides in the health insurance battle. Opponents of compulsory health insurance argued that private protective institutions adequately supported sick workers. They also believed that voluntary protection was a virtue in itself, and far preferable to the government interference that compulsory health insurance would require. But defenders of compulsory health insurance insisted that the patchwork system was a dismal failure at meeting the economic and medical needs of the populace. All types of existing protection, from voluntary insurance to factory health clinics, had significant restrictions and drawbacks for their users. Most important, the majority of Americans had no access at all to these limited benefits.

MUTUAL AID AND SELF-HELP: FRATERNAL SOCIETIES

Fraternal societies — voluntary groups organized by religion, ethnicity, or similar affiliation — were the most common providers of insurance and relief before the New Deal. According to historian David Beito, "literally thousands" of these societies, also known as lodges, "dotted the American landscape" between 1900 and 1930. Low-income workers were far more likely to receive benefits from a fraternal order than from other charity or welfare institutions.[12] At the time of the health insurance battle, about 30 percent of workers obtained some coverage by fraternal methods in the large industrial states of California, Illinois, Ohio, and Pennsylvania. The number of workers covered in New York was probably smaller.[13]

In addition to providing benefits, native white fraternal societies such as the Freemasons and Odd Fellows were known for their elaborate secret rituals and their valorization of "brotherhood" and masculinity.[14] The very concept of fraternalism was based in exclusion. However, this type of exclusion could be practiced not just by prosperous white males but also by middle-class blacks, Jewish immigrants, and women workers. African Americans and women forbidden to join the large mainstream fraternals formed their own, separate branches, while smaller societies proliferated among ethnic and working-class groups in the nation's cities. For example, there were large, all-black branches of the Knights of Pythias and the Order of Odd Fellows. These black fraternals, Beito points out, "owed [their] origin[s] to the exclusionary racial restrictions of the parallel white organization."[15]

Fraternalism, as the name implies, was primarily a male endeavor. Of the 690 charity applicants interviewed by Russell Sage researchers in 1917, 124 men and only 3 women belonged to some type of benefit society.[16] Those fraternal organizations that admitted women members at all, according to the Russell Sage study, "allowed only those who were wives and widows of members to join . . . [and] these women were not even admitted on the same basis as men. The women for the most part were eligible only for the death and burial benefits."[17] In addition to upholding their purpose as havens of masculine solidarity, fraternals were wary of signing up women members because of their higher sickness rates.

Even those few societies that paid sickness benefits to women refused to cover conditions identified as "female problems," including pregnancy and childbirth. When David Jacobs applied to join the Jewish Progress Mutual Aid Society, which normally provided benefits to the wives of its members, he was required to sign a special agreement: the society admitted Jacobs to membership but "as a single man, merely deriving benefits for myself. This agreement is made, due to my wife being in a pregnant condition. . . . I will not hold the PMAS responsible for any benefits occurring under the laws of the Society for my wife Rose Jacobs."[18]

As with African Americans, this discrimination led women to start their own lodges. Most were branches of existing male orders. The Women's Benefit Association of the Maccabees, an affiliate of the Knights of the Maccabee, had over 231,000 members in 1920. The women Maccabees were one of the few fraternal societies that offered maternity benefits.[19] The all-white Independent Order of Odd Fellows had women's branches that were known as Rebekah Lodges; the Sojourna Household of Ruth was an all-female adjunct to the black Grand United Order of Odd Fellows. (It should be pointed out, however, that many African American fraternals included members of both sexes.[20])

Despite their diversity, most fraternal and mutual aid societies had a great deal in common that made them a useful source of protection for some Americans but entirely inaccessible to others. All fraternals, including the black and women's associations, had stringent requirements for membership. For example, most societies had age limits and charged higher rates to older members since they were more likely to use sickness or death benefits. The most common rule was that no one over forty-five years of age was eligible for membership in a fraternal.[21]

Voluntary societies offering benefits required a medical examination for membership in order to exclude those in poor health.[22] Those who passed the examination were then required to pay an initiation fee of one or two dollars, followed by monthly dues payments. Fraternal dues averaged ten dollars a year, with some societies charging as little as two dollars and some as much as twenty-two annually.[23] In return, members received a modest cash benefit when they could not work because of illness. In New York City, payments to beneficiaries of fraternal sickness funds averaged five dollars a week. Brief illnesses were not covered; most societies would pay benefits only for sickness lasting at least one week. And there were maximum as well as minimum limits placed on benefits. A typical example is the Sojourna Household in New York City, which in 1914 made payments of four dollars a week for the first six weeks of a member's illness, dropping to two dollars for the next six weeks and nothing thereafter.[24] These restrictions meant that most fraternal insurance did not cover long-term disability.

While benefits tended to be meager, the fraternal mission often led to great generosity above and beyond the stipulated benefits of membership. Societies could vote to give special "gifts" or "extra aid" to members whose sickness exceeded the time limit. The Sage study found that one fraternal had contributed a total of three hundred dollars to a member with a prolonged illness.[25]

Most societies also paid a death benefit. The largest fraternal lodges maintained substantial reserve funds and were able to pay death benefits of up to five hundred dollars, which would include some money for the member's family in addition to funeral expenses. But the majority of societies paid a much smaller amount, often just enough to provide a modest funeral. For the poorer ones, regular dues might not be enough to pay for the lump sum required in the case of a member's death. Women of the Sojourna Household, for example, were charged a "death tax" when one of their number went to "join the great household above."[26]

To receive benefits and remain in good standing, members of fraternal orders were held to certain standards of behavior. The Workmen's Benefit Fund of New York forbade its members on the sick list to "drink spiritous liquors, frequent saloons, club rooms or places of public amusements." This may seem as much of a stricture against malingering as a moral imperative—anyone frequenting such places was obviously not sick enough to stay in bed—but the fund made exceptions for visits to the more upright venues of "public reading rooms, museums of art and public parks."[27] Official gatherings required decorous behavior; during a meeting of the Progress Mutual Aid Society, Brother Joseph Lesser was fined 25 cents "owing to an ungentlemanly remark passed to the President during the course of the meeting."[28] To fall behind on dues payments was a grievous violation of the fraternal code, and members who did so were held up to public shame. The Salamanca Rebekah Lodge, a women's fraternal in upstate New York, for example, spent part of every meeting reading the names of those members in arrears on their dues.[29]

David Beito argues that fraternal societies exhibited the "middle-class morality" more often attributed to organized charity, particularly by creating distinctions between the "worthy" and the "unworthy" when it came to paying out benefits.[30] Members claiming sick benefits had to be prepared for careful scrutiny and a surrender of privacy. The Ceres Union, a Jewish society, announced the names of its sick members on the front page of its monthly bulletin.[31] A claim of sickness invariably prompted a visit from the "sick committee." These committees resembled the "friendly visitors" of organized charity. They visited sick members to offer solace, but they also "aggressively investigated eligibility."[32] Any evidence that a member was not as ill as claimed could lead to the immediate termination of benefits. When a committee member from the Sojourna Household visited the home of Sarah Porter, who made a sickness claim in November of 1917, she "found her up bed made and dressed and she didn't recommend her sick aid."[33]

Despite its surveillance role, the visiting committee could be a welcome sight to the bedridden. Visitors offered invaluable "friendly assistance, [and] the expression of condolence" as they carried out the fraternal mission of comforting the sick.[34] One member of the American West Indian Ladies' Aid Society was profusely thankful for such visits: "For the four and a half years of my mother's illness there hasn't been a day that some one did not come in to give her a word of cheer and comfort." Another member offered "my sincere thanks and appreciation for your very kind and thoughtful gift of flowers during my recent illness, also to those members who called to see me. . . . Bless the work of this organization."[35] Members also eagerly awaited the arrival of the visiting committee because they came bearing the benefit payment. It is easy to imagine the dismay of a sick member of Sojourna Household, confined to her bed in April of 1917, when the friendly visitor arrived and realized she had forgotten to bring the benefit check. The Household considered fining the visitor, Sister May Miles, for her forgetfulness but in the end accepted her excuse—that she had been distracted while visiting other sick members.[36]

Fraternals carried out their mission of camaraderie and sociability in other ways as well. When the Russell Sage Foundation studied fifty-five benefit societies, it found that in thirty of them "every member who was married while connected with the society was entitled to a wedding present."[37] The preprinted forms used by the Salamanca Rebekah Lodge to record the minutes

of its meetings each closed with this affectionate message: "No further business appearing Lodge closed in due form, with love to all."[38] Fraternal societies
sometimes functioned as extended families for their members.

But as in families, the sociability of fraternals also had a compulsory element. The Sojourna Household denied benefits to a member in 1915 not only
because her illness was not covered by the society, but "moreover the Sister has not being [sic] to meeting for quite some time."[39] The minutes of the
Ceres Union are filled with complaints about a lack of member participation
in meetings and lodge activities — perhaps indicating that, in this society at
least, members saw the lodge's benefit function as more important than the
social one.[40]

Most fraternal societies provided some sort of medical care for their members. The societies saw the doctor's primary role as providing a certificate con-
firming the beneficiary's ill health rather than offering extensive bedside assistance. The Sojourna Household was typical in requiring each member to
"present a medical certificate from a doctor, with a notarized seal, for each
week she was sick."[41] Fraternals took this requirement seriously; members of
the Progress Mutual Aid Society found themselves denied benefits if they failed
to obtain a doctor's certificate or sent in one that had not been notarized.[42]

Even when society physicians — known as "lodge doctors" — provided treatment, the quality of care was often questionable. According to sociologist
Paul Starr, "the more successful doctors were generally unwilling to take such
work."[43] The Sage study reported that "most of the [benefit society] physicians
felt that their remuneration was so poor that they could not afford to give as
careful medical attention to lodge members as to private patients." Only one of
the doctors surveyed bothered to keep records on his fraternal patients.[44] The
Progress Mutual Aid Society paid its doctors $1.50 per patient per year, which
was the average rate paid by fraternals but considered by the medical profession to be "unconscionably low."[45] The disaffection of lodge physicians may
have been the reason that Brother Fieger of the Progress Mutual Aid Society
waited in vain for the society's doctor to appear at his sickbed in November
of 1913. The society's minutes recorded, "Bro. Fieger reported that though he
had called on the society's Brooklyn Doctor to visit him at his home owing
to his inability to go out, the Doctor failed to call, and it was necessary to call
upon a strange physician. Bro. Fieger made no claim on account of this non-
attendance, merely calling the attention of the Society to the neglect in looking
after the Society's sick members."[46]

Reformers often cited the poor quality or sheer lack of fraternal medical
care in arguing that voluntary societies inadequately met the needs of their
constituents. Even more important to the reformers' position was the weak

financial state of most fraternals. Many voluntary societies were poor in resources and frequently ended up insolvent and unable to pay their members any benefits.

Only a few large fraternal societies employed professional accountants. More often, an organization's finances were supervised by a volunteer committee or not supervised at all.[47] Fraternals were criticized for not keeping adequate medical statistics on their members that would enable them to minimize claims.[48] A society's financial weakness could leave sick members without benefits. When a New York laborer came down with typhoid fever in 1917, he expected help from his two Italian benefit societies but received payments from only one; the second society admitted that its "treasury was too low to pay any benefits."[49]

Unexpected large claims could empty a society's coffers and force it deeply into debt. In 1919 the Catholic Mutual Benefit Association of Hornell, New York, had liabilities in excess of its assets in the amount of $364,477.71. This fraternal had failed to adjust its members' contributions to face the vast increase in the death rate brought on by the influenza epidemic and the First World War. The New York State Insurance Department investigated the Catholic Association and allowed it to levy additional assessments on its members to make up for the losses.[50] Such emergency assessments were so frequent that one New York benefit society voted in 1920 to raise its dues to a relatively high twenty dollars a year in the hopes that the increase "forever will do away with the obnoxious assessments and levies."[51] Fraternals' financial weakness was ammunition for reformers seeking to replace voluntary insurance with a compulsory system based on sounder actuarial principles.

TRADE UNION AND EMPLOYER SICKNESS PLANS

Some wage earners in the Progressive Era also received sick pay or medical care, but rarely both, through their union or employer. Funds run by labor unions differed from fraternals' in that sickness benefits were provided automatically with union membership. The benefits were only part of the package of protection that unions offered workers, and in the eyes of union leaders they were less significant than organizing and bargaining for better wages and conditions. There is no doubt, however, that funeral and sickness benefits offered strong incentives for workers to join those unions that provided them.

The American Association for Labor Legislation estimated in 1916 that about one-quarter of unionized workers "belong to unions which give sickness benefits." With only slightly over 5 percent of American workers in labor unions, this meant that the number covered by union benefits was extremely small.[52] Some labor organizations, like the International Typographical Union, provided a death benefit but not coverage for sickness. Union plans almost never provided medical care; only one of the trade unions studied by the AALL had its own doctor.[53]

There were some important exceptions, however. Both metal and coal miners set up an extensive network of union-owned hospitals throughout the American West beginning in the 1890s. In 1913 the International Ladies' Garment Workers' Union (ILGWU) established the Union Health Center at its New York City headquarters in response to the high incidence of tuberculosis among its members. As well as being the first, the ILGWU Health Center was also the most impressive clinic of its kind in the country, boasting free daily examinations for workers, X-ray equipment, a laboratory, a drugstore, and specialist physicians.[54]

Union health and sickness benefits attracted workers to membership and cemented their loyalty to the organization. Company-based mutual benefit funds carried out a similar function for employers. Employers who offered health benefits hoped to reduce worker turnover and discourage unionization.[55] Factory plans were particularly restrictive, often involuntary, and usually controlled by the employer. Most allowed only workers over a certain wage level and under a certain age to join. They required a minimum amount of service before employees could receive benefits, and the benefits ended when a worker left the company, no matter how long his or her employment. This last restriction led to hardship for a New York driver who had paid dues to his employer's benefit society for years. He briefly left the company to take a day job that would allow him to be with his new wife. Upon returning to his old employer and rejoining the benefit society, he became ill and found to his dismay that "he was not entitled to a sick benefit because he had not made the requisite number of consecutive payments." The driver ended up seeking charity help.[56]

Employer benefit plans differed in some important ways from those of fraternals. Most employer-run societies enrolled members of both sexes. In fact, working women in New York State were far more likely to be members of an employer benefit plan than a fraternal society. A study by the New York State Factory Investigating Committee found that 328 of 462 women employed in New York City department stores paid dues to a company mutual aid society, while only 22 were members of fraternals. But a few companies had separate organizations for male and female employees, and several employer plans excluded "sickness or disease peculiar to females."[57]

Company plans in the Northeast made no attempts to appeal to workers' ethnic identities, but those in the South and West behaved more like fraternals

with their explicit practices of racial exclusion. One Kentucky factory benefit society described itself as "a voluntary organization for Mutual Benefit of
the White employees. . . . [T]his Association shall be composed only of white
people." And the Southern Pacific Company's Hospital Department enrolled
all employees "with the exception of . . . Chinese."[58]

Like fraternal societies, employers' aid associations exercised a social function for their members. Company benefit societies sponsored parties, ball
games, and other "wholesome recreation[s]" not only to channel workers'
energies but also, historian Andrea Tone argues, to increase employer control
over private life.[59] That such activities could be coercive as well as pleasurable is
evident in the bylaws of a Brooklyn factory aid society, which stipulated, "All
members of this society will be required to purchase tickets not exceeding 50c,
for all picnics and entertainments which have been ordered by the society."[60]

Factory aid associations differed widely in their organization and financing.
Some required all employees to join, while others were completely voluntary.
Some company benefit societies were financed entirely by worker dues, and
some split the cost between workers and employer. At a few large companies,
including Western Union and American Telephone and Telegraph, employers
absorbed the full cost of the benefit society and required no worker contribution at all.[61] Employer administration and financial support of benefit plans
meant employer control of the plans' operations. In one Midwestern factory,
for example, the employer paid 25 percent and workers 75 percent of contributions to a benefit society, but the company controlled 100 percent of the
administration of the plan.[62] Even a company that made no contribution at
all to its relief plan still retained administrative control; the Westinghouse Air
Brake Company's relief committee was composed of equal numbers of workers
and company managers, but the fund was supported entirely by worker contributions.[63]

Employer-sponsored mutual aid was intended to provide sickness and/or
death benefits and rarely included medical care. A study of 382 benefit societies
found that only 46 of them provided medical attendance, and the cash benefits
were too small for most members to retain a doctor's services: "Members of associations in which the disability benefits are $5 or $6 a week stated that medical attendance very often alone cost them that much."[64] Those employers who
did take an interest in providing workers with medical care initially tended to
be industries with a high injury rate. Railroad companies were among the first
to establish company hospitals, which were used to treat passengers injured on
the railroad's property as well as injured railroad workers. Company medical
care was also common in the mining and timber industries.[65] During the 1910s,
an increasing number of employers in the Northeast established work site clin-

ics and hired their own physicians and nurses. The growth of "industrial medicine" was partly a response to the movement for workmen's compensation; employers hoped to improve workplace hygiene and quickly treat on-the-job injuries, reducing compensation claims and absenteeism. Factory clinics and physicians also performed medical examinations of job applicants.[66]

In 1920 the National Industrial Conference Board (NICB), an employer group, conducted a study of company-sponsored medical care in New England. It found a wildly diverse array of services, ranging from minimalist to elaborate: A few workers trained in first aid made up the entire medical program at one small Massachusetts factory, whereas the 15,000 employees of the General Electric Company in Lynn, Massachusetts, could take advantage of a factory clinic with separate waiting rooms for men and women, on-site X-ray and laboratory services, and four full-time physicians.[67]

Company health services offered significant advantages to workers. Some provided rooms with couches for exhausted employees to rest, nurses to visit sick workers in their homes, and glasses to correct poor eyesight, or they subsidized the cost of overnight stays in a hospital to which the employer made regular contributions. Many employees used these services with enthusiasm and even pleasure. The women workers at one Massachusetts dress factory, for example, made its poorly supervised dispensary into a social gathering spot where they could take off an hour from work with friends.[68]

But workers also had good reason to dislike company medicine. The same visiting nurses who made free house calls were also required by the employer to report on the condition of absentees.[69] Exams for physical fitness that at one factory would lead to correction of medical problems could result in the employee's dismissal at another. Workers objected to payroll deductions for medical care "because they naturally distrusted doctors paid by the company," whom they saw as spies for employers seeking to eliminate poor health risks.[70] Southern timber companies made deductions from already minuscule paychecks to pay for doctors whom most workers never saw.[71] While the average worker's attitude toward company health services was likely ambivalent, union leaders consistently denounced such benefits as coercive and undemocratic.

COMMERCIAL HEALTH AND LIFE INSURANCE

Throughout the nineteenth century, insurance companies that provided life, fire, accident, and most other types of insurance refused to cover sickness, which was thought to be too risky and hence unprofitable. But in 1894 the Health Insurance Company of Philadelphia began attaching a rider to its accident policies that covered eight epidemic diseases, and other companies soon followed. The private health insurance business grew between 1900 and 1918, increasing from half a million dollars in premiums to over twelve million. But the expense and heavy restrictions of the coverage still made it unpopular relative to other insurance services.[72] Commercial health insurance was severely limited, excluding sufferers of the major diseases of the day (including tuberculosis, bronchitis, diabetes, and venereal disease),[73] and extremely expensive. One contemporary writer estimated that individuals with private health insurance policies paid "more than twice in premiums what they receive in benefits. . . . [I]ts excessive cost places [health insurance] beyond the reach of the great majority of the people of the United States."[74] As a result, very few wage earners carried private health insurance policies.[75]

But low-income workers were not strangers to the insurance business. Horror at the prospect of a pauper's funeral led large numbers of working families to buy "industrial insurance," life insurance policies sold by commercial companies whose agents collected the premiums through weekly visits to workers' homes. Industrial insurance did not provide sickness coverage, only the crucial funeral benefit upon the death of the insured.[76] Although the weekly payments were small, cumulatively the policies were very expensive because of the high cost of collections. The importance of the funeral benefit, however, meant that workers continued scraping to pay for policies that they could ill afford. Premium payments proved "a real burden" on a family budget, and one 1907 New York study reported, "Several women said 'insurance keeps us poor.'" Even so, working families saw the insurance policies as a priority. One impoverished woman interviewed for the Russell Sage study, whose husband had been jailed for nonsupport, "stoutly averred that she 'wouldn't give up [the insurance] for anything.'" Noting that some families used the death benefit to offset some of the costs of the fatal illness, the Sage study commented, "[T]hese policies furnish a sort of post-mortem sickness insurance, dismal enough and scarcely adequate."[77]

USING AND "ABUSING" CHARITY MEDICINE

Workers in the Progressive Era found it difficult to pay for medical care. A 1917 survey of wage earners in Rochester, New York, by the Metropolitan Life Insurance company found "only 63 percent of the employees too sick to work were seeing a physician, while only 45.3 percent of those sick but able to work were under professional care," partly due to "the relatively high cost of medical assistance."[78] While the cost of medical care was modest compared with later in the century, working-class families with little or no savings could easily exhaust their resources paying doctors' fees during times of sickness.

Although the public system of charity medicine was intended to serve the very poor, wage earners in New York were avid consumers of the services of free health clinics, known as dispensaries, and the outpatient departments of hospitals. The dispensary occupied a prominent position in the nation's health care system from the late eighteenth century until the 1920s. In addition to providing free medical services to the poor, dispensaries were central to the education of physicians.[79] Attendance at a dispensary clinic a few hours a week was a significant part of a doctor's training, and physicians vied for the most prestigious dispensary slots. One 1919 study estimated that in New York and Boston, the cities with the largest number of dispensaries, between 25 and 40 percent of all local physicians were on dispensary staffs.[80]

Following industrialization and the late-nineteenth-century flood of immigration, dispensary use exploded, particularly in urban centers. One public health physician estimated in 1919 that over a million people were visiting New York City dispensaries each year,[81] and the demand seemed to be continually growing. The trustees of Gouverneur Hospital Dispensary reported that patients were "coming in increasing numbers," with attendance doubling from 1906 to 1913. Another dispensary had to start charging fees in 1918 in order to reduce the throng of patients overwhelming its services. At the New York Post-Graduate Hospital, the demand for free prescriptions rose by 40 percent during 1915.[82] Dispensaries in Northeastern cities became so crowded during the 1910s that by the end of the decade the public health committees of both the New York Academy of Medicine and the Rockefeller Foundation advocated charging fees for clinic admission to relieve the pressure.[83]

While high numbers of unemployed and destitute people accounted for part of the increase, another reason for the growing demand on dispensaries was the increasing willingness of the working poor to seek out charity medical services. One researcher found that 40 percent of low-income workers' families in New York City took advantage of free medical assistance.[84] Dispensary "abuse," as the use of free medical care by the nondestitute was known, had been a major concern since the 1890s, when it first came to the attention of medical journals; but it was clearly on the increase after 1910.[85]

Some observers attributed the growing demand on dispensaries to the surprising public belief that free care was often superior to that obtainable in private doctors' offices. Advanced laboratory equipment and X-ray machines were more likely to be found in a dispensary, especially one attached to a hospital, than in the office of a small private practitioner in a working-class neighborhood.[86] Many New York City dispensaries, such as the Eye and Ear Infirmary, offered specialized services that would otherwise be out of the reach of the average patient. A New York Academy of Medicine study noted that "the dispensary has ceased to be a place where the indigent come for relief and medicines. The large masses of people have come to regard it as the only institution where the services of the specialists can be obtained."[87]

Dispensaries were not all well equipped, however. In many cases, over-crowding, absentee doctors, haphazard care, and decaying facilities made dispensary treatment a harrowing experience. Administrators at the Gouverneur Hospital complained that physicians repeatedly failed to show up for their free clinics, and they were finding it "extremely difficult to control properly the attendance of the unpaid doctors in the dispensary." Gouverneur's physicians may also have been reluctant to put in their hours at the free clinic because of the overwhelming crowds. During just one morning in 1914, two doctors at the Gouverneur dispensary saw a total of 162 patients.[88] And despite their free services, dispensaries almost seemed designed to make it difficult for working people to use them. They were open for only a few hours a week and usually during working hours, making clinic visits a hardship for workers. In New York City dispensaries, "morning hours from ten to twelve and afternoon hours from two to four are most frequent. . . . [T]here are in all not more than ten institutions maintaining evening clinics." Since dispensary patients were not allowed to make appointments, they had to arrive early without any guarantee of being seen during the clinic hours. Usually "the patients are obliged to assemble before 9 A.M. or 2 P.M., and then to wait often the whole morning or afternoon," which meant the loss of a full day's wages.[89]

Patients also had to face a barrage of questions, forms, and surveys to determine their incomes and whether they were eligible for dispensary care. Some dispensaries employed social workers who visited patients' homes to confirm their claims of destitution.[90] Many patients took offense at what they saw as an invasion of privacy and the implication that free medical care was the equivalent of charitable relief, with its accompanying stigma. At the request of several dispensaries, New York's Charity Organization Society made visits to patients' homes to determine their incomes and reported that some patients "resented our visits as intrusive and have not recognized the propriety of investigations by this Society."[91]

There were a few other options available to individuals who were unwilling or unable to use dispensaries but still had difficulty affording doctors' fees. Most private physicians continued their profession's venerable tradition of reducing or waiving their fees for low-income patients, although there is evidence that this practice was starting to decline.[92] And not all physicians were unwilling to charge large fees to the poor. Peter Smith, a worker in the New York City street-cleaning department, suffered from chronic indigestion. He went to see a doctor who had advertised a cure for exactly his condition.

"The doctor first of all exacted a $25 fee for five weeks' treatment which consisted chiefly in giving the patient several bottles of a 'special' medicine." Smith followed the regimen, but his symptoms continued, and then the doctor demanded another twenty-five dollars to complete the treatment. Smith, who earned fifteen dollars a week, "lost confidence in the medical profession [and] worried along on patent medicines."[93]

Wage earners who could not afford physicians' fees also turned to less expensive, usually female, practitioners like nurses or midwives. Families who purchased industrial insurance policies from the Metropolitan Life Insurance Company received regular visits from visiting nurses hired by the company in the hopes of prolonging the lives of beneficiaries (thus reducing claim payments).[94] The growth of hospital obstetric clinics did little to reduce the demand of New York's Italian and Jewish women for attendance by traditional midwives. Self-treatment with assorted patent medicines remained extremely popular among all classes, but especially wage earners. African Americans brought folk medicine from the South to northern cities. W. E. B. Du Bois reported that in Philadelphia, for example, "root doctors" had a thriving practice. Black households, according to medical historians Joel D. Howell and Catherine G. McLaughlin, maintained "a tradition of self-medication" until "well into the 1920s, often practiced by older women who were skilled in the art of folk medicine."[95]

At the beginning of the twentieth century, New York probably offered more ways for people to get medical care than anywhere else in the nation. Besides private care, most towns in the state, and of course New York City, had developed far more public health programs and more dispensaries and clinics than other areas of the country. New York was "no microcosm";[96] many Americans, especially if they were black or lived in rural areas, had little or no access to formal medical care or public health programs.[97]

New York City had the nation's first city health department; by the turn of the century, it offered an astonishing array of services and programs: "laboratory diagnosis of communicable diseases, the production and free distribution to the indigent of vaccines and serums, mandatory registration of all cases of tuberculosis and venereal disease, an active program of health education, and physical examinations and treatment of schoolchildren."[98] For many New Yorkers, their first contact with the public health system came when they were children undergoing a mandatory school exam; their last may have been involuntary confinement to the Riverside Hospital wing for the "recalcitrant tubercular."[99]

Even in those parts of the country, like New York, with many ways to obtain inexpensive treatment, sick people continually ran up against financial barriers when they sought medical care. The network of public health and charity assistance fell far short of meeting the demand. For example, tuberculosis was so common among low-income individuals that free sanatoriums had long waiting lists.[100] Lillian L. Foster of Wareham, Massachusetts, wrote to New York's Charity Organization Society in 1916 to ask for help in entering a local sanatorium because she could not afford the thirteen dollars it charged weekly. She had been ill "for a long time, have had many M.D.[s] and spent my little all" when she read in a newspaper that "Rockefeller left a large amount to help the poor." "Can you use just a small amount for me?" she asked. "I do not ask for a cent for some luxury[,] no no[,] only to get my health."[101]

Emil Bollhausen's decline into sickness and poverty, which began this chapter, was far from an exceptional story. Many workers who took sick fell through the gaping holes of the haphazard American safety net. Even New York's varied health care institutions could not prevent the slide into poverty of workers without wage protection; their sickness was likely followed by destitution, with charity and relief as the last resort. A New York cook was another case in point. He had "held very good positions" until April of 1915, when "he took a heavy cold and was unable to go on with his work because people [were] unwilling to employ a cook with a severe cough." The cook entered a Brooklyn hospital and after his discharge found himself homeless. He lived at the Municipal Lodging House until making his way to the Cornell Dispensary for medicines, where he was referred to the Salvation Army Home for destitute tuberculosis patients.[102] Countless similar stories of economic and physical decline are found in contemporary records, but they refer only to the poor who came into contact with organized charity; those who were denied assistance or lacked even the resources to seek it filled the paupers' graves at potter's field.

The inability of benefit societies, insurance companies, and charity medicine to sufficiently protect workers from sickness and poverty gave Progressive reformers a powerful argument in favor of compulsory health insurance. These institutions never assisted more than a minority of Americans. To those who contended that voluntary associations precluded the need for state involvement in worker protection, Progressives countered that such an inadequate patchwork system could not substitute for a more centralized plan with guaranteed benefits. Indeed, the Russell Sage study concluded that the very existence of private benefit societies "stand[s] as a tangible expression of a keenly felt need, a feeble instrument for performing a duty beyond its own powers."[103]

People's experiences with private benefits and charity medicine would shape their responses to the campaign for compulsory health insurance. Some had financial and personal stakes in the existing institutions. Most fraternal orders and commercial insurance companies were extremely hostile to the AALL's plan because compulsory health insurance, which excluded private benefit associations from participation, would eliminate their need to exist.[104] Some trade unions with sickness funds and employers with company benefit plans resented the AALL's threat to their power to maintain worker loyalty by providing benefits.

Negative experiences with the patchwork system could also serve to turn its users against the idea of compulsory health insurance. Even the most loyal members of fraternal lodges sometimes resented the intrusion of the friendly visitors into their homes and might have feared similar supervision under a government system. Factory workers loathed their employer plans' compulsory medical examinations and thought that exams under state health insurance would blacklist the less robust. Physicians who detested the low pay of lodge practice warned that the entire medical profession would be similarly degraded if forced to practice for the state.

But compulsory health insurance could also retain some of the best features of voluntary societies and relieve the pressures that made mutual aid and charity medicine unworkable. Some principles of compulsory insurance were similar to those underpinning fraternal and trade union associations. The worker contributions required by the compulsory plan, especially, echoed fraternalism's concerns with mutualism, self-reliance, and democratic control of benefit funds. A few labor unions with sickness and death benefits actually welcomed proposals for compulsory health insurance because their own plans were becoming too expensive and unmanageable, and they preferred to devote their resources to organizing rather than mutual aid.[105] Health insurance would relieve dispensary crowding and pay doctors for services they had previously given without charge or at reduced rates. Patients clamoring for dispensary care and waiting patiently for charity medical services would likely be grateful for the free doctor's visits that compulsory health insurance would provide.

Reformers who condemned the inadequacy of the patchwork system faced the task of convincing all those involved in it—doctors, employers, fraternalists, unions, and workers—that the system's replacement with compulsory health insurance would be in their interests. Throughout the coming battle, the existing system of provision, its virtues and shortcomings, would continue to serve as ammunition for both sides of the debate and to shape Americans' responses to proposals for compulsory health insurance.

2

Crafting a Solution to the Sickness Problem

THE AMERICAN ASSOCIATION FOR LABOR LEGISLATION

High above the streets of Manhattan, several stories removed from New York's shops, factories, and docks, a world apart from its hospitals, dispensaries, and fraternal orders, men and women in white collars labored to solve the economic problem of workers' sickness. The sixteenth floor of the imposing Metropolitan Life Insurance Tower housed the national headquarters of the American Association for Labor Legislation, sponsor of the nation's first compulsory health insurance proposals.

Academic economists Richard Ely and Henry Farnam founded the AALL in 1906 as the American branch of the Geneva-based International Association for Labor Legislation. The AALL defined itself as a bureau of "experts" rather than a political organization, and its objective was the "conservation of human resources" through labor legislation, which intended to protect American workers from the worst excesses of industrial capitalism. John R. Commons, the famous labor economist at the University of Wisconsin, became the organization's first secretary. Commons's protégé John B. Andrews was appointed executive secretary in 1909, when the association moved its headquarters to New York City and the Metropolitan Life building. The AALL's new office was run by Andrews and his future wife, Irene Osgood, another Commons student. The organization's national membership never grew to much more than 3,000, but the AALL's journal, *American Labor Legislation Review* (*ALLR*), was widely circulated and cited as the major source of information on labor laws throughout the Progressive Era. The association's board members ranged from settlement house leader Jane Addams to insurance executive Frederick Hoffman to American Federation of Labor president Samuel Gompers.

The AALL's academic economist leaders and their commitment to the ideals of expertise and efficiency shaped the organization's direction. AALL founders Ely and Commons had briefly embraced socialism in the 1880s, and they were threatened with dismissal from university jobs because of their political views.[1] Their subsequent caution led them to modify their ideologies and those of their organization. The AALL disavowed socialism and instead committed itself to preserving the capitalist system by curtailing its abuses. AALL leaders insisted that employers would benefit from labor laws as much as workers would, for increased worker security would lead to greater efficiency on the job and hence higher productivity. And a secure worker was a contented one. Labor legislation would lessen the threat of rebellion and revolution that menaced American business. The gospel of efficiency and stability, more than ideals of social justice, informed the AALL agenda.

AALL leaders believed that the country's salvation lay in creating a system of protection for wage earners—a "security state," in the words of historian David Moss.[2] In the AALL's vision, the state's role would be regulatory, not redistributive. AALL reformers agreed with many in the Progressive Era who thought that direct relief to individuals increased pauperism and dependency. In addition, providing relief implied that damage had already been done, that an individual was being rescued from an intolerable situation. The AALL instead argued for the prevention of such conditions before they occurred. While workmen's compensation, for example, would pay workers injured on the job, it also would create a financial incentive for employers to increase workplace safety and prevent future accidents. The AALL envisioned a system of labor legislation and regulation that would encourage employers to make rational choices, improving the lives of workers and reducing the need for direct relief.

The AALL saw itself as a disinterested party mediating between the two poles of capital and labor. While businessmen and trade unionists were motivated by economic interests, AALL leaders thought that their own advocacy of scientific methods and expertise implied detachment from the political chaos and struggles of the day, and certainly detachment from private interest. It was true that no AALL reformer stood to benefit materially from the success of labor legislation, except for the possibility of employment on new investigatory commissions or regulatory agencies. But this did not mean that the AALL lacked interests. Unlike many elite reformers who had independent incomes, John B. Andrews and many of the AALL staff depended on the organization's ability to attract wealthy donors to its cause so that their salaries might be paid, and much of Andrews's time was spent raising money. The AALL's fund-raising prowess was tied to its legislative successes and its ability to maintain public respect as a "disinterested" source of expert opinion in a time of social turmoil.[3]

The AALL's agenda was tied to the interests and status of its leaders. As Kathryn Sklar has written, the AALL's "heart and soul . . . was middle-class."[4] Like other middle-class Americans of the day, AALL reformers feared both working-class unrest and the unbridled power of big business. These reformers had a personal interest in social stability, which their policies intended to achieve. Entirely white and overwhelmingly Protestant, the association's leaders also shared the middle-class Progressive belief in "Americanization" as the solution to the threat of immigrant racial difference. Labor legislation, AALL reformers argued, would go a long way toward Americanizing foreign workers and giving immigrants a stake in the capitalist economy.

In their endeavors, AALL reformers may have sought security and some financial gain, but more than anything they sought a prominent role in public life. Countering the public perception of academics as isolated from the workings of society, the AALL wanted economists and social scientists to have a major role in the crafting of legislation and the operation of government. AALL leaders desired not just to achieve status[5] but also to exercise control and to enjoy power. Neither captains of industry nor producers of market goods, middle-class reformers insisted on the value of their skills and expertise to running a modern society. In its demands for nonpartisan commissions and boards to design and administer labor legislation, the AALL envisioned a government of experts with autonomy from the political system. Even as they continued to insist on their own objectivity, the reformers' desire for control and autonomy was something they shared with other interest groups of the day, including their greatest enemies. But their illusion of detachment made it more difficult for the AALL to comprehend the role of conflicting interests in society and to gauge the reactions of interest groups to legislative proposals.

The AALL's vision of disinterested expertise as the solution to social strife would prove inadequate to the task before it. Believing themselves above the crass struggle for advantage, the AALL's leaders failed to prepare a strategy to meet the opposition of interest groups that mobilized against the legislation. With research and expertise its only means of persuasion, the AALL was unprepared for the fierce ideological and political battle that the health insurance campaign would provoke.

The AALL's ideologies and interests shaped its legislative program. Its leaders' belief in the efficacy of modern medicine, along with their concern for the conservation of labor power, put the protection of workers' health at the top of the AALL agenda. Recent advances in medical science added to reformers' faith in the possibilities of seemingly unlimited scientific progress and in the ability of experts to solve the problems of human life. As one Progressive said, "Just as physicians study the diseases which attack the physical body so social workers are studying the diseases which attack the social body, are trying to learn their causes and are seeking the means for their prevention."[6] Combining medical and social advances would lead to a new era in which rational expertise would vanquish the twin evils of ill health and economic insecurity.

The AALL addressed worker health in all three of its major campaigns of the 1910s: for elimination of poisonous phosphorus in the workplace, compensation for workplace injuries, and worker health insurance. The first two of these campaigns were extraordinarily successful. After the AALL initiated, drafted, and introduced the proposals, the use of phosphorus in match factories was banned by federal legislation in 1912, and thirty-three states adopted workmen's compensation laws by 1915.[7] Fresh from these victories, AALL strategists in 1915 felt the nation was prepared to adopt what they saw as the logical next step in worker protection: compulsory health insurance.

Established in Germany as early as the 1880s, compulsory health insurance had spread throughout Europe in the years before World War I. AALL reformers were especially encouraged by the adoption in Britain of the National Insurance Act in 1911, which covered almost all British employees and provided them with sick pay, medical and hospital care, and disability and maternity benefits. Glowing testimony from British workers and physicians — and American visitors — gave John Andrews and his colleagues confidence that a similar system of health insurance would be greeted in their own country with enthusiasm.

Compulsory health insurance meshed with the AALL's ideals and vision of the economy. A worker's health was of value not just to the individual but to the employer, and to the nation as a whole. AALL member Dr. Alexander Lambert told a group of women physicians, "The greatest capital that a workman or that a professional man . . . has is the possession of that degree of health which enables him to go each day and do his work thoroughly." Compulsory health insurance would conserve the valuable "capital" of laborers' health. And American workers badly needed health conservation: their poor physical condition was the subject of widespread comment and debate before and during the war. Physicians expressed shock at "the wretched physique of the great majority of those who carry on the production of the world." Sickly workers threatened to undermine strong economies and nations.[8]

Worker illness led not only to lost productivity for business but also to economic losses to the workers themselves. Wage earners suffered from a higher proportion of sickness, and they were also the "least able to bear" the cost of wage loss and medical care.[9] In the AALL's view, the insurance principle would allow the unequal burden of ill health to be spread more evenly among the population. A cash benefit for those who missed work due to illness was just as important as the medical service health insurance would provide.

Compulsory health insurance also opened another avenue for the AALL's belief in the prevention of social ills. Just as workmen's compensation created a material incentive for employers to improve safety, health insurance, reformers thought, placed a monetary value on sickness prevention in the workplace. The fewer sick workers, the lower the employer's premium payment. Because workers contributed, they too would be strongly motivated to conserve their health, and free access to medical care would further reduce the frequency of sick days.

In 1914 the AALL's Social Insurance Committee began drafting model legislation for compulsory health insurance. The model plan was designed for adoption by individual states, not the country as a whole. As David Moss points out, reformers in the Progressive Era "assumed that nearly all social insurance and protective labor laws would have to be enacted at the state level."[10] Since health insurance did not involve interstate commerce, it was likely that the courts would impose constitutional constraints on the implementation of national legislation.[11] AALL leaders settled on the state-by-state strategy for health insurance that had worked so well for workmen's compensation.

The Social Insurance Committee was chaired by Edward Devine, director of the New York School of Philanthropy, and its members included an economist, a sociologist, two insurance experts, a librarian, two statisticians, and a physician.[12] Not surprisingly, the Social Insurance Committee was entirely white, and initially exclusively male. Missing from the membership roster were any representatives of the group to be covered by health insurance: industrial workers. Nor were any employers included. The committee was a forum for the middle-class experts and intellectuals who could avoid the interest-group bickering of those who stood to benefit and lose from health insurance — or so the AALL believed.

The Social Insurance Committee agreed on a list of basic standards for a health insurance system, including the necessity of compulsion; joint contributions from workers, employers, and the state; provision for both sick pay and medical care; time limits on benefits; disability insurance; and administration by local mutual funds under public supervision. After the addition of three new members in 1915 (two physicians and the committee's first and only woman member, nurse and settlement worker Lillian Wald), the Social Insurance Committee published a tentative draft of a bill for compulsory health insurance. This model bill proposed a system of local mutual funds, made up of contributions from workers (two-fifths), employers (two-fifths), and the state (one-fifth), supervised by a state health insurance commission.[13]

The legislation was built on the two pillars of medical care and wage replacement for sick workers. It would provide eligible workers — those earning under $100 a month — with free medical services, including physicians' visits, surgery, nurses, drugs, and supplies; hospital care could be elected in place of part of the cash benefit. Medical coverage included the dependent wives and children of the insured, and did not exclude maternity care (as did most existing types of insurance). In addition, workers would receive cash payments equal to two-thirds of their weekly wages for up to twenty-six weeks of sickness.[14] The amount of two-thirds was chosen because too much cash benefit might encourage malingering, while less "would entail sacrifices of food and shelter."[15] Compulsory health insurance would also pay the insured a maximum of fifty dollars as a funeral benefit.

The model bill of the AALL's Social Insurance Committee was the basis for discussion of health insurance for the rest of the decade. It was distributed throughout the nation and debated in state legislatures considering the establishment of health insurance commissions.[16] In the only two states where health insurance became a live political issue, California and New York, health insurance proposals followed the model bill's precepts. Although the AALL's bill would eventually undergo alterations in New York, it remained unchanged in its basic premise of coverage for certain workers only. Insurance for the middle class and the unemployed was never seriously considered. Agricultural and domestic workers, too, were excluded from the plan.

MEANINGS OF EXCLUSION

The model bill's provisions, and especially its exclusions, reflected the assumptions of both the AALL and the emerging welfare state. The bill's limitation of coverage to workers earning less than $1,200 a year was based on similar restrictions in the German and British health insurance systems, which the AALL saw no reason to modify. Coverage of low-income workers only was clearly expedient, since they were the group with the least access to medical care; those with higher incomes could presumably pay for doctors, while the very poor were allowed treatment in dispensaries and through physician charity. The unemployed were not included in the system because of the AALL's firm belief in the importance of the worker's financial contribution to the coverage. The limitations were also important to the AALL's scheme for administration, which would become unwieldy if it were forced to include white-collar employees, professionals, and the self-employed on the insurance commission.

The exclusion of higher-income workers and the unemployed from health insurance proposals led to charges that the AALL was promoting "class legislation" that would increase the divisions and antagonisms in American society. Fear of "class legislation" helped defeat the health insurance referendum in California, wrote one AALL supporter, who suggested expanding coverage to avoid a repeat of the California debacle: "I wonder if in future all such plans for social betterment would not better include every member of the political body."[17] But the AALL resisted such (infrequent) suggestions to extend coverage to the middle class because "it was thought they should provide for themselves."[18] It wasn't just that the better-off *could* financially survive times of illness; they *should* do so as a mark of their respectability and class standing. Despite its attempts to portray health insurance as an honorable social provision supported by worker contributions, by confining coverage to industrial workers alone the AALL still reinforced notions of middle-class autonomy and worker dependence. In the coming battle, its opponents would use this contradiction to decry social insurance as "class legislation."[19]

The nonworking poor, on the other hand, were thought by AALL strategists to be the proper objects of charity, not labor legislation. "It is not the function of health insurance to take care of the dependent classes," read an AALL pamphlet, "but to prevent people from dropping into them."[20] In arguing for the exclusion of the very poor and the unemployed from health insurance, the AALL did not invoke distinctions between the deserving and undeserving, as they later did with unemployment legislation.[21] Instead, the reformers argued on the basis of need. They expressed strong faith in the ability of charity medicine to take care of the destitute and unemployed, while portraying the employed as the group with the greatest need for health insurance. AALL supporter John A. Lapp told an audience that after health insurance for industrial workers passed, "The humanitarian impulse will still find a field for action among the very poor who are below the insurance line."[22]

Casual and seasonal workers received similar treatment in the legislation. Compulsory health insurance, according to Irene Osgood Andrews, "is not intended to and will not reach the man who is . . . casually employed. . . . Such a person is a case for charity or poor relief."[23] The omission of casual and domestic laborers fit a historical pattern in the United States that left temporary, agricultural, and domestic workers without the protection of social insurance programs until well after World War II. Since these occupations were dominated by nonwhite workers, their exclusion from legislation was also part of reformer and governmental neglect of the concerns and needs of black Americans.[24] The AALL certainly contributed to this neglect. Even though its legislation did not explicitly discriminate based on race, the organization never proposed laws to protect agricultural or domestic laborers.[25] This omission seems particularly striking since both domestic and agricultural workers were included in the British National Insurance Act.[26] By leaving out these occupations, reformers participated in the exclusion of the nation's most powerless workers from the emerging welfare state. Had AALL strategists talked at all about health coverage for the agricultural sector or for African Americans, they might have set a precedent for discussion of the issue, and possibly for the inclusion of the poorest black Americans in later legislative proposals. The AALL's silence on race was deafening, but its exclusion of agricultural and domestic workers from labor legislation spoke volumes.

AALL leaders never spoke explicitly about excluding black workers from the health insurance plan.[27] The reformers likely shared the racial assumptions of most whites of their era—they had no qualms about appointing scientific racist Frederick Hoffman to the Social Insurance Committee—but they rarely referred to the race question in their correspondence and publications and their actions were not driven by overt racism.[28] The best explanation for AALL's apparent lack of concern for blacks is the organization's overriding concern with industrial workers—a category of workers that the AALL envisioned as white. Even though increasing numbers of African Americans entered industrial jobs during the Progressive Era, discussions of these black workers never appear in the AALL's records.[29] The *American Labor Legislation Review* reflected the invisibility of black industrial workers to the AALL. Fifty-four photographs of American wage earners appeared in the *ALLR* between 1910 and 1920. Only one of the images pictured a black worker, a cooper who was photographed standing alone among his barrels.[30] His isolation is striking, especially since *ALLR* photographs repeatedly depicted white workers in large groups, in factories, workshops, and cafeterias. The black barrel-maker was portrayed as the AALL saw black industrial workers: as a rare exception to the rule of African American agricultural and domestic labor, an exception that the reformers could easily ignore.

The AALL also showed little interest in recruiting New York's black Progressive organizations to its cause.[31] Because the AALL did not as a rule reach out to them, it is impossible to say whether African Americans might have supported the concept of compulsory health insurance. But a single piece of evidence offers a tantalizing hint that some did: in 1920, John B. Andrews spoke on health insurance to the Roosevelt Republican League, a group of "negro women" who "by an almost unanimous rising vote endorsed the measure." Apparently this was the first and last time the AALL approached a black organization about health insurance.[32]

IDENTIFYING ALLIES AND ENEMIES

The AALL launched a political campaign for the adoption of compulsory health insurance at the beginning of 1916. Its leaders decided to propose health insurance bills in three states: New York, Massachusetts, and New Jersey. In New York, a bill for compulsory health insurance was introduced on January 24 by state senator Ogden L. Mills and became known as the Mills Bill. New York's Senate Judiciary Committee held public hearings on the Mills Bill in March 1916, attracting a variety of speakers to Albany. Physicians made a strong showing at the hearing. At this point, they exhibited diverse opinions on the desirability of health insurance, not least because the AALL's model bill had left open the question of medical organization and the payment of physicians.[33] The state medical society then recommended that the New York legislature appoint a commission to study the question of health insurance before bringing the bill to a vote. Mills obligingly withdrew his bill and introduced a new one to set up an investigatory commission. The commission bill passed in the senate in April 1916 but was subsequently killed in committee in the assembly.[34] The AALL would reintroduce its health insurance legislation in New York in 1917, 1918, and 1919, but it would not come to a vote until 1919.

Compulsory health insurance received a major blow in 1918 with the failure of the California health insurance referendum. A bill based on the AALL's model had been proposed by the California Social Insurance Commission, but the legislature decided that the state's constitution had to be amended first. California voters soundly defeated the health insurance amendment in a public referendum on November 6, 1918, with 133,858 votes for and 358,324 against.[35] Although the AALL was not heavily involved in the California campaign, leaving the organization and lobbying efforts to the local Social Insurance Commission, the West Coast defeat provided important lessons for the New York reformers. Right before the referendum, John B. Andrews received an urgent telegram from California health insurance activist Ansley K. Salz: "Opposition better organized and financed than any previous fight on any other measure. House to house canvass and real financed publicity campaign being made by Christian Scientists, insurance companies and most of the doctors spreading deliberate falsehood . . . situation getting worse all the time."[36] The California experience foreshadowed the alliance of interest groups (the Christian Scientists excepted) that the AALL would face in its New York campaign.[37]

As the AALL bills wound their way through the legislative process in New York, Andrews and his colleagues worked to solidify support for health insurance and to win new allies. In this task, the AALL was both aided and hindered by its complex relationships with a variety of interest groups. Interactions between the reformers and the medical profession were particularly fraught with difficulty. The AALL's failure to woo physicians early in its campaign later came to haunt it, as New York physicians emulated their California counterparts in their vocal opposition to health insurance.

When Dr. Alexander Lambert joined the AALL's Social Insurance Committee in 1916, he was ideally positioned to build a bridge between the social scientists and the American Medical Association. Lambert was already influential in the AMA, and he became its president in 1918. But Lambert's strong belief in the ideals of compulsory health insurance failed to persuade his colleagues in the medical profession. Initially favorable to health insurance, the AMA by 1920 had condemned it in no uncertain terms.[38] While the reasons for this change of heart are complex, the AALL's troubled relations with the medical profession undoubtedly played a part. The few doctors on the Social Insurance Committee gave AALL policy makers an inaccurate picture of physicians' ideologies and interests. Besides Lambert, the only physicians involved in drafting the AALL's health insurance legislation were Isaac Rubinow, a socialist (and nonpracticing physician), and S. S. Goldwater, who had been the health commissioner of New York City.

A reformer, a socialist, and a public health physician—the AALL doctors could hardly have been less representative of the physicians of the New York state and county medical societies, who tended to practice in small towns or rural areas. These physicians distrusted government and resented the "meddling" of big-city doctors and reformers in their affairs. Although a big-city doctor himself, anti–health insurance crusader Dr. Eden V. Delphey echoed the sentiments of countless upstate New York practitioners when he said that AALL reformers "have, by birth and environment, not been in a position to know the wishes, needs, aims and ideals of those whom they wish to uplift; nor of the trials, troubles and tribulations of the physicians who have worked among these people in the past."[39] The AALL's decision to leave medical organization out of its initial bill was intended to leave room for physicians' suggestions, and indeed the legislation changed continually and dramatically in response to doctors' demands. But it also enabled physicians to accuse the reformers of neglecting the needs and desires of their profession.

The AALL had a complicated and generally uncomfortable relationship with organized labor. Despite the presence of national labor leader Samuel Gompers's name on its stationery, the makeup of the AALL membership, consisting mainly of middle-class social workers and academics, left the organization vulnerable to charges of elitism. Rather than speaking for labor, scoffed a manufacturers' journal, the AALL merely represented the voices of a "small coterie of college professors."[40] John B. Andrews was particularly sensitive to these accusations, informing critics that "[t]he Association in fact has a much wider influence than is generally appreciated . . . over one hundred trade unions, for example, are subscribers to [our] publications."[41] But the AALL's reputation for slighting labor opinion only worsened when Gompers resigned from the association in 1915 because, according to his friend Ralph Easley of the National Civic Federation (NCF), he was "tired of the socialistic stuff they were putting out."[42] In a series of angry attacks, Gompers renamed the AALL "American Association for the Assassination of Labor Legislation" and condemned its leaders as "our benevolent 'intellectual' self-assumed guardians" and "barnacles" on the labor movement.[43] Gompers's resignation was often invoked by the AALL's opponents (and is still cited by historians) as the prime example of the organization's inability to mobilize labor support.[44] The labor movement in the Progressive Era, however, consisted of a far broader constituency than that represented by Gompers or his American Federation of Labor. Other major labor leaders, such as William Green of the United Mine Workers, Rose Schneiderman of the International Ladies' Garment Workers' Union and the Women's Trade Union League (WTUL), and James Lynch of the New York State Federation of Labor (NYSFL), saw labor legislation as a central part of their movement's agenda, worked closely with the AALL, and became enthusiastic supporters of compulsory health insurance.

There is no doubt, however, that the AALL could have done much more to garner support among labor. Its Social Insurance Committee never included any worker representatives. Nor did it solicit opinions from any union leaders during the drafting of the health insurance bill, an oversight that would later come to haunt the organization.[45] AALL leaders often bordered on arrogance in their assumptions that labor would automatically approve of any legislation that the reformers initiated. Andrews and his colleagues put so much faith in scientific and academic expertise that they missed myriad opportunities to consult those whose knowledge of labor issues came from direct experience. Gompers's resignation was, of course, a most public humiliation and a powerful blow to the AALL's ability to argue on behalf of labor. Opponents of the reform agenda found it easy to attack the AALL on the grounds that the organization failed to represent the true voice of American labor—a theme that would arise often during the health insurance campaign.

The AALL repeatedly asserted that its legislation addressed the needs of both labor and industry. Like trade unionists, however, business leaders were skeptical of the reformers' claim. The AALL was initially complacent about employer support for health insurance because of the extent of business cooperation it had received in the campaign for workmen's compensation. Historians agree that workmen's compensation succeeded so rapidly not simply through the efforts of reformers and labor but because American business eventually came to support the measures. Manufacturers wanted the cumbersome and expensive liability system replaced by a more efficient and predictable method of insuring workers, and powerful business organizations like the National Association of Manufacturers and the NCF were among the most enthusiastic supporters of workmen's compensation. Commercial insurance companies also advocated social insurance for workplace injuries because they were offered a profitable role in the system as insurance carriers.[46]

The AALL told its supporters in 1916 that they need not be concerned about employers opposing health insurance, since business's positive experience with workmen's compensation meant they understood how labor legislation "is a good thing for them as well as for their employees."[47] That assessment was overly optimistic, to say the least. Aside from a favorable early report by a committee of the National Association of Manufacturers (which was later altered to recommend voluntary, not compulsory, insurance),[48] employers' organizations were uniformly hostile to the health insurance proposal. The AALL's optimism left it unprepared for the active opposition of major employer organizations, including the NCF, the National Industrial Conference Board, and the Associated Manufacturers and Merchants of New York State (AMM). The latter organization declared in 1915 that health insurance was "an uneconomic proposition . . . perhaps so ingeniously drawn as to constitute a most dangerous sophism, but in the light of practical experience opening up possibilities for fraud and malingering such as we have not been called upon to face in our history." Throughout the campaign, the AMM's attacks on compulsory insurance and the AALL were so virulent that John Andrews came to call the organization "the obnoxious state employers' association." Industrialists decried the AALL as a group of leisured nonproducers meddling in business affairs. One New York factory owner referred to the reformers as "chair warmers" and "the swivel chair gang who are after the jobs [health insurance] will produce."[49]

The opposition of commercial insurance companies to compulsory health insurance came as less of a surprise to the AALL. The funeral benefit provision of its model bill would wipe out the industrial business that brought the insurance industry such high profits.[50] And the AALL already had an extremely strained relationship with the insurance industry. Frederick Hoffman, a vice president of the Prudential Insurance Company, made an ugly break with the AALL over health insurance in 1916. Hoffman, a prominent statistician of industrial disease and a promoter of scientific racism, sat on the AALL's Executive, Industrial Hygiene, and Social Insurance Committees and was a strong supporter of the AALL's campaign against phosphorus poisoning. But the organization's turn toward compulsory health insurance forced Hoffman to choose between the AALL and loyalty to his commercial employer. In the Social Insurance Committee, he objected to the proposed standards for health insurance because of their exclusion of commercial insurance companies from the system. He continued to fight this provision of the bill until finally resigning from the AALL "in disgust" on April 10, 1916.[51] On the heels of Gompers's defection, Hoffman's resignation was another embarrassing blow for the reformers; now the representatives of two interest groups with major stakes in health insurance legislation had publicly rejected the AALL. Once the AALL's allies, Gompers and Hoffman went on to become its most outspoken enemies.

As a New York–based organization, the AALL was part of the largest charity and reform community in the nation. New York was home to such prominent and influential philanthropies as the Charity Organization Society, the Association for Improving the Condition of the Poor (AICP), the Russell Sage Foundation, and the Rockefeller Foundation. Although the charity sector was not always on the side of social legislation — its initial opposition to mothers' pensions is an important case in point[52] — the AALL enjoyed cordial relations with New York philanthropies based on ideological affinity. New York's scientific charity leaders shared with the AALL a self-identification as "experts" and a preference for the prevention of poverty over its relief. The Association for Improving the Condition of the Poor supported compulsory health insurance because of the encouraging results of workmen's compensation, which had "remov[ed] many families completely from the necessity of relief by either private or public agencies," leading charity workers "to believe that an extension of this principle to sickness insurance would be wise."[53]

Although New York's organized charities occasionally made public statements in favor of health insurance, and the Charity Organization Society's Edward Devine headed the AALL's Social Insurance Committee, charities served the AALL more as sources of statistics than of active political support. The studies of the AICP and the Russell Sage Foundation were instrumental to the AALL's attempt to prove the link between sickness and poverty. AICP leader John Kingsbury announced that illness was a factor in 4,809 of 6,423 families assisted by the charity in 1917.[54] One 1916 AICP study of charity cases found "a fundamental trouble" among the families: *no money laid up for emergency*"; an emergency almost inevitably involved health problems.[55] The AICP's identification of wage loss during illness as a major factor in charity dependency reinforced the arguments of health insurance advocates.

But publicly, charity support for health insurance was muted. The only charity leader to testify at an Albany hearing on the AALL's bill was J. J. Weber of the State Charities Aid Association, in 1917. Weber claimed that his organization had "taken a neutral position" on the proposal but favored the creation of a health insurance commission. The rest of his testimony was devoted to a presentation of sickness statistics in New York State. No charity leaders other than Devine participated actively in the health insurance campaign.[56]

The AALL could expect more vocal political support for its proposal from another influential group: New York's socialists. Although the AALL's professed goal was to curb demands for social revolution by making capitalism more efficient, some prominent socialists saw little contradiction between their own ideals and support for the AALL's ameliorative measures. The Socialist Party had been the first American organization to endorse the principle of social insurance as early as 1900. Meyer London, the New York Socialist elected to the U.S. House of Representatives in 1916, introduced an unsuccessful bill in Congress to create a health insurance investigating committee.[57] Another Socialist, Isaac Rubinow, author of the important text *Social Insurance* (1913), was on the AALL's Social Insurance Committee and, even after a move to Palestine, kept tabs on the health insurance battle through a warm and lively correspondence with John B. Andrews. The AALL also had strong ties to some Socialist trade unionists, most notably Pauline Newman of the ILGWU. Newman was an outspoken defender of compulsory health insurance who testified at New York Assembly hearings, made numerous speeches, and wrote articles supporting the AALL's bill. Rather than being put off by the AALL's gradualism, Newman thought that advocacy of protective laws and other "immediate demands" was an essential first step on the road to socialism. She maintained a commitment to social revolution while working for concrete reforms, in her union and in alliance with the reformers of the WTUL and the AALL. Explaining her commitment to both reform and revolution, Newman later said that workers "didn't want to wait that long before socialism would come and make all the changes—they wanted something NOW."[58]

Even though the AALL professed to defend capitalism, the programs it advocated for doing so, particularly health insurance, could be construed as socialistic for their intervention in the economy, and were condemned as such by the organization's opponents. Indeed, founders Commons and Ely had professed socialist beliefs in their youth. AALL leaders thus spent a great deal of time defending themselves against charges of socialism and Bolshevism. But their sensitivity to Red-baiting by their opponents, perhaps surprisingly, did not lead them to engage in such tactics themselves by purging the organization's socialist members or disavowing its radical supporters. For example, Pauline Newman was among the AALL's most sought-after speakers, and AALL leaders eagerly used her words in the association's health insurance propaganda. And at the height of the Red Scare in New York, John Andrews wrote to Isaac Rubinow expressing sympathy for his "Socialist brothers" who had been expelled from the assembly.[59] Rubinow's presence in the AALL was perpetual ammunition for opponents who sought to discredit the AALL for its ties to socialists, but Andrews continued to stand by one of his organization's most dedicated and well-informed members. The ideological differences and antagonism between the AALL and its more socialist-minded supporters that would later split the social insurance movement into advocates of the "American plan" versus state centralization were far less evident in the health insurance movement of the 1910s.[60] The AALL's struggle to deflect accusations of Red sympathies during the campaign for compulsory insurance never included a disavowal of its socialist allies.

FEMALE EXPERTISE: THE WOMEN OF THE AALL

The AALL shared some affinity with another major branch of the Progressive movement: the women's reform network that advocated measures to protect women and children. Cooperation between the AALL and prominent women reform leaders was frequent. Margaret Dreier Robins, head of the WTUL, was both an AALL member and a major financial contributor to the organization. Lillian Wald, founder of the Henry Street Settlement and the National Organization for Public Health Nursing, was a member of the AALL's Social Insurance Committee and corresponded regularly with John B. Andrews. The AALL's alliance with women's groups would reach its height in 1919, when the WTUL, the New York Consumers' League, and the New York Woman Suffrage Association would adopt compulsory health insurance as part of their legislative programs for women workers.

Some recent analyses of the AALL have emphasized the contrast between the organization's emphasis on "male expertise and power" with the grassroots strategies of female-dominated Progressive organizations like the National Consumers' League (NCL) and the National Congress of Mothers. Certainly the AALL's tactics differed greatly from those of the more activist and participatory women's groups, and the organization was far from a bastion of gender equality. But the regular collaboration between the AALL and women reformers, as well as the presence of women in some influential AALL staff positions, make pigeonholing the AALL as a "male" organization incorrect.[61]

While prominent female reformers like Robins, Wald, Crystal Eastman, and Jane Addams cooperated closely with the AALL, some lesser-known women worked tirelessly on the AALL staff, drafting legislation, creating publicity, and lobbying. Although the (pre–Lillian Wald) all-male Social Insurance Committee is usually credited with drafting the AALL's model health insurance bill, much of it was actually based on the research of Olga Halsey, a young AALL staff member whom Andrews hired because of her expertise on the subject of European health insurance. As a student in England, Halsey had written a graduate thesis on Britain's National Insurance Act. John Andrews was impressed by Halsey's formidable expertise and her command of the technical details of health insurance, describing her as "trained, experienced, and entirely trustworthy," and he left many of the research and propaganda tasks of the health insurance campaign in her hands.[62]

Halsey has escaped notice by scholars and little is known about her life.[63] She was born in upstate Unadilla, New York, in 1889. In 1896 her father, F. A. Halsey, moved the family to New York City, where he took a position in the Department of Mechanical Engineering at Columbia University. Halsey was influenced both by her father's academic achievements and by her mother Stella's volunteer work with the Harlem Council of Women, a club dedicated to philanthropy and social reform. Mother and daughter would bridge two worlds of women's reform activity: charity work and professional expertise. Olga Halsey entered Wellesley College in 1912, where she studied with the noted educator and reformer Emily Green Balch. She next enrolled in the London School of Economics for graduate studies, writing her master's thesis on the British National Insurance Act. In Britain, she also produced a comparative study of British and German health insurance at the behest of the AALL. Shortly after Halsey's return to the United States in 1915, John Andrews hired her as a "library research investigator" for the AALL, and she spent the next two years working almost exclusively on the health insurance campaign.[64]

In many ways, Halsey's ideas and her career resembled those of the quintessential male Progressives. Trained as an academic social scientist, she shared the AALL's faith in science, expertise, and the European model. In her work for the AALL she proved capable of producing both meticulous research and persuasive propaganda. Like many Progressives, Halsey was part of a transatlantic network of reformers and continually looked to Britain's emerging welfare state for inspiration.[65] Halsey's knowledge of the British National Insurance Act was incorporated into versions of the AALL's health insurance bill, and her

Olga Halsey, ca. 1908 (Division of Rare and Manuscript Collections, Cornell University Library).

Irene Sylvester (*The Survey*,
September 13, 1919; photograph
courtesy of The University Library,
University of Illinois at Chicago).

continuing research created the knowledge base for the entire health insurance campaign. AALL records are filled with Halsey's reports, ranging from subjects like "Medical Benefit Arrangements in Germany and Great Britain" to "Sickness in Twelve Industries in New York State" and "Childbirth Protection."[66] Halsey was an important liaison between the AALL and prominent American and British reformers. Among her regular correspondents were Sidney and Beatrice Webb, Vida Scudder, and leaders of the British Women's Trade Union League. Halsey also carried on an eloquent correspondence with the health insurance plan's major supporters and detractors. She wrote nearly every piece of health insurance propaganda found in the AALL papers from 1916 through 1918. Her replies to major health insurance opponents like Samuel Gompers and the NCF were filled with statistics and research findings and rarely veered onto the emotional or sentimental territory supposedly claimed by women reformers.[67] As Linda Gordon points out, female Progressives could embrace statistics and expertise as eagerly as their male counterparts.[68]

One of the AALL's most public, visible jobs was held by a woman. As chief lobbyist for its legislation, the AALL employed Irene Sylvester, who relentlessly hounded politicians to support labor legislation while she dispatched reports from Washington and Albany describing her interactions with lawmakers. In contrast with Halsey's earnestness, Sylvester often displayed a cutting wit and an amused contempt for the AALL's foes. Writing to John Andrews from the New York State House in 1919, Sylvester said that her work there was easier because she had become a familiar face, "and the doorkeepers know me and help me spot unfortunate victims!" She described how she "chided" a health insurance opponent and concluded that the AALL should "let the doctors hang themselves."[69] Like Halsey, Sylvester was from a privileged background and had a graduate education in social science. She attended Mount Holyoke College and held a master's degree in labor relations from Columbia University. As a graduate student, she lived with other women Progressives at the Greenwich House Settlement in New York City. Sylvester worked for the AALL as a researcher and lobbyist from 1915 to 1923 (during this time she married and took her husband's last name, Chubb). She was the AALL's chief Washington lobbyist for one of its greatest victories, the Federal Employees' Compensation Act of 1916.[70] Sylvester was not marginal but a central figure in the AALL's legislative campaigns. As a lobbyist, she presented legislators with the female face of the AALL.

Irene Osgood Andrews, John Andrews's wife and like him a former student of John R. Commons, also played a major role in the organization. Thoroughly trained in social science methodology, Irene Andrews had conducted the AALL's investigation of phosphorus poisoning as an equal partner with her husband. The nationwide ban on phosphorus in manufacturing was not the only outcome of the study: historian Christopher Sellers credits both Irene and John Andrews with pioneering an American method for investigating industrial disease.[71] Unlike Halsey and Sylvester, Irene Andrews also had a child, but hiring a full-time nurse for their young son enabled both Andrewses to devote time to the AALL.[72]

For Halsey, Sylvester, and Irene Andrews, their identity as experts, as much as their identity as women, shaped their experiences. Their academic training and social science backgrounds allowed them to participate in an arena dominated by men. But their gender still set them apart; their expertise translated into influence but not into real power. John B. Andrews and the AALL's various committees made all the most important strategic decisions for the organization. None of the AALL women served as a voting member on the Social Insurance Committee, even though Halsey often attended as a expert adviser. All three women were paid staff, rather than voluntary AALL members; hence all were employees of Andrews, and as female employees their work was often devalued. If historians have never given Halsey credit for her contribution to the health insurance legislation, neither did the male leaders of the AALL— Halsey even wrote correspondence to which Andrews signed his own name. And when Halsey's contribution *was* recognized, her gender led AALL opponents to call her expertise into question. Upon hearing of Halsey's reports on British health insurance, Frederick Hoffman sneered that they had been written by "some little girl."[73]

In other ways, however, the AALL women's gender gave them an advantage. They could draw upon their womanhood to reach out to the influential Progressive women's network in a way that male reformers could not. Female staff served as the AALL's liaisons to New York women's groups, moving easily between the AALL offices and organizations like the Consumers' League and the New York Maternity Center Association (Irene Andrews was a board member of the latter). Sylvester worked with upstate women's club leaders, many of whom were alumnae of Mount Holyoke and other women's colleges. Their subsequent familiarity with the issues facing women gave AALL women a kind of "female expertise" that led them to advocate legislation for women workers more passionately than did their male counterparts. Olga Halsey, Irene Sylvester, and Irene Andrews were staunch supporters of the maternity benefit provision of the health insurance bill, one of the most controversial parts of the legislation, and they would all invest greater effort than male AALL members in arguing for and defending maternity payments, to both women workers and the wives of insured men. While the AALL leadership did not turn a blind eye to women's concerns, only to its women experts were they ever a top priority.[74]

THE AALL AND INTEREST POLITICS

Throughout the health insurance campaign, the AALL exhibited a somewhat naive faith in the power of rational public discourse to sway the public. Unfortunately, the AALL's coolheaded language of expertise—or, as Kathryn Sklar puts it, "the association's determination to remain scientifically objective and above the political fray"[75]—was no match for the fiery rhetoric of its detractors. The distance between the AALL's rhetoric and methods and those of its opponents was glaringly obvious at the 1917 New York Senate Judiciary Committee hearings on the health insurance bill. In front of a standing-room-only crowd in the senate chamber, the AALL's opponents began a vociferous attack on health insurance. A parade of physicians admonished their colleagues to unite against the legislation that, they argued, would threaten their profession's autonomy and incomes. Two hours and twenty minutes later—forty minutes longer than the time allotted for opposing remarks—Dr. Eden Delphey rose and declared, "If I had the tongues of angels, could I speak with words of flame, it would not be sufficient to depict the iniquity and the insanity and the danger of the bill."[76] A shaken John B. Andrews then presented a careful, well-reasoned speech, followed by statistical testimony from public health and charity officials. The AALL was clearly unprepared for the bravado of its opponents, a deficiency that was not lost on the audience in the senate chamber. The leader of New York's AMM gloated over the AALL's lackluster performance in Albany. "Between you and me," Mark Daly wrote to another health insurance opponent, "don't you think they were absolutely flabbergasted by the intensity and strength of the opposition[?] I never in my life saw John Andrews so much at a loss."[77]

The AALL's weak performance in Albany highlighted the shortcomings of the reformers' political strategy in the health insurance campaign. Solid expertise and statistical backing had little effect in the face of such passionate opposition; as Kathryn Sklar points out in her analysis of the AALL, "Scientific objectivity, unaided, did not win political contests."[78] Yet the AALL was strongly opposed to involving itself in partisan politics and to mobilizing a constituency for its proposals. While the organization acknowledged the importance of political maneuvering by positioning its lobbyist Irene Sylvester in the State House, the AALL made no effort to involve ordinary citizens in its cause, or to engage in grassroots political strategies like petition campaigns or mass meetings. It was not the AALL but its allies in the labor movement and women's organizations who would eventually rise to the political and strategic challenges posed by the foes of health insurance.

Looking back on the 1915–20 health insurance campaign, the AALL's Isaac Rubinow concluded that the organization had not understood how many powerful group interests would be threatened by compulsory health insurance. A later historian agreed that Andrews and his colleagues "consistently underestimated the strength and resolve of their opponents."[79] Belated in its response to the criticism of physicians, the AALL was also unprepared for the assaults from conservative labor leaders, employers, and the commercial insurance industry. The reformers miscalculated the ability of diverse groups of opponents to unite in a passionate defense of their interests against the threat of compulsory health insurance. They also lacked a viable political strategy to combat the opposition. And the AALL could not have predicted how a world war and revolution in Russia would irrevocably shape the course of its crusade for health insurance.

3

A Dose of Prussianism

EUROPEAN ORIGINS AND
AMERICAN IDENTITIES

Throughout their crusade for compulsory health insurance, American reformers hailed the success of social insurance in Europe. The AALL's 1916 pamphlet, "The Need for Health Insurance in America," informed readers that the health of German workers had substantially improved since the introduction of "sickness insurance" in the 1880s. Social welfare measures had strengthened the German economy and, significantly, the German military: "Hundreds of thousands, now fighting on the field of battle for the fatherland, may trace their health and capacity to the timely and proper treatment received with the aid of sickness insurance."[1]

For American Progressives, the establishment of programs such as health insurance in many European countries set a convincing example for the United States to follow. The American Association of Labor Legislation used the models of the nascent British and German welfare states to convince politicians and the public of the need for similar legislation at home. Opponents of Progressive reform, however, turned the European example against its advocates, insisting that European welfare measures were not only unsuccessful but also un-American. While reformers saw America as a slower-moving partner of Europe in a transatlantic trend toward enlightened state intervention, their opponents declared that European social programs threatened American values. Because of the program's genesis in Europe, groups that opposed compulsory health insurance could portray it as an essentially foreign system, forcing supporters to defend their proposal's compatibility with the American way of life.

The propaganda of both advocates and opponents of health insurance embodies a struggle over the meaning of "Americanism" and American identity.[2]

"British Workman's Social Insurance Protection Compared with American Workman's. Which umbrella would *you* prefer on the inevitable 'rainy day'?" (*American Labor Legislation Review* [1910]; photograph courtesy of The University Library, University of Illinois at Chicago).

Conceptions of Americanism played an important part in the health insurance debate for several reasons. The AALL's campaign coincided with both the great immigration wave from eastern and southern Europe and the entrance of the United States into World War I, which led to widespread discussion of supposed racial and cultural differences between Europeans and Americans. Coinciding with the flowering of racial "science," concern with the difference of immigrants and foreign nations and the uniqueness of America became a central theme in discussions about the welfare state. As wartime sentiment gave rise to a hatred of anything German, the AALL's campaign also suffered because of compulsory health insurance's origins in Germany. And the health insurance campaign occurred at a time of heightened labor radicalism, when the American socialist movement was still a political force to be reckoned with. Even though the AALL's health insurance plan arose from the impulse to preserve capitalism by increasing workers' security, opponents were quick to label it socialistic. The fierce antiradicalism of the postwar Red Scare, which condemned social reform efforts as un-American and Bolshevik, dealt a stunning blow to health insurance.

But it was not just the timing and context of the campaign that left health insurance open to charges of un-Americanism. The nature of the proposal itself was also important. Compulsory health insurance *was* more "socialistic" than other reforms. It would tax workers and employers, replace much private and charity medicine with state-supervised physicians, and put most of the commercial insurance industry out of business. Health insurance, far more than other Progressive reforms like workmen's compensation and mothers' pensions, would directly affect the incomes and autonomy of powerful groups. These groups — employers, physicians, insurance companies, and organized labor — had a material stake in the outcome of the health insurance battle. The AALL's opponents found in the rhetoric of Americanism and antiradicalism a mighty weapon against health insurance that would allow them to define their own economic interests as central components of American identity.

This chapter describes the inspiration American reformers took from European social insurance systems, and the subsequent attempts of their opponents to label health insurance essentially foreign and un-American. Although this chapter concentrates on Americanism as an ideology and a rhetorical strategy, Americanist discourse was more than just words. It was closely related to the material interests of those who employed it, as following chapters will show. In addition, the rhetoric and ideology of Americanism would eventually achieve the power to manipulate not just public opinion but the political process itself.

AMERICAN INVESTIGATIONS OF EUROPEAN HEALTH INSURANCE

When the New York health insurance campaign began in 1915, ten European nations already had some form of compulsory insurance for workers' illness, most notably Germany and Great Britain.[3] The German health insurance system, the first in the world, was established by Chancellor Otto von Bismarck in 1883. The "Iron Chancellor's" pioneering social reforms, which included old-age pensions and accident and unemployment as well as health insurance, were critical to his project of national unification and the suppression of radicalism. Social insurance for Bismarck was the "bait" that would accompany the state's "whip" of repression against German socialism, for the reforms followed his banning of the Social Democratic Party. The German emperor summarized Bismarck's strategy in his opening speech to the 1881 Reichstag: "[T]he cure of social ills must be sought, not exclusively in the repression of Social-Democratic excesses, but simultaneously in the positive advancement of the working classes."[4] Despite its genesis in the highest levels of government, the German health insurance system was remarkably decentralized. Bismarck's program required all workers under a certain income, and their employers, to contribute jointly to a medical care and sick pay fund. Benefits were administered by local mutual funds organized by factory, occupation, or region; each fund was run by a board comprised of employers and workers. The state made no financial contribution at all; its only role was to supervise the funds.[5]

By 1911, the sickness insurance plan covered 77 percent of all German employees. While Germany's autocratic system made it difficult to gauge popular feelings with any accuracy, evidence emerged that most Germans, even those with major complaints against the system, had come to support compulsory sickness insurance.[6] Employers said that while a few workers abused the system by making false claims, sickness insurance benefited the employer through increased worker productivity. Insurance coverage, by relieving the worker of the dread of wage loss during illness, contributed to a "feeling of confidence [that] increases his productive power and his efficiency," according to one German industrialist.[7] The Social Democrats, who had bitterly opposed the law in 1883, became some of its staunchest supporters a decade later. The German labor movement, although its members paid a heavy share of the premiums, not only praised the system but also argued for its expansion.[8] German physicians, who threatened to strike because so many were excluded from practicing in local panels, won a significant victory in 1913 when their national organization was given a major voice in the administration of sickness insurance.[9]

In Britain, Chancellor of the Exchequer David Lloyd George proposed his national insurance plan after a brief visit to Germany in 1908. Influenced by an impoverished childhood, as a politician Lloyd George distinguished himself by his tax reforms, which attempted to address Britain's glaring economic inequalities. Alongside Lloyd George's sincere commitment to alleviating poverty, his Liberal Party also saw social insurance as a way to improve the physique and the efficiency of the British working class, to maintain the dominance of the empire, and to "make socialism less likely."[10]

When he announced his health insurance plan, Lloyd George described himself as "driving an ambulance wagon" to the rescue of British society. With the help of Winston Churchill and Sir William Beveridge, he persuaded the British Parliament to approve the National Insurance Act in 1911. The system that emerged differed from Germany's in several important respects. Unlike the German model, the state as well as the worker and employer contributed to the sickness insurance funds. And, because of pressure from Britain's large private insurance sector, including fraternal ("friendly") societies and commercial insurance companies, the system would be administered by "approved non-profit societies." (This was an important difference from the later American proposals, which would exclude private insurers from participation.)[11]

As in Germany, early skepticism of British national insurance was later replaced with general, if qualified, public support. Employers and labor complained about their compulsory contributions, and the medical profession threatened to sabotage the system by refusing to participate. But by 1919, a representative of the British Ministry of Health could write, "To those of us who have been associated with State Insurance from its commencement in 1912 and who can recall its unpopularity in the early days, the change in the attitude both of employers and workers is astonishing. I doubt if any one of us in 1912 was sanguine enough to suppose that such a complete revolution in public opinion could be accomplished in comparatively so short a time."[12]

The greatest change of heart was on the part of the British Medical Association (BMA). Even though Lloyd George had agreed to most of the medical profession's major demands, including free choice of doctor and the independence of physicians from friendly society governance, in 1911 the conservative leadership of the BMA collected over 27,000 signatures of doctors who threatened to boycott the system unless further concessions were made. But this rebellion was short-lived because general practitioners (the majority of the profession) who worked under National Insurance began reporting higher incomes, thanks to the regular payments they now received. Soon the rush of physicians to join the system turned into a "stampede."[13] In 1921, the secretary of the BMA reported that "I can confidently say that not one doctor in 1,000 who is doing National Health work would willingly go back to the old system."[14]

After the passage of the British National Insurance Act, American reformers began to cross the Atlantic to study health insurance. As historian Daniel T. Rodgers demonstrates, the makers of American social policy kept close watch on European developments, and American Progressives were enthusiastic participants in a transatlantic network of reformers.[15] The AALL's Isaac Rubinow published a book in 1913 titled *Social Insurance*, which included an evaluation of European insurance schemes and became the standard reference work on the subject. In 1914 Olga Halsey, who was living in Britain, accepted the AALL's assignment to write a comparative study of the German and British health insurance systems. Not surprisingly, AALL reformers used these reports to argue for the adoption of similar legislation in the United States. America, Rubinow complained, was "twenty-five years behind more progressive countries" in welfare-state development; there was "scarcely a country in Europe without some well-defined policy" for insuring workers against illness. And Halsey's report, which argued that the German model was more democratic and efficient than the British because it was decentralized and excluded private insurance carriers, was used as the basis for the AALL's 1915 model bill for health insurance.[16]

The European health insurance systems received some favorable attention from American publications. The Progressive journal *World's Work* was extremely critical of German social insurance because of its association with Bismarckian autocracy, but it published a rhapsodic account of Lloyd George's reforms in 1912, calling the chancellor "our contemporary George the Dragon Slayer" for fighting the "dragons" of poverty and ill health. Lloyd George's government was "remaking the conditions of human life in England—insuring a nation against sickness and two million workers against unemployment," and "realizing a vast scheme of social regeneration." The piece concluded, "Certainly America has much to learn from what has been done in the mother country."[17] The *Literary Digest* reported that "poverty is robbed at a single stroke of one of its worst terrors" by the British Insurance Act, and it quoted a London journal's praise of Lloyd George: "He makes laws as the Romans made roads—for all time."[18] The *Journal of the American Medical Association* (*JAMA*) reflected the initial reaction of American physicians to British health insurance, which was fairly positive. Although skeptical of the insurance act's "socialistic nature," *JAMA* reported that Lloyd George's measures were improving the health of the British working class and predicted that the adoption of similar legislation in the United States was inevitable.[19]

Although American Progressives looked eagerly to Germany and Britain for models, the creation of European health insurance systems offered little useful precedent for the reformer-initiated legislation advocated by the AALL. Unlike Europeans, American reformers could not agitate for nationwide social insurance because they were limited by the American federal structure to state-level campaigns.[20] Also, both British and German health insurance had been established by powerful political leaders, not by reformers. Germany's Bismarck imposed his system from above. In Britain, reformers and the labor movement were more active participants in democratic governance but Lloyd George still played the crucial role in the passage of health insurance. American politicians, on the other hand, were far behind reformers in their advocacy of social insurance. Although Theodore Roosevelt had expressed support for such legislation during his Progressive Party campaign, the only political leader to independently introduce health insurance legislation (actually, a resolution in favor of an investigatory commission) during the Progressive Era was the Socialist congressman Meyer London, whose efforts failed in the U.S. House of Representatives in 1916. Those elected officials who supported compulsory health insurance were followers of reformers rather than initiators of legislation. Governor Hiram Johnson of California and state senator Frederick Davenport of New York both wielded their influence to work for the adoption of the AALL's health insurance proposals, but they would give up the fight very quickly in the face of strong opposition. Most American politicians were either indifferent or actively hostile to social insurance initiatives. But the absence of political leadership did not dissuade the AALL from its belief that the United States would quickly follow the European example and adopt compulsory health insurance. AALL leaders believed that the activities of reformers like themselves would fill the leadership vacuum, that they could play the part of a Bismarck or a Lloyd George and lead the nation into a new era of enlightened social policy. It was not yet clear to them how quixotic those beliefs were.

Also, with the exception of the early response of the BMA, the European experience did not entail significant, sustained organized opposition to health insurance. Because most workers, reformers, businesses, and even physicians eventually rallied behind the German and British systems, Europe offered no model for the kind of interest-group opposition that would finally frustrate the AALL's campaign in the United States. Opposition from the commercial insurance industry, which would play such a huge role in New York, was barely a factor in Britain and Germany.[21] And American interest groups also had a uniquely powerful weapon in the form of ideologies of Americanism. Both Bismarck and Lloyd George had succeeded in portraying compulsory health insurance as a component of national greatness and racial uplift, and as an *alternative* to socialism. But in the United States, opponents of health insurance would portray the measure as essentially hostile to an American identity that precluded state involvement in business and in the lives of individuals. The ideological power of antistatist Americanism, wielded by materially powerful interest groups, made the American battle for health insurance inherently different from its European precedent. The reformers' inability to recognize this difference made their task even more formidable.

No sooner had American discussion of European health insurance begun than a barrage of negative reports on the implementation of the British Insurance Act appeared. A committee of the National Civic Federation released a study in 1914 claiming that national insurance had damaged the quality of medical care in England.[22] *JAMA*'s early support eroded, and American medical journals began to lament the "pauperization" of British physicians under the National Insurance Act. Not only physicians but also the recipients of British health insurance benefits were demoralized, according to insurance executive Frederick Hoffman. "The fine spirit of the English working classes, at one time the finest people of that type in the world, is gone, entirely gone" since the passage of the National Insurance Act made them dependent on the state, Hoffman lamented.[23]

The German system of "sickness insurance," according to health insurance opponents, was also a massive failure. Sickness and mortality rates remained high, and social insurance pauperized German workers and encouraged fraudulent claims for sick pay. Typical of opponents' anti-German rhetoric was a pamphlet produced by a New York insurance association denouncing Bismarckian social insurance as "Skillful Measures which Bind [workers] to the Soil as effectively as the serfs of the middle ages." The pamphlet went on to quote a former U.S. ambassador to Germany who claimed to have received letters from German workingmen "begging me for steerage fare to America" because "their insurance payments were so large that they could not save money out of their wages."[24] Compulsory health insurance, according to the leader of the New York State manufacturers' association, "has made of the working men and women of Germany . . . spineless creatures dominated by the will of an autocracy, their independence and initiative sapped."[25]

With opponents trumpeting the flaws, both real and imagined, of European health insurance, reformers soon found themselves on the defensive. It was true that German sickness rates had increased slightly since the introduction of health insurance, but the AALL argued that this was due to increased *reporting* of illness, and was thus an indication of the system's success.[26] Unable to assert that overseas health insurance systems were faultless, reformers instead underscored the popularity of social insurance among the European public despite its flaws. The AALL referred repeatedly to the BMA's and British employers' support for health insurance and circulated a statement from the British Manufacturers Association declaring, "We believe that in spite of many weaknesses in the organisation of this [National Insurance] Scheme, that in the main it is one which confers many benefits on the Assured, and we are convinced that any proposal to repeal the Act would meet with very considerable opposition." Most important, the admitted shortcomings of European health insurance did nothing to threaten its survival and expansion. Once a nation adopted social insurance, neither politicians nor the public seemed willing to return to the times of individual responsibility for sickness. "Already some dozens of countries in Europe have successfully instituted and maintained such health insurance," reported the *New York Herald* in 1916, "without in a single instance a confession of failure or abandonment of the effort to solve this serious problem."[27]

Conflicting interpretations of European health insurance went head to head in a clash between the National Civic Federation and the AALL's Olga Halsey. The NCF, an alliance of American employers and conservative labor leaders, condemned the British system in no uncertain terms, calling it inefficient and financially unsound.[28] Its 1914 report concluded that "the present impression [of compulsory health insurance] is most unfavorable, and the prospects are gloomy both for the taxpayers and [for] the insured." [29] Halsey, fresh from her studies of the British National Insurance Act, used the pages of the *American Labor Legislation Review* to refute the NCF's hostile report.

The NCF and Halsey relied on similar evidence to come to very different conclusions. Medical treatment under British National Insurance, according to the NCF, was "a *menace* to the health of the people" because the system of capitation, whereby doctors received payment based on the number of patients treated, led to hasty and slipshod service. "Worse than insufficient," the NCF continued, medical service in Britain was actually "*dangerous*." Halsey, in contrast, praised the medical provisions of the act. Capitation had almost doubled the income of British physicians, she wrote, attracting huge numbers of doctors to join the scheme; the resulting accessibility of treatment was leading to a "higher standard of medical care for the working man." [30]

Both Halsey and the NCF agreed that the British provided medical care and sick pay for the very poorest workers who needed relief the most. Halsey lauded the "diminution in pauperism . . . attributed to the insurance act." She cited figures demonstrating that relief payments and demands on charity funds had dramatically decreased in British urban centers since the introduction of national insurance. But, judging the same phenomenon, the NCF report lamented that the Insurance Act was "drying up the sources of private and voluntary relief" throughout Britain.[31]

The two reports also offered contrasting views of the effect of health insurance on the British character — and on British manhood. The NCF criticized the "possible lowering of the national character" occasioned by the Insurance Act. Health insurance, said the NCF report, compelled "large numbers of industrious and self-respecting workingmen to become wards of the State" and threatened "to destroy the virile elements" of the English personality. While the NCF equated receiving insurance benefits with "pauperization," Halsey retorted that health insurance eliminated pauperism and increased workers' self-respect. Reminding readers of England's "democratic and individualistic" nature, Halsey also suggested that the Insurance Act could be credited to the manliness of Lloyd George, whose "commanding leadership" had brought the act to fruition.[32]

Halsey conceded that the National Insurance Act had many flaws. She was particularly concerned about the failure of actuaries to correctly predict the rate of sickness, which meant that the insurance funds had to dip continually into their reserves to meet the demand for payments. But the system's drawbacks need not be a deterrent to developing health insurance legislation in the United States, Halsey insisted; indeed, the British experience obliged Americans to create an improved system. "If even a cumbersomely conceived plan of health insurance can improve health, decrease pauperism, and forge an effective weapon against tuberculosis," concluded Halsey, "are not we Americans challenged to devise a system which will function more perfectly in our war against poverty and disease?"[33]

But the NCF's report concluded that it would be disastrous for the United States to attempt to duplicate Britain's Insurance Act. Not only was the British system medically and financially unsound, but British conditions were too different from those in the United States to allow comparison. American workers were too well-off to require such a system, while in Britain "the poverty prevailing among the masses must be on a scale and at a depth unknown in the New World." According to the NCF, British workers were so low paid that the Insurance Act "is a boon to them," but prosperous American workers would reject similar assistance from the state. America was also exceptional in its racial diversity. The "race question" in the United States, argued the NCF report, thwarted the adoption of a national insurance system. Unlike Europe, with its racially homogeneous population, the United States had "three distinct levels of poverty—the level of the white native born, that of the immigrants, and that of the colored race—each associated with its own level of wages, opportunity, and industrial education." No national insurance system, said the NCF, could "possibly be adapted to these incongruous social elements."[34] Where European governments had called for "race preservation" to cement national unity and to bolster arguments for social insurance, the NCF used the United States' racial and cultural amalgam as a weapon against health insurance proposals.

As the health insurance debate in New York heated up, the authors of these dueling reports hastened to discredit each other. Halsey derided the composition of the NCF committee that had produced its study, which included an insurance executive, an employer, and a conservative labor leader. These men were already biased against health insurance, said Halsey, because of their "connections and preconceived ideas."[35] In Halsey's view, the business-oriented NCF was clearly incapable of producing a favorable report on legislation that would threaten the economic interests of its members. In turn, NCF member Frederick Hoffman doubted that Halsey, being a woman, could be a competent researcher. "[S]ome little girl goes over and comes back with a new wonderful report," Hoffman laughingly told a meeting of the NCF, yet the AALL expected its foreign investigations to be taken seriously. In addition to mocking Halsey's youth and her gender, Hoffman argued that it was the AALL's stance on health insurance, not the NCF's, that was rooted in self-interest; the reformers were "social idlers . . . who speculate in other peoples' interests at other peoples' expense" and who coveted positions for themselves in the administration of health insurance.[36]

THE USES OF AMERICANISM

The AALL's model bill incorporated aspects of both the British health insurance system and the German one. As in Britain, the plan required contributions from the state as well as from employers and workers. In other significant ways, however, the proposed system looked more like Germany's. AALL leaders thought the state administration of the British plan too centralized, and instead adopted the German model of administration through local mutual funds. They also rejected the British precedent of including commercial insurers and friendly or fraternal societies in the system. Olga Halsey argued that the private insurance societies were inefficient, making the administration of health insurance cumbersome and arbitrary.[37] These decisions led to political trouble for the AALL on two fronts: Rejecting the inclusion of insurance companies aroused the bitter enmity of American fraternal orders and the insurance industry, which faced elimination under the AALL's plan. And by incorporating so much of the German system, the reformers opened themselves up to charges of emulating the enemy. As *The New York Times* reported (with great understatement) in 1917, "It is not popular, just now, to go to Germany for models." [38]

Anti-German sentiment had been swelling in the United States since the outbreak of the First World War. Fear of a German American conspiracy to support the kaiser gave rise to a campaign for "One Hundred Percent Americanism," whose adherents called for the banning of German American organizations and German-language publications. Highly publicized examples of supposed disloyalty, such as the *Year-Book of the German-American for 1918*, which unfavorably compared "the dangers of Anglo-Saxon individualism with the blessings of German collectivism," convinced many individuals that the American way of life was under threat and that "there was something fundamentally wrong with the Teutonic soul." [39] Health insurance advocates faced the delicate task of pushing a German model while downplaying its origins.

It was not long before opponents linked compulsory health insurance to the hated Germans. Manufacturers, insurance companies, the American Federation of Labor, the National Civic Federation, and the American Medical Association joined forces to brand insurance proposals "Prussian" and "un-American." The New York Board of Trade blasted the AALL's bill, insisting that "the ultra-paternalistic insurance methods in vogue in European countries were not needed here." New York's superintendent of insurance declared that reformers were trying to "establish . . . in America the autocratic, imperialistic German system—the 'blood and iron' policy of Bismarck." AFL leader Samuel Gompers condemned the deduction of insurance payments from workers' paychecks as "too autocratic." An anti–health insurance pamphlet depicting the German kaiser with the caption "Made in Germany. Do you want it in California?" helped opponents defeat the West Coast health insurance campaign.[40]

In the face of the aspersions cast on their patriotism, insurance advocates adopted various strategies that attempted to reconcile their use of European models with American ideals. When it became clear that emphasis on the German system would damage their cause, supporters of health insurance played on the American public's pro-British sympathies. After the outbreak of war in Europe, Lloyd George was the most widely admired of foreign statesmen, and reformers used the example of the British system to argue that compulsory health insurance could happily coexist with capitalism and democracy. Irving Fisher of the AALL reminded Americans that health insurance thrived "in England, the most liberty loving of nations, the home of laissez-faire."[41] California governor Hiram Johnson acknowledged that health insurance originated in Germany, "but its conspicuous success has been in England and its most enthusiastic advocate has been the great democratic statesman of Great Britain—Lloyd George."[42] The *New York Globe* assured its readers, "Lloyd George . . . has been the chief exploiter of the idea of health insurance, and any dose of Prussianism that gets by his palate others may safely swallow."[43] Reformers expended considerable energy emphasizing the British origins of health insurance, but their reliance on the German model, and the context of wartime jingoism, still left them open to charges of "Prussianization."

Since they could not deny the European origins of their proposals, reformers turned instead to arguments that social insurance was compatible with, and would even strengthen, traditional tenets of Americanism. Compulsory health insurance, they insisted, could cater to the uniqueness of the American character. Liberty and individualism, for example, were central to American identity. But these ideals were undermined when an individual was threatened by sickness or disease. Frederick Davenport, one of the New York Senate sponsors of the health insurance bill, mocked his opponents' Americanist rhetoric, saying sarcastically, "Those persons who shed crocodile tears about the downfall of personal liberty through compulsory health insurance . . . are very amusing. The personal liberty of being sick without being well cared for—how precious it is!" Responding to accusations that health insurance would erode initiative,

Davenport thundered, "I can't think of individual initiative being developed in the suffering and agony of uncared for illness. I can't think of individual initiative being developed in a man who remembers at home he has a sick wife who isn't being well taken care of." [44] Sickness and economic insecurity, not health insurance, were the greater threats to personal liberty. In Davenport's view, health insurance would make Americans freer by relieving them of the fear of not being able to pay for medical care. With its guarantees of income protection and doctors' visits, health insurance would safeguard the essentials of the American character against the debilitating threat of ill health.

Health insurance advocates and their opponents clashed most frequently over the question of an increased role for the state in health care, and whether such intervention could be compatible with American values. A druggist who attacked health insurance in the pages of a pharmaceutical industry journal queried, "Is there any more reason for the State to sell health insurance or drugs or medical service than for it to sell shoes or groceries or clothing?" Compulsory health insurance, by involving the government in such transactions, was a clear manifestation of "Rank Socialism." [45] AALL supporter John A. Lapp countered that the objection to the state's role in health insurance "is an objection against government itself, that we cannot manage our own affairs through the State. I have greater confidence in our ability under democracy to solve our problems than that." [46] Rose Schneiderman of the Women's Trade Union League went even further; she argued for a definition of Americanism with state protection of working people at its center. Schneiderman, testifying in support of health insurance at a New York Assembly hearing, told her audience that "this country's greatness" could be measured by its commitment to improving the condition of its working people: "I say that it is highly American to take care of the people who work for you." [47]

Not all backers of health insurance, however, agreed on the desirability of state involvement. Frederick Davenport emphasized the decentralism of the health insurance proposal, which would keep the government's role to a minimum. The New York bill's "great strength," according to Senator Davenport, "is in the fact that the State has almost nothing whatever to do with it, but matters of health are discussed and administered and paid for in little mutual, democratic establishment, trade and community units," making the AALL's proposal "the very reverse of Prussianism." [48] The contrast between Lapp's, Schneiderman's, and Davenport's appraisals of the state reveals a fissure in the reformers' definition of Americanism and hence in their rhetorical strategy. Some tried to argue for an Americanism that left room for an expanded state role, while others accepted their opponents' interpretation of government as a menace to liberty and stressed the minimal involvement of the state in the health insurance plan. This confusion prevented a unified ideological stance on the part of reformers and left them more vulnerable to attack.

Health insurance supporters, then, were unable to agree on either a definition of Americanism or a coherent approach to defending their proposal's compatibility with the American way. Their opponents, on the other hand, seemed increasingly to speak in one voice as they denounced health insurance's foreign nature. Repeatedly, opponents argued that U.S. conditions differed too much from Europe's to allow application of either the German or the British model. The poverty and squalor wrought by industrialization were widely perceived as particularly European problems, and newspaper reports of industrial unrest overseas promoted, in Daniel Boorstin's words, a "vision of Europe where dissension, misery, and oppression were endemic — a natural antithesis to America."[49] Insurance proponents were forced to defend the very idea that the United States had grave industrial problems comparable to Europe's. Reformers struggled against notions of exceptionalism that defined the American economy as essentially different from, and superior to, that of other industrial nations.

America was exceptional, according to health insurance opponents, not simply for its wealth but for the liberty and independence of its working men. America's working classes were more dignified than Britain's or Germany's, and so neither needed nor desired state assistance. The New York Board of Trade's report condemning health insurance argued that only "the pauperized condition of the laboring and lower classes [in Europe]" made social insurance necessary.[50] The higher wages of the American workingman led to greater self-reliance. Compulsory health insurance was unwarranted, announced the NCF, "because the economic condition of the average American workman enables him to provide for medical attendance and pecuniary support during sickness in his own way and at his own cost."[51]

Ralph Easley, head of the NCF, was particularly incensed that Olga Halsey's reports on European health insurance were being used as a basis for the New York proposal when, in his mind, European conditions were irrelevant to American needs. In a long letter to Halsey, Easley condemned the AALL's equation of European and American conditions. Wages in the United States were dramatically higher than in Europe, he informed her, food and clothing were cheaper, and housing was larger and more plentiful. And the vast immigration from Europe to the United States, Easley concluded, "refutes completely any attempt to show that poverty exists in this country as in Europe." Halsey retorted that opponents of health insurance were blinded by Americanism. Her reply to Easley mocked the "false American pride which prevents our looking at the facts and discovering that here, as in England, there are large numbers of people who cannot make adequate provision for themselves."[52] For opponents, acknowledging the hardships faced by American workers not only would bolster arguments for health insurance but also would undermine their image of a prosperous America.

One of the most frequent arguments employed by opponents of the New York health plan was that social insurance was a product of the stratified European class system. America, they insisted, was a classless society. Social mobility in the United States, according to the AFL's J. W. Sullivan, prevented the creation of permanent economic classes. The American and the European, said Sullivan, "simply live in two different worlds. . . . The expectation of the poorest man here is that things will be better by and by," while Europeans never dreamed of escaping their class status.[53] Class, like compulsory health insurance, was a foreign import that threatened the American way of life. As Frederick Hoffman put it, "We have no labor class. We have a labor element but no class in which anyone is born and stays in it as in England and Germany." The imposition of health insurance would serve to divide Americans and create a "dependent" working class like Europe's, insisted Hoffman: "The moment you establish social insurance whereby a class can get free doctors from the state you will have a class different from the free and independent American we now know."[54] Even those opponents who acknowledged the existence of an American working class rejected any comparison with the European class system. The representative of a fiercely anti–health insurance fraternal order proclaimed, "An immense gulf separates our splendid laboring classes in the United States from the poverty-stricken, brow-beaten lower classes of Germany who so gratefully accepted the sop of social insurance thrown to them by the astute Bismarck."[55]

By emphasizing America's difference from Europe, and particularly its supposed lack of a class system, opponents of health insurance hoped to deflect positive reports of foreign social insurance and discredit reformers' invocation of the European example. They even contended that admirers of European social insurance exhibited questionable loyalty to their own nation. The National Fraternal Congress stated this most bluntly when it declared, "There should be but two classes in this Country—the American and the un-American."[56] The un-American, of course, were those who advocated compulsory health insurance.

Not only were European social programs unnecessary, according to opponents, but they were also a threat to the American character. Social insurance both created and was a product of peculiarities of the European nature against which Americanism could be defined. In the birthplace of health insurance, Germany, autocracy ruled over a populace pathetically dependent on the state. This view of the German character had wide currency. The magazine *World's Work*, for example, reported in 1913 that in Germany, the "land of super-orderliness," state paternalism was noticeably eroding "frugality, independence, efficiency, and initiative." Testifying before the Massachusetts Social Insurance Commission, an American physician who had practiced in Vienna explained the support of the Austrian medical profession for state insurance: "In the central powers, Germany and Austria, it is merely the question of obedience which is manifested in all walks of life." Samuel Gompers informed readers of the *American Federationist* that "[i]n the German people there is a spirit that results from training to recognize the sanctity of authority and acceptance of commands and regulations." He went on to contrast German obedience to the American traditions of liberty and independence: "This is far different from the spirit and the genius and the ideals of the American people. It is a difference of race psychology."[57] A coalition of manufacturers, physicians, and insurance companies known as the New York League for Americanism (NYLA), which would play a major role in the defeat of the AALL's proposal, described compulsory health insurance as a "*racial custom . . . fundamentally anti-American and not in harmony with our high ideals and free institutions.*"[58]

The perception of Germans as racially distinct from Americans was one weapon in the rhetorical arsenal against health insurance. Ironically, late-nineteenth-century racial science had claimed that democratic society had originated in Germany, making the Teutonic races superior to all others. With the outbreak of war in Europe, however, public discourse in the United States increasingly stressed German racial difference from other Anglo-Saxons.[59] Germans' supposedly distinct characteristics—militarism, obedience to authority, and, crucially, their embrace of a welfare state and compulsory health insurance—made them a unique, and uniquely abhorrent, race. With the image of a hostile and alien Germany looming large in the public mind, opponents of the welfare state promoted an Americanism that stood in stark contrast to German "racial" traits. For German American insurance executive Frederick Hoffman, the rejection of compulsory health insurance became a facet of his American identity.

THE CASE OF FREDERICK HOFFMAN

Frederick Ludwig Hoffman, NCF member and vice president at the Prudential Insurance Company of Newark, New Jersey, was also the author of the influential 1896 study *Race Traits and Tendencies of the American Negro*. Hoffman was a renowned medical statistician and pioneer in public health research, a president of the American Statistical Association and a founder of what later became the American Lung Association and the American Cancer Society.[60] Less remembered are his racial theories and his campaign against compulsory health insurance. Since he was a proponent of "racial science," a chief propagandist opposed to compulsory health insurance, *and* a German American, Hoffman's story reveals much about the connection of ideas about race and American identity to opposition to the emerging welfare state.

With *Race Traits and Tendencies* Hoffman had established himself as a foremost practitioner of scientific racism. His book, jammed with statistical tables, set out to offer numerical "proof" of African American racial weakness and inferiority. Hoffman emphasized excess mortality and incidence of tuberculosis and syphilis among blacks, calling African Americans a race in danger of "dying out with loathsome diseases" whose very existence posed a threat to the white race. In his conclusions, Hoffman discounted any social or cultural explanations for the hardships besetting American blacks, instead claiming explicitly that race was always determinative. "Given the same conditions of life for two races," he wrote, "the one of Aryan descent will prove the superior, solely on account of its ancient inheritance of virtue and transmitted qualities which are determining factors in the struggle for race supremacy."[61]

Throughout his career, Hoffman continued to argue that race was the elemental force shaping individuals and nations. "Race . . . is fundamental and not explained away by academic discussion," he wrote, "and the more the factor of race is considered as elementary to certain social and economic and political problems, the more likely it is that we shall arrive at safe and sound conclusions." Poverty, for example, could be explained by eugenic rather than social factors. The "poor derelicts on the scrap heap" that reformers often invoked in their arguments for health insurance, fumed Hoffman, "are in poverty, always have been in poverty, and that condition is congenital in many of them."[62]

Although his theories were vehemently opposed by prominent black leaders, most notably W. E. B. Du Bois, Hoffman's racial investigations elevated him to prominence in the field of statistics and his eventual appointment as a vice president of the Prudential Insurance Company.[63] At Prudential, he continued to analyze what he saw as inherent racial differences, using his statistical skills to compile mortality tables assessing the insurability of various races. Having devoted much of his career to scientifically "proving" that certain races were more prone to disease and high mortality rates, Hoffman's "expertise" was valued by an insurance industry that sought to eliminate poor risks for life insurance.

Starting in 1881, Prudential had reduced benefits to black policyholders paying the same premiums as whites due to "excessive mortality." Other insurance companies followed suit. When New Jersey, in response, passed antidiscrimination legislation in 1894, Prudential simply stopped selling policies to blacks. As Hoffman put it, "The Prudential Insurance Company to-day makes no effort to obtain colored risks at rates which it feels would be prejudicial to the business as a whole."[64] Prudential would not deny a policy to an African American who wanted one. Instead, the company actively penalized agents who signed up black clients. As a result of Prudential's efforts to eliminate black policyholders, by 1900, Hoffman wrote, "very little business of this class [blacks] is now written by Industrial companies, and practically none by the Prudential." The insurance industry used Hoffman's studies of racial difference to justify its discriminatory treatment of particular racial groups, Asians as well as blacks, and Hoffman continued to defend Prudential's exclusionary policies for the rest of his life.[65]

Beginning in 1915 Hoffman became preoccupied with a new crusade. Prudential gave Hoffman free rein to devote much of his time to fighting the compulsory health insurance campaign. In addition to extensive lecturing and working with various groups opposed to health insurance (see Chapter 5), Hoffman also made several trips to Europe, at Prudential's expense, to compile reports condemning European health insurance systems. Hoffman became the nation's single most active and influential opponent of compulsory health insurance. He explained his motivations: "In so far as our right to oppose compulsory health insurance was concerned, it was the duty of every American to oppose German ideas of government control and state socialism."[66]

Here, however, Hoffman faced a problem: he was himself of German origin, born in northern Germany, and had lived there until age nineteen. Hoffman knew that his patriotic credentials could be called into question by those who condemned German Americans as potentially disloyal and autocratic. With discussion of German difference so widespread, Frederick Hoffman was in danger of falling victim to the same discourse on racial determinism to which he had so significantly contributed.

Hoffman believed, however, that he could overcome his racial heritage, modify his German-ness, and become more fully American. Indeed, he had spent most of his life doing so. He noted in his memoirs that he had been "brought up in the German language and under the domineering influence of German minds" but through struggle and self-discipline was able to free himself "from intellectual serfdom." To do so he "absorbed . . . the best thoughts of the English race, modified by the American point of view." After his arrival in New York in 1884, Hoffman devoured American dime novels and Westerns, which he credited with strengthening his belief in rugged individualism.[67] He wrote poetry throughout his life, and in a poem reminiscing about his youth, he reflected on his early rejection of German identity:

I resented Prussian methods
that determined to enslave
My every aim and purpose,
From the cradle to the grave.

Hoffman titled his self-published poetry collections "Verses of a Wanderer," no doubt expressing his sense of rootlessness as an immigrant who so resoundingly denounced his heritage.[68]

For Hoffman, the surest path to Americanization lay in political activity. During the war, he proclaimed, "It is for Americans of German birth and ancestry to do even more than their required share in behalf of the national cause." In an article titled "On the Duty of Americans of German Birth," Hoffman called upon fellow German Americans to "square their conduct with their oath of allegiance and to prove themselves worthy of the priceless privilege of American citizenship in behalf of the cause of national defense against a foreign foe."[69] Hyphenated Americans should prove their loyalty with patriotic activity, and also by renouncing the cultural and political influence of their homelands. "I feel that the greatest hindrance to Americanization," wrote Hoffman, "is the reading of foreign-language newspapers. . . . It is lamentable to observe the deep and profound interest of foreigners in political affairs in their own country."[70] Hoffman's superpatriotism was so well publicized that he was approached by George Creel, head of the federal Committee on Public Information, to conduct an anti-German speaking tour "directed at the more or less disloyal remnant of German people in this country."[71]

Opposing compulsory health insurance became for Hoffman not just a defense of his employer but part of his denunciation of German culture.[72] To Hoffman, the drawbacks of compulsory health insurance in Germany confirmed the deficiencies of his homeland. In his widely circulated publications, including *Failure of German Compulsory Health Insurance* and *Facts and Fallacies of Compulsory Health Insurance*, Hoffman condemned German health insurance as autocratic "state socialism" and argued repeatedly that increased German sickness rates were due to worker malingering and shoddy medical service under the system. He attacked the AALL's health insurance plan as "in conformity to the one of Leipzig," and he blamed favorable reports on European health insurance on "the insidiousness of the German propaganda."[73] Hoffman's opposition to compulsory health insurance, as he described it, was "patriotic."[74] His zealous campaign against health insurance bolstered Hoffman's crusade for self-Americanization. His embrace of the tenets of private property and self-reliance meant that he had thrown off the shackles of his German heritage and was free to fight the threat of Prussianism embodied in proposals for social insurance.

Indeed, opposition to the welfare state played an important role in Hoffman's racial theories. "Inferior" races could redeem themselves to a certain extent, according to Hoffman, by spurning assistance from the government. State help was the greatest threat to racial soundness, weakening the genetic stock and leaving races unfit for Darwinian survival. Hoffman was particularly enamored of the example of American Indian tribes, who in his view were victims of "[t]he most subtle agency of all, governmental pauperism . . . [which] did what neither drink nor the poisons of venereal disease could do," bringing the Indian race to the brink of extinction. Charity or welfare would only worsen the condition of weaker races; Hoffman prescribed self-reliance and vigorous resistance to government encroachment as the only true path to racial uplift. In the case of African Americans, Hoffman admonished, "Instead of clamoring for aid and assistance from the white race the negro himself should sternly refuse every offer of direct intervention in his own evolution." [75]

But in the end, Hoffman would not grant other races the same malleability he reserved for his own German people. The determinative power of race meant that non-Aryans, no matter how earnest their desire for racial improvement, were strictly and permanently limited by their biology. Hoffman never rigorously applied his own brand of racial analysis to the question of German hereditary difference. But it is apparent from his writings that while he conceded Anglo-American intellectual and moral supremacy, Germans were still members of the Aryan "race" and thus superior to other racial groups. In Hoffman's view, since German Americans were white they were inherently capable of improving themselves by studying Anglo-American language and ideas, by vigorously supporting the war effort — and by rejecting compulsory health insurance.

WARTIME AMERICANISM

Many Progressives saw the entry of the United States into World War I in April of 1917 as an opportunity for an expanded state role. Irving Fisher of the AALL wrote in 1917, "The war has at last started us out of our Rip Van Winkle slumber, and we are now passing through a period of national self-examination." [76] The AALL immediately sought to capitalize on the chance to portray health insurance as part of the war effort, distributing 23,000 copies of its pamphlet "Labor Laws in Wartime" in 1917. The pamphlet warned against allowing wartime pressures to weaken existing labor legislation. Social legislation, reformers argued, was necessary not so much to protect workers as to insure industrial and military efficiency: according to the AALL, "Health insurance is in essence a preparedness measure."[77]

The military draft made public new data on the poor physical condition of inductees and raised fears of a decline in the quality of American manhood.[78] In rebuttal to Frederick Hoffman's attacks, reformers were quick to point out that the robust health and world-famous efficiency of German soldiers stemmed from their care under a system of state sickness insurance. "If some one wants to know why Germany is startling the world with her capacity for sustained fighting," Idaho's Republican senator William Borah wrote to the AALL, "let him look into the manner in which Germany has taken care, organized and made efficient her whole people for the last number of years."[79] Not only was the enemy strengthened by social insurance, but so too were the United States's formidable allies. New York labor leader James Lynch wondered whether opponents of compulsory insurance "realize or appreciate who are the soldiers that are to-day opposing the advance of the Hun, who are the soldiers that are attaining the fields of France with their life blood, who oppose the onward march of the Prussian . . . who but the wage earners of England who are under a health insurance act."[80]

U.S. engagement in the European war gave reformers the opportunity to compare American soldiers, who daily faced danger on the battlefield, to the nation's workers, who labored under the threat of injury and death on the factory floor. If the American public were to understand "that in this country the annual loss of death and lives among our industrial workers is not far behind that caused by the greatest war in history," stated a report of the U.S. Public Health Service, the adoption of health insurance would quickly follow.[81] Since success on the battlefield required "that the health and efficiency of the soldier actually in the war shall be conserved to the highest point," argued James Lynch, "why is it not true that the health of the industrial soldier in the trenches at home, in the factories, should also be conserved to the highest point[?]"[82] An AALL mailing asked New York politicians, "Why not celebrate the return of 'New York's 27th' by passing the 'Davenport-Donahue Health Insurance Bill'? Show the boys that you are as interested in their health as *workers* as you were as *fighters*."[83]

But with the triumph of the United States and its allies in 1918, opponents of health insurance gleefully attributed the German failure to Teutonic race and culture, including the Bismarckian welfare state. Some even went so far as to suggest that "Germany lost the war because she had Compulsory Health Insurance." "You have but to look at the fall of the Great German Empire," an insurance salesman warned, "to remind you, of what Paternalism has done."[84]

In return, reformers indignantly condemned their adversaries' exploitation of war hysteria. "It is with regret that we note the characterization of health insurance as 'Prussian' and 'socialistic,'" commented James Lynch, "because we realize this is simply an attempt to prejudice the minds of the people through the securing of space in newspapers for such sensational statements, obtaining prominence simply and solely because of the great war."[85]

But the war's end did not dim the patriotic rhetoric of health insurance's opponents. After the 1917 Russian Revolution, anti-German sentiment increasingly became conflated with the newest threats to Americanism: Bolshevism and domestic radicalism. Frederick Hoffman was as zealous a hater of Bolshevism as he was an enemy of Bismarckian autocracy. He concluded one of his overseas investigations with the observation that in Britain, "Bolshevism was directly incurred by National Health Insurance" because it made workers dependent on the state. Health insurance opponents' propaganda simultaneously invoked anti-German and anti-Bolshevik fears. "Behind this bill is an organization called the American Association for Labor Legislation," trumpeted an oft-quoted pamphlet of the anti–health insurance Professional Guild of Kings County, "MADE IN GERMANY as a part of the Infamous Kultur and imported to this country by a Russian disciple of Bolshevism and I WON'T WORK-ISM"[86] (the latter accusation likely referred to AALL member Isaac Rubinow's socialist and immigrant background). The strongly conservative leader of a women's fraternal society also accused reformers of the twin crimes of Prussianism and Bolshevism, declaring that the health insurance proposal "strikes at the very roots of our State and National institutions. For it is a well-known fact that the plan of Compulsory Health Insurance was conceived in Socialism [and] born in Germany."[87] Bismarck's original intent in creating social insurance—to take the wind out of radicalism's sails—was entirely disregarded as opponents equated health insurance and socialism. Whether Prussian or Bolshevik, autocratic or socialistic, compulsory health insurance, opponents inevitably concluded, was essentially un-American.

The diverse and often contradictory arguments of health insurance opponents made their patriotic rhetoric appear highly irrational in the eyes of AALL reformers. As a result, the backers of health insurance initially did not take Americanist arguments very seriously. Reformers ridiculed the opposition's overblown nationalism—one AALL pamphlet mocked that "the characterization of health insurance as Prussian or Bolshevist was invented by certain people who feared that their own patriotism needed advertising"[88]—but spent little effort putting forth their own beliefs about Americanism. The AALL was generally uncomfortable arguing on any grounds other than rationality and efficiency, and passionate debates over national identity certainly fell outside these boundaries. In the volatile political atmosphere wrought by war and revolution in Europe and civil unrest at home, the AALL's own rationalism left it at a rhetorical disadvantage. The AALL did not rise to the challenge of fighting explicitly for a definition of Americanism that could encompass compulsory health insurance.

Reformers instead dismissed Americanism as a smokescreen for the material interests of their opponents. Health insurance supporter Rose Schneiderman said of those who called reforms "Socialistic" or "pro-German," "These gentlemen will oppose anything that will spell progress for the worker, which will touch their pocket. . . . Whenever anything is introduced that means welfare for the great majority of people they are always here calling upon the flag." [89] Schneiderman was absolutely correct in her assessment of the economic motives of her opponents. But Americanism was not *just* a smokescreen. For opponents of health insurance, their definition of Americanism was inseparable from the defense of private medicine and private property, as subsequent chapters will show. Reformers also misunderstood the force of Americanism itself. In a time of war and the Red Scare, assertions of American exceptionalism would carry not just emotional but also political power.

4

The Worst Insult to
the Greatest Profession

MEDICAL PRACTITIONERS
AND HEALTH INSURANCE

At the beginning of their campaign, reformers were optimistic about the attitude of the providers of medical care toward compulsory health insurance. Both the American Medical Association's journal and its president praised health insurance in 1916 as "a great movement" and "the next step in social legislation."[1] Public health physicians and nurses' organizations spoke out in favor of the plan. When the Medical Society of the State of New York approved the principle of compulsory health insurance that same year, the American Association for Labor Legislation seemed to have captured doctors' support for its bill.

But just one year later, the health insurance campaign was overwhelmed by a deluge of opposition from the smaller county medical societies throughout New York. Furious local doctors forced the state medical society to rescind its favorable resolution, and physicians emerged as the most frequent and vocal spokesmen against health insurance at Albany hearings and in the press. The swelling of grassroots opposition among the profession, in New York and elsewhere, led the AMA to make an about-face and condemn health insurance by 1920.[2] The medical profession's journey from cautious support to outspoken denunciation shows how a profession defined and then defended its own interests in response to the challenge of health insurance. Most doctors came to see the plan as a threat to their incomes and autonomy, interests that were often inseparable in their minds. The medical profession then defined these interests as tenets of true Americanism. And the health insurance campaign spurred physicians to unveil another rhetorical strategy, one that they would employ throughout the rest of the century: the argument that government intervention in physicians' autonomy and incomes would lead to a reduction in the quality of medical care.

The AALL's model bill for health insurance, although clearly stating that "medical service, supplies, necessary nursing and hospital care" would be included, deliberately left out any specific provisions for the organization of medical service or the payment of doctors under health insurance. The three physicians on the Social Insurance Committee—S. S. Goldwater, Alexander Lambert, and I. M. Rubinow—and the one nurse, Lillian Wald, agreed to postpone deciding on the medical profession's role in the system until the AALL had gathered a larger sample of medical opinion on health insurance.[3] The AALL believed that omitting medical provisions from its bill would allow for the greatest possible participation of physicians in later drafts. The support of the medical profession was critical for the success of health insurance, and AALL staffers knew it would not be easy to secure. Doctors had been left out of the framing of workmen's compensation laws, and many were none too pleased with what they saw as their subordinate status in the compensation system.[4] In Britain, physicians had nearly derailed Lloyd George's plans by threatening to withhold their services under the new National Insurance Act. However, the British Medical Association's eventual capitulation led the AALL to believe that American physicians, too, would come to see the benefits of health insurance, especially if they were given a prominent role in the formulation of the plan.

As Ronald Numbers and Gary Land demonstrate, American physicians had been discussing European health insurance in their journals for a number of years, and most coverage was guardedly positive. The *Journal of the American Medical Association* (*JAMA*), for example, carried reports that "physicians were benefitting financially" under British national insurance, even though the system's impact on the quality of medical care was mixed (encouraging malingering and hasty treatment, but increasing working-class access to "proper medical care").[5] The strongest message sent by the medical journals before 1917 was that the United States would inexorably follow Europe in adopting a health insurance system. Physicians were advised not to oppose the inevitable but to "make themselves heard" and to cooperate with reformers and legislators in formulating a plan for health insurance.[6]

Physicians' perceptions of the inevitability of health insurance sprang not just from the existence of European precedents, but from the context of rapid changes in American medical practice during the first two decades of the twentieth century. The prestige of the medical profession was growing significantly because of the rising standards for medical education, as well as the increased public faith in the power of medical science to cure disease and prolong life. The closing of for-profit medical schools, stricter licensing requirements, and attacks on eclectic and homeopathic physicians drastically reduced the number of American medical practitioners throughout the 1910s.[7] At the same time, the AMA consolidated its role as the preeminent national organization for physicians, unifying the medical profession as never before.

But doctors' economic position was still far from secure. Poorly compensated general practitioners felt threatened by competition from growing numbers of specialists, public health physicians, visiting nurses, fraternal society and contract doctors, and dispensaries. The medical profession also faced a widening gulf between the growing demand for medical care and the public's ability to pay for it. Fewer physicians, more specialists, and medical advances were leading to significantly higher medical costs. As a result, immigrants, workers, and the urban and rural poor — among those most in need of medical care — found doctors' fees increasingly out of their reach. These rapid medical and economic changes encouraged leaders of the profession to argue that some form of reorganization of medical practice was inevitable.[8]

One of the strongest advocates of this position was Frederick R. Green, head of the AMA's Council on Health and Public Instruction. Author of many *JAMA* articles on health insurance, Green wrote in 1915 of "the certainty that such laws will be enacted within a few years." Ronald Numbers points out that Green had a long-standing friendship with John B. Andrews, which undoubtedly contributed to the AMA official's eagerness to publicize the AALL's health insurance bill. In early 1916 Green persuaded the AMA to create its own committee on social insurance to study the issue, and to hire the AALL's I. M. Rubinow as executive secretary. When this new AMA committee opened an office "in the same building that housed the AALL," physician cooperation with the AALL seemed assured.[9]

PHYSICIANS FOR HEALTH INSURANCE

One reason the AALL was unprepared for the later opposition of physicians was because the doctors with whom they worked most closely had little in common with the upstate practitioners who would come to dominate the debate. The three physicians on the AALL's Social Insurance Committee represented the most zealously Progressive wing of their profession. Dr. Alexander Lambert was head of the AMA's Judicial Council, a clinical professor of medicine at Cornell, and a close friend of Theodore Roosevelt. Dr. S. S. Goldwater, a major figure in urban public health, had been New York City's commissioner of health, the assistant superintendent of Mount Sinai Hospital, and the president of the American Hospital Association. And Dr. Isaac Rubinow was an outspoken socialist and no longer a practicing physician.[10] Although Lambert would eventually reverse his position on health insurance as president of the AMA, the AALL could count on Goldwater and Rubinow's active support throughout the campaign.

Rubinow later suggested that the health insurance debate divided physicians into two camps: "institutional" physicians, or those in public health, university teaching, and hospital work, who supported health insurance, and local general practitioners, who opposed it.[11] While this is too sharp a dichotomy, there was a definite association between a public health orientation and support of health insurance. New York City, a center of public health activity, was home to many physicians who believed strongly in government's duty to distribute the advantages of medical progress. As Goldwater put it, compulsory health insurance was the only way for working people to enjoy the benefits of medical science. "Civilization cannot get along without" medical care, said Goldwater, but "it is as clear as day that the workers are not getting any such service today and that they cannot afford to purchase it out of their own resources." Dr. B. S. Warren of the U.S. Public Health Service thought that health insurance "would prove to be the greatest public health measure ever enacted" because it would "place adequate medical relief within the reach of all."[12]

The massive expansion of public health activities in New York City during the first two decades of the twentieth century had given rise to new thinking about the role of the state in national health. Dr. Samuel Kopetzky of the state medical society reflected these views when he argued on behalf of health insurance: "The health and happiness of its citizens is properly the care of the State and the act provides the means for this care." Many public health measures in use in New York already involved a great deal of state involvement and even compulsion, including physical examination of schoolchildren, compulsory reporting of infectious disease, and compulsory vaccination. Kopetzky argued that compulsion was an essential element of many institutions that benefited the public: "If [health insurance] is un-American because it is compulsory," he said, "then compulsory education, compulsory vaccination, compulsory income tax are all, also, un-American."[13] Public health physicians' comfort with state involvement in medical care helps explain why so many of their profession supported compulsory health insurance. Haven Emerson, Goldwater's successor as commissioner of the New York City Department of Health, endorsed health insurance, as did the Public Health Committee of the New York Academy of Medicine. Numerous officials of the American Public Health Association and the U.S. Public Health Service, many state public health officers, and the *American Journal of Public Health* all supported the AALL's proposal.[14] In addition to their commitment to expanding access to medical care, some public health officials thought that health insurance would be a boost to their profession because of the possibility of utilizing existing public health agencies in the administration of the plan.[15] Public health physicians may also have approved of health insurance because, unlike private practitioners, they were accustomed to working for salaries rather than fee-for-service and so were not threatened by possible changes in physician payment under health insurance.

Like Goldwater, some superintendents of major hospitals spoke out in favor of health insurance. The reason for their support was straightforward: the bill would provide hospitalization benefits to all the insured and so add greatly to hospital revenues. These funds were badly needed because hospitals provided so much uncompensated care to the poor. "[U]nder Health Insurance," hospital administrator John Lapp told a 1918 meeting of the American Hospital Association, for the first time "hospitals should receive enough to cover their total cost." Hospital leaders argued that the flow of insurance money would be to the public's benefit as well as hospitals'. As Thomas Howell, superintendent of New York Hospital, put it, "Health insurance will supply funds from which to improve and expand hospital services."[16]

Industrial medicine was a growing branch of public health work, and many industrial physicians—M.D.s who specialized in treating industrial workers and studying industrial disease—could be counted among the supporters of health insurance. Industrial physicians already had experience with reorganized medical services, and some found in this experience a solid argument for social insurance. A doctor for the Pennsylvania Railroad Company argued that company medical practice was a good precedent for compulsory health insurance: "The service that has been rendered these men by the large corporations is a proof that people are able by [prepaid health plans] to take care of their families during sickness."[17] Industrial physicians' familiarity with the health and income problems facing workers led some, like Utah physician C. E. McDermid, to see compulsory health insurance as essential. Dr. McDermid had been a private physician before turning to industrial practice. As the physician for a mining company with a health plan, McDermid concluded that workers' health benefited considerably from access to medical care. His "experience as an industrial surgeon" led him to believe there was "a crying need of [health insurance] legislation."[18] Alice Hamilton, one of the founders of the field of industrial medicine, was also a supporter of the AALL's plan. Hamilton thought that since workmen's compensation laws could never be extended enough to "cover all of the occupational diseases," only compulsory health insurance would force employers to reduce disease hazards in the workplace.[19]

Industrial physicians' experience with many aspects of reorganized medical service included salaries rather than fee-for-service payment and the exchange of professional autonomy for financial security. As a result, some of them had different conceptions of the role of the medical profession than did private doctors. The Pennsylvania Railroad physician felt that his private-practice colleagues' opposition to health insurance was based in greed: "It looks to me as though the doctors have chosen the wrong profession from which to make a living. It looks as if the whole thought were to protect the doctor and not to protect the public."[20] Not all industrial physicians, however, were so oriented toward public service, nor did they look so kindly upon compulsory health insurance. Since many were employed directly by companies, loyalty to those who paid their salary led them to oppose the AALL's plan. One industrial physician, for example, conducted a study of company-sponsored health care for a major employers' group that was intended to discredit arguments for health insurance.[21] Several company doctors spoke against health insurance at the 1920 meeting of the Conference of Industrial Physicians and Surgeons. As Christopher Sellers notes in his history of industrial medicine, industrial physicians' allegiance to their employers could preclude a commitment to workers or to broader social concerns. This diversity of opinion among such physicians may have contributed to the American Association of Industrial Physicians and Surgeons' refusal to take a stand on health insurance.[22]

Since two of the best-known women doctors of the time — Alice Hamilton and S. Josephine Baker, of the New York City Bureau of Child Hygiene — supported health insurance, it would be tempting to suggest that their gender might have led female practitioners to embrace the AALL's plan. As Regina Morantz-Sanchez argues, women physicians tended to be far more social-minded than their male colleagues.[23] However, this did not hold true in the case of health insurance. While the American Medical Women's Association, the preeminent national organization for women doctors, did not appear to take a position on health insurance, the Woman's Medical Society of the State of New York was decidedly opposed. The society's legislative committee said of health insurance in 1919, "[This] committee not only did not endorse this bill, but actively opposed it. . . . The bill is a long step toward State Socialism." In the absence of any further discussion of the issue in the *Woman's Medical Journal*, it is possible only to speculate on the reasons for the New York women's opposition. The Women's Medical Society represented private physicians with less of a public health orientation than Hamilton and Baker. As a result, the society's anti–health insurance statement mirrored the values of male-dominated private medicine. Rather than setting out an independent women's position, the legislative committee simply quoted the male president of the Medical Society of the State of New York, who said that doctors' "means of livelihood [would be] largely confiscated and their incomes greatly reduced" under the AALL's plan.[24] Like their male counterparts, women physicians' public health or private practice orientation influenced their stand on health insurance.

Women practitioners and their medical societies were devoted to eliminating gender discrimination in the medical profession, and this too may have eclipsed their concern with social insurance. Legislation that did not specifically attack male dominance of the medical field was of little interest to women doctors besieged by a quota system and pervasive discrimination. It could even have posed a threat to them. Dr. Alice M. Johnson, a Columbus, Ohio, physician, reflected women doctors' priorities when she declared at the AALL's 1917 annual meeting, "[U]nless you put in this [health insurance] bill something about there being no discrimination against women physicians they will be utterly annihilated in Ohio. . . . Unless they are guaranteed the same rights as other physicians they will be excluded from service under health insurance." Alexander Lambert replied that physicians would all have equal rights to join the system, but this reassurance clearly fell short of the specific antidiscrimination wording that Johnson demanded for women doctors.[25]

The overwhelming importance of discrimination also partly explains the lack of interest shown by African American physicians in health insurance. There was not one mention of the AALL's plan in the *Journal of the National Medical Association*, the black physicians' journal, for the entire period of the health insurance campaign. The AALL's neglect of blacks' concerns, of course, and its failure to approach the National Medical Association (NMA) or any of its representatives, must bear the brunt of the blame for this (see Chapter 2). But it is also possible that African American physicians' concern with race discrimination precluded any interest in health insurance legislation. The NMA's *Journal* was far from apolitical, and it took a strong stance against Jim Crow laws and against discriminatory barriers within the medical profession even as it ignored social insurance. Also, their disfranchisement led African Americans to concentrate on creating their own mutualistic health and welfare institutions rather than advocating state involvement, at least until the New Deal era.[26] Fighting racism continued to be the NMA's priority throughout the century. (African American doctors' silence on health insurance was not permanent, however. In the 1960s, the NMA would become a consistent supporter of Medicare and universal health insurance.[27])

NURSES AND COMPULSORY HEALTH INSURANCE

With much of their attention focused on converting doctors, reformers took little notice of another group of medical professionals: nurses. The nursing profession seemed favorably disposed toward health insurance, especially since the American Nurses' Association (ANA) endorsed the AALL's plan in 1916. Renowned nurse and reformer Lillian Wald, who sat on the AALL's Social Insurance Committee, thought that nurses were ideally poised to prepare the citizenry for health insurance. Unlike most physicians, many New York nurses already had worked under a kind of insurance system, namely the visiting nurse service of the Metropolitan Life Insurance Company, which had existed since 1909. Wald told her fellow nurses that families holding Metropolitan policies were becoming accustomed to the idea of insurance coverage that included nursing, and "the public has a right to expect that out of the actual, practical experience of the nurse some important social insurance plans will be perfected."[28] For a while it seemed that nurses might provide the AALL with an important source of support. Labor leader Pauline Newman told a convention of nurses in 1916 that she had "yet to hear that nurses are opposed" to health insurance, "and there may be a good reason for that. You know conditions because you . . . come in contact with [working people], you are doers and not observers only."[29]

As Newman and Wald pointed out, nurses' work often brought them into close proximity with the poor and led them to a sharp awareness of inequities in medical care. Nurses, said Boston nursing leader Mary Beard, "have felt so very personally and so very keenly the need that comes to the families they nurse when there is sickness." She and many other nurses supported compulsory health insurance, Beard testified, since many of their patients "are unable to pay for the care they get . . . because there is not any money out of the low wages earned to pay for the care of the sickness that comes to the family. This we see every day and all the time."[30] The head of Chicago's visiting nurse association wrote to John B. Andrews that she was "very much interested in this question of health insurance" since the "vast majority" of her patients made under the $1,200 a year that would make them eligible. Health insurance, said the nurse, "can't come any too quickly in Illinois or elsewhere, to please me."[31]

At least one nurse with experience among the poor even thought the bill did not go far enough. At the 1918 annual meeting of the New York State Nurses' Association (NYSNA), a nurse named Miss Quinlan criticized the health insurance proposal because "farmers and servant girls . . . are not even considered in it." One of the very few participants in the health insurance debate ever to object to—or even mention—the exclusion of agricultural and domestic workers, this nurse argued that her profession had a special interest in such groups because so much nursing work was concentrated in medically underserved rural areas. "Now, with all the work that is expected of the nurses in the rural communities," continued Quinlan, "I think [it] would be of vital interest that these two classes be protected."[32] Her comment—ignored by both the nurses' association and the AALL—highlights how nurses' responses to the health insurance proposal were rooted in circumstances particular to their profession. Nurses' low pay made their services more affordable than those of physicians, and nurses were often the only medical practitioners in remote areas.[33]

In 1916, a joint committee of nurses appointed by the ANA endorsed the AALL's health insurance bill. These nurses were especially pleased that the legislation included nursing for the insured, because it meant that compulsory health insurance would increase the demand for their services.[34] One member of the ANA committee, nurse Martha M. Russell, told her colleagues that "the passage of [health insurance] laws opens a wide opportunity for us to nurse many persons whom we have been unable to reach. . . . The private duty nurse will find that her work will ultimately be increased."[35] The AALL's Miles Dawson agreed, advising a meeting of New York nurses that compulsory health insurance would "very greatly increase the use of trained nurses both in hospitals and out of them, and . . . enlarge the visiting nurse system enormously."[36]

Although compulsory health insurance would provide the insured with the services of both physicians and nurses, in some ways the legislation treated nurses differently from doctors. The position of the nursing profession under health insurance was unique, since its members were the only group that would be both practitioners *and* beneficiaries. Physicians were defined as professionals in the bill and hence would not be covered by the insurance, while nurses were treated as workers eligible for coverage. There was a good reason for this: like the low-income people they cared for, nurses found it difficult to pay for their own medical treatment. The financial position of most women in the nursing profession was as precarious as that of industrial workers. Noting that health insurance would automatically include a majority (if not all) of the nursing profession, those who "earn habitually less than $1,200 a year," *The American Journal of Nursing* endorsed the AALL's plan in its editorial pages. "We know of no group of people who are more entitled to such aid than nurses," continued the journal, for "their work is for the health of the community, and . . . we believe that all public health workers whose salaries are inadequate should be beneficiaries."[37]

Like industrial workers, nurses lost income when they became ill. Also, nurses faced a greater risk of illness than the general public because of their close contact with the sick. The ANA established a relief fund to assist nurses who succumbed to illness. This fund paid a small cash sickness benefit and in a few states endowed hospital rooms, but it was inadequate to meet the need among the ANA's members. In a plea for contributions at a meeting of the NYSNA, one nurse said that the relief fund "cannot do as much as they would like." In 1916 the fund was assisting six nurses, "getting very little, some five, six, fifteen dollars a month, but that little stands between them and actual privation, difficulty and distress."[38] Financially strapped, organized nurses could not provide the benefits that their constituency required, and compulsory health insurance would relieve them of this burden.

The nursing profession officially endorsed compulsory health insurance, and nurses had many reasons to support the legislation. Yet nurses actually did little to push for passage of the bill. The timing of the campaign partly accounts for nurses' lack of active support. During the years of the health insurance agitation, both the ANA and the NYSNA were primarily concerned with professionalization issues, especially the passage of the Nurses' Practice Acts, which would set minimum educational requirements for nurses.[39] The struggle for professionalization in the face of many obstacles, including the resistance of physicians and politicians, absorbed most of the nurses' time and energy, leaving little room for consideration of health insurance. With a Nurses' Practice Act in front of the New York Assembly during the same years as the health insurance bills, organized nurses chose to prioritize their own legislation over the AALL's.[40]

But the AALL's neglect of their concerns must share the blame for nurses' lack of enthusiasm. The nursing profession has fought an uphill battle for recognition and respect, and its relationship with the AALL was no exception. Although Lillian Wald was on its Social Insurance Committee, the AALL did not consult a single nurses' association during the drafting of the New York bill. To make matters worse, the AALL refused to put a nursing representative on the commission that would oversee the health insurance system. When Mary Beard asked the AALL to add a nurse to the commission since physicians, employers, and workers would all be represented, she was quickly rebuffed. "A nurse on the Commission is considered undesirable," replied the Social Insurance Committee, "because it would overload the Commission with representatives of other interests [and so] would not be an efficient administrative body."[41] Since physicians were to be prominently represented on the commission, the AALL sent the message that doctors were the backbone of its health insurance system, while nurses were to be pushed to the margins. The reformers showed little awareness that nurses played a crucial role not just in patient care but also in medical decision making.

Nurses were also deeply offended when the AALL decided to allow the service of "attendants," or nurses' aides, as part of health insurance coverage. This was a direct blow to nurses' professionalization struggle. The provision prompted an angry letter from the head of the New York State Organization for Public Health Nursing, who asked Andrews, "Do you consider it just or right that the registered nurse, who at the beginning of her nursing training must have an efficient preliminary education, spend three years in a hospital, after that take a post-graduate course in Public Health Work, be put on the same footing as the woman who is called an attendant, who has only had two or three months practical work?"[42] The AALL's reply to this and other complaints was that because attendants were trained and would only work under the supervision of a registered nurse, it was "undesirable to restrict nursing under health insurance to registered nurses."[43]

Health insurance also seemed a threat to nurses' professionalization because of its definition of nurses as workers eligible for coverage. Even though many nurses thought this coverage could only benefit their colleagues, some were angered that the bill treated nurses as wage earners rather than as professionals. One nursing leader wrote to Andrews that "nurses in general would very much dislike to be included in any such measure which did not apply equally to physicians, dentists and teachers." The AALL seemed to consistently treat doctors with more respect than nurses. New York State Nurses' Association activist Beatrice Stevenson noted that the AALL's bill referred to physicians' medical societies by their correct titles, but the NYSNA was simply called "A State Nurses' Association. . . . [I]t seems to me that we should be entitled to that same recognition given the doctors' professional guilds," she complained. This sort of omission on the part of the AALL did not give nurses confidence that their professionalization concerns would be addressed by the health insurance bill.[44]

Given the strong sentiment in favor of health insurance among nurses, they may have worked for health insurance more actively had the drafters of the bill shown more sensitivity to their professional concerns and taken better advantage of their support. But the AALL made no effort either to organize the nursing profession or to ask for its assistance in working out the details of the bill. It seems that the AALL simply did not perceive nurses as medical professionals deserving the same consideration as physicians. AALL leaders could court voluntary women's groups as authorities on social welfare, but they fell short of seeing nurses as authorities on medical matters. The result was neglect of the nursing profession. No AALL staff member approached nursing organizations until 1919, when Miles Dawson made his speech at the NYSNA annual meeting. Lillian Wald, despite her early involvement, stopped actively supporting the health insurance campaign by 1920, possibly reflecting her disillusionment with the reformers (or at least the AALL's failure to court her continuing participation.)[45] The AALL was too obsessed with winning over another group of practitioners—the physicians—to notice that by taking nurses for granted, they were alienating a natural constituency.

THE RISE OF MEDICAL OPPOSITION

In 1916, the Medical Society of the State of New York, representing doctors throughout the state, agreed to work closely with the AALL in drafting the medical provisions of the health insurance bill. By the end of the year, physicians and reformers were able come to an agreement on the organization of medical service under health insurance. The AALL and the Medical Society decided that all New York physicians would be eligible to join panels from which the insured would have free choice of physician. In turn, physicians would have the "right to refuse patients." The agreement stipulated a maximum of five hundred insured families or one thousand individuals for each panel physician. These provisions met several major concerns of the medical profession, which had criticized European panel systems for forcing doctors to treat too many patients, and which also feared that health insurance would end free choice for both patient and physician. Physicians' apprehensions about patients' malingering and insurance commissioners' abuses of power were addressed by plans to appoint salaried medical officers to supervise insurance claimants and to ensure strong representation for doctors on the New York health insurance commission.[46]

On the issue of physician payment, however, there was only conflict. Physicians demanded a fee-for-service system, but the AALL deemed this too expensive and — crucial to the reformers' vision of efficiency — too unpredictable. Instead, the AALL preferred the British method known as capitation, or payment based on the number of patients treated. Many physicians have historically disliked capitation because they would not be compensated for each service they performed; as New York City physician Dr. Eden Delphey asked, "Should not the patient pay more if he gets more?" Rather than bowing entirely to physician demands, the AALL agreed to a compromise that included both capitation and a modified fee-for-service system. This seemed to be enough for the council of the state medical society, which in December 1916 officially endorsed the medical provisions of the health insurance bill, giving the AALL the ostensible "support of the most powerful and influential medical organization in the state."[47]

However, as Ronald Numbers shows, rather than encouraging further physician support, the state medical society's endorsement opened the floodgates of opposition. It was one thing for well-informed urban medical leaders to endorse health insurance, but capturing the allegiance of New York's rank-and-file practitioners was another matter. In the winter of 1917, dozens of upstate medical societies passed strongly worded and virtually unanimous resolutions against compulsory health insurance. Seemingly in succession, doctors from the counties of Erie, Albany, Livingston, Monroe, Richmond, Dutchess-Putnam, Schenectady, and Cayuga, among others, voted their opposition.[48] When news of the health insurance plan reached private practitioners, their response was not to study the bill's complexities but to immediately reject its main principles. In 1915 and 1916 some physicians had described health insurance as inevitable and even desirable, but the majority of medical opinion soon reflected the statement of an upstate doctor, that health insurance was "the worst insult that could be offered to the greatest profession." By 1917 medical leaders were estimating that "nine out of ten physicians would . . . with their present knowledge of the subject, be opposed to health insurance."[49]

What explains the great divergence of opinion between the AALL's physician supporters and the rest of the medical profession in the state of New York? First, the public health physicians and reformist leaders of the AMA and the state medical society were simply not representative of the majority of their profession. As Isaac Rubinow pointed out, virtually every physician associated with the AALL's plan had a public health, academic, or institutional orientation, and these physicians' interests and ideologies were shared by some leaders of the state medical society. The county medical societies represented instead small-town, rural, upstate general practitioners who were more politically conservative and felt far more threatened by health insurance than their reformist counterparts.

Paul Starr points out that during the 1910s "academic and private physicians began to diverge and represent distinctive interests and values."[50] The same divergence was true of private physicians and their professional brethren in urban public health and institutional work. General practitioners had long condemned public health physicians and their programs as unfair competition. Eden Delphey, for example, who represented general practitioners in the Medical Economics Society, "resented" AALL member " 'Goldwater's encroachments on the territory of the practicing physicians.' "[51] Public health work was also ideologically suspect in the eyes of conservative physicians. Dermatologist William Cunningham, author of the anti–health insurance article "A Bolshevik Bolus," claimed that the venereal disease clinics of the Public Health Service were "the entering wedge of Bolshevik medicine" and reflected the desires of "reformers who seek the subjugation of medicine to the dictation of salaried institutionalists."[52] The "salaried institutionalists" resented as competitors by private practitioners included not just public health physicians but also academics like Alexander Lambert, industrial physicians, and the staff of dispensaries and hospitals, all of whom were well represented on the official bodies in favor of health insurance.

Members of New York's county medical societies also resented that public health–oriented leaders had approved health insurance without consulting them. Their anger found an immediate outlet in political mobilization. It was no coincidence that so many county societies condemned health insurance almost simultaneously during a three-month period in early 1917. Apparently much stimulus to local organizing came from Dr. James F. Rooney of Albany, an upstate leader of the Medical Society of the State of New York who opposed the organization's endorsement of health insurance. Rooney meant business when he announced, "If the profession is to save itself [from health insurance] it must organize, as it has never organized before."[53] The Albany doctor was all over upstate New York in January of 1917, when most of the county societies passed their anti–health insurance resolutions. Rooney's political mobilization of upstate doctors took many forms: during January alone, he organized a public meeting on health insurance in the state capital, spoke at the meeting of the Albany County medical society, and lobbied doctors' groups as far west as Rochester. His lobbying was instantly effective. The Medical Society of the County of Washington, for example, passed its anti–health insurance resolution on January 4 after "a letter was received from Dr. Rooney" and "a telephone message was received from Dr. Rooney."[54] Throughout the health insurance campaign, Rooney would continue to act on his belief that "the only attitude for the medical profession to take is that of 'no compromise.' "[55]

The county medical societies' resolutions against health insurance revealed not just a divergence between private physicians and public health/institutional physicians but also a breach between rank-and-file doctors and their statewide leadership. County doctors were furious at the members of the Medical Society of the State of New York who had worked with the AALL on the health insurance bill. The medical society of Erie County, for example, "instructed its delegates to oppose the candidacy [for state office] of any person who had formerly been active as a proponent of the Mills Bill."[56] And the county societies had real power to back up their threats. County medical societies had a crucial role in both the state society and the national AMA: they elected the statewide leaders, who in turn elected doctors to the AMA's powerful House of Delegates.[57] On January 22 the Medical Society of the County of New York passed a resolution condemning the state society's endorsement of the AALL's bill. And on March 3, the Council of the Medical Society of the State of New York rescinded its approval of health insurance. Samuel Kopetzky, who had chaired the state society committee that endorsed the bill, was removed from his committee position and replaced by an anti–health insurance doctor.[58]

All of the AALL's early cooperation with state medical leaders had proven futile. In 1916, reformers thought they had reached an understanding with the medical profession. The concessions that followed were supposed to appease medical concerns about fee payment, physician representation, and free choice of patient and physician. Yet the provisions that emerged from the negotiations only aroused the opposition of private practitioners. Why did most New York physicians interpret health insurance as a violation of their own interests?

INCOME, AUTONOMY, AND AMERICANISM

Doctors' opposition seems especially puzzling since general practitioners may have had much to gain economically from health insurance. The average doctors' financial status during the Progressive Era was still quite insecure. While specialists were commanding higher and higher fees, most general practitioners of the time could expect an income not significantly higher than that of a prosperous industrial worker.[59] Adding to physicians' economic difficulties was the custom of providing uncompensated charity care to the poor.

The AALL and its supporters argued that health insurance would improve the economic status of physicians. Those doctors who gave free or low-cost services to poor and working people would find their fees increasing, because health insurance would pay them the same amount regardless of a patient's income. Dr. Kopetzky argued that "under the proposed bill the fees of medical men . . . would be increased." Senator Frederick Davenport, sponsor of the 1919 health insurance bill, agreed that doctors under health insurance "are in a better position, because they do not lose anything from bad debts or charity in their practice." These claims rested on solid evidence; in Britain, general practitioners' incomes had risen dramatically since the introduction of national health insurance.[60]

But most New York physicians simply did not accept arguments that health insurance would improve their financial status. Ronald Numbers and other historians have argued that the incomes of American doctors were rising steadily throughout the 1910s, weakening the financial case for compulsory health insurance.[61] Also, British experience did not provide an accurate comparison with the American medical system; British medicine both before and since national insurance had been dominated by general practitioners, while in the United States the number of specialists had markedly increased since the turn of the century. Specialists' higher incomes were indeed threatened by health insurance, and even general practitioners were incorporating more specialization into their practices and hence were able to start charging higher fees.[62]

Growing physician incomes were a reality, but New York doctors never mentioned this in their discussions of health insurance. Without evidence, it is difficult to say to what extent the average practitioner was aware of these broad structural changes in medicine, and how much this awareness shaped attitudes toward health insurance. A more convincing explanation for doctors' rejection of reformers' claims about medical incomes is that most New York physicians firmly believed that health insurance would *lower* their incomes — not just because their own incomes were already increasing, but because medical leaders deliberately spread frightening rumors about doctors' fees under health insurance.

The lack of specific medical provisions in the health insurance bill left the field wide open for speculation about how much doctors would receive. No sooner had the campaign begun than a rumor spread like wildfire that doctors would receive the appallingly low amount of twenty-five cents for office visits and one dollar for home visits under health insurance. This was an "outright lie," as one reformer called it, but an effective one.[63] The source of the rumors was uncertain, but physician leaders had no qualms about spreading them among their profession. The editor of the *Journal of the Medical Society of New Jersey* declared to a conference of industrial physicians that a report that he held "in his hand" (but whose origins he did not explain) proved a chilling fact: "I am afraid that instead of the medical men of Pennsylvania reaping $5,400 a year from health insurance . . . the sum that they would get would be more like $400."[64] Rumors led physicians to believe that compensation under health insurance would be "a mere pittance,"[65] threatening not only the financial well-being of doctors but also the quality of medical care. "In talking with reputable physicians," wrote one doctor to health insurance sponsor Davenport, "I am convinced that the best would be driven out of business [by health insurance] . . . for they would not submit to the paltry salaries that would be paid physicians appointed to the positions provided by this legislation."[66] (This doctor demonstrates how unfamiliar physicians were with the actual provisions of the bill, which stipulated that only the medical supervisors, not the practicing physicians, were to be salaried.) In 1919 John Lapp tried to correct the false impression that doctors would be paid twenty-five to fifty cents per visit under health insurance; he promised they would receive around $2.50 for a home visit, but the rumors had spread so rapidly it was too late to deny them.[67]

The AALL thought the rumors would be put to rest as specific medical provisions were added to its plan. The final version of the bill would have allowed the county medical societies to set their own fee schedules for health insurance — surely a major concession to doctors' fears.[68] But physicians remembered the rumors first. Once the horror stories about fees were spread, it was nearly impossible for the AALL to reassure doctors that health insurance would be in their economic interest.

The AALL struggled to meet physicians' demands, but the one thing it could not offer them was continuing autonomy. No matter how many benefits health insurance offered the profession, the system by definition had to take away some of doctors' freedom to act independently from outside controls. By imposing new forms of organization and payment on the medical profession, health insurance required some surrender of physician autonomy. This loss of autonomy was at the center of physicians' opposition to health insurance. Dr. John P. Davin, former pharmacist and representative of the Medical Society of the County of New York, announced that health insurance "would . . . make us bondmen to the State, instead of free and independent practitioners of medicine."[69] And the Medical Society of the State of New York condemned the system because under health insurance "the practitioner would be . . . in the final analysis subject to lay dictation as to means and methods of practice."[70]

Autonomy—the freedom for physicians to choose their own patients, work hours, fields of specialization, courses of treatment, and fee schedules—had long been an essential principle of American medical practice. And, as Paul Starr notes, "For many physicians . . . concerns about autonomy have outweighed strictly financial considerations."[71] This helps explain why even many doctors who had studied the bill closely and discounted rumors about lower fees chose to oppose health insurance. However, there was really no dichotomy between autonomy and fees, because autonomy was inseparable from the protection of physician incomes. Opponents of health insurance argued that only physicians should be allowed to set medical fees. The Schenectady County Medical Society objected to health insurance because "the fees of physicians employed under the Act will be fixed finally by [a] Commission, of whom only one will be a physician."[72] Complained one doctor, "No banker or merchant would expect to succeed if outsiders were allowed to control his business."[73] When a Dr. Patterson, president of the Rennselaer County Medical Association, was asked by Senator Davenport, "What do you doctors want anyway?" he replied, "Leave us alone. Have your insurance if you will, but leave us out of it." Davenport then asked him, "Do you mean that doctors should be allowed to charge what they like?" "Certainly," retorted the physician. Autonomy invariably included doctors' freedom to set their own fees.[74]

Doctors under health insurance would lose control not only over their payment, opponents argued, but also over their time. Without the barrier of the fee separating doctor and patient, physicians would be forced to provide endless medical care on demand. "Inasmuch as all medical services are to be free to the insured persons, will they not call on the doctor very much more frequently, even for trivial matters, than now? Has that been considered in your estimate of the statistics?" Eden Delphey demanded of the AALL.[75] Once medical care became a right of citizens rather than a prerogative of physicians, the medical profession would lose its power to accept or deny patients; the patient rather than the doctor would be in control. Dermatologist William Cunningham warned fellow practitioners that under health insurance "the doctor must respond to any amount of work that may be laid upon him by [the insured]. He is to be at his beck and call, and he cannot refuse to comply."[76] (This statement ignored the concessions to physician choice in the AALL's bill.)

The question of charity medicine also confirms the cardinal importance of autonomy to the medical profession. Private physicians still provided a great deal of uncompensated care to patients unable to pay. Doctors sometimes romanticized their profession's role in charity care and overestimated its ability to address the needs of the sick poor, as did insurance opponent Dr. G. Franklin Bell, who proclaimed that he had "never yet seen anyone in our town who did not get medical attention when he needed it" because of the "humane sentiment of my brother practitioners."[77] Still, charity care was expected of most American physicians, and too much uncompensated work clearly contributed to keeping down physician incomes. Reformers argued repeatedly that health insurance would solve this difficulty. "The act," said Dr. Samuel Kopetzky, "takes the greater burden of public charity off from the shoulders of the medical profession."[78]

But, rather than welcoming the prospect of relief from charity care that health insurance would offer them, physicians defended free care as a component of professional autonomy. The New York County medical society's Dr. John P. Davin fumed, "Confiscation by the State of the ancient heritage of the medical professions, the care of the sick poor, is without right, reason, or justification."[79] Physicians wanted to care for the poor as a matter of choice, not compulsion. Dr. John D. Bonnar of Buffalo argued that poor patients were currently "taken care of . . . by the free-will offering of the State and nation," but "when it is made compulsory . . . then it is obnoxious to the freedom and democratic spirit of the people of this State and nation."[80] Argued Dr. William Cunningham, "When a man gives away his services he retains his self-respect; when a man sells them at a ruinous reduction he feels that he has become a bargain counter remnant of his former self."[81] These physicians preferred the financial losses of charity care over the loss of autonomy under health insurance. Autonomy would allow physicians to continue to control the amount of free care they would give, and to whom.

Physicians' belief that health insurance threatened their incomes and their autonomy mobilized the medical profession against the AALL's plan. But, like other interest groups, doctors had to proceed carefully in defending their interests lest their opposition be perceived as professional selfishness and greed. To meet this challenge, New York medical societies launched a rhetorical campaign against health insurance that tied doctors' professional interests to the concept of Americanism.

Physicians' earliest attacks on health insurance opened with Americanist rhetoric. The first doctor who spoke at the 1917 Albany hearing on the Mills Bill told the assembled crowd that "it is entirely un-American to propose this." Dr. Patterson of Rennselaer said that his organization had first adopted a resolution against health insurance "on account of its medical features" but it was quickly followed by another resolving that "we were opposed to it as independent American citizens."[82] Health insurance, doctors agreed, violated the American principles of liberty and property rights. Dr. John D. Bonnar of the Erie County medical society thought that because of its compulsory nature, health insurance "is autocratic and not democratic. It strikes at the root and foundation of the fundamental law of our land: life, liberty and the pursuit of happiness."[83] The Medical Society of the County of Schenectady resolved that "this legislation is an immediate institution of State socialism, and an abrogation of the rights of the individual to the control of his own life and property."[84]

But doctors did more than draw on language of patriotism to serve their cause. Physicians went beyond existing Americanist rhetoric to construct their own version of national identity, with physicians' interests at its core. Traditional tenets of the medical profession became the centerpiece of the definition of Americanism promoted by the medical foes of health insurance. In the crucible of the health insurance debate, physicians' autonomy and incomes were imbued with patriotic significance.

Physicians' construction of Americanism encompassed the right of doctors to the freedom to earn income unencumbered by forces outside the medical profession. The highly vocal physician Dr. John O'Reilly of the Professional Guild of Kings County linked Americanism with the defense of physicians' earnings when he assailed the health insurance bill as "Un-American, Uneconomic, Unfair, Un-Scientific and Un-scrupulous. . . . [Doctors, dentists, and druggists must] defeat this pernicious legislation which threatens the dignity of their Professions [and] the security of their income."[85] "As medical men and as citizens, we object to having our fees fixed for us by the State," wrote the New York Physicians' Association to each assemblyman. "The real AMERICAN working man does not ask for or desire this State charity."[86] A representative of the western New York Federation of Physicians "declared that nobody would set his fee and that before he submitted to this invasion of his rights, he would cease the practice of medicine."[87]

To opponents of health insurance, doctors' autonomy was not simply a component of a professional code; it was part and parcel of the American way. At the 1917 hearing in Albany, Dr. Eden Delphey told assemblymen that "this country fought the Revolutionary War in order to acquire self-government and I believe in self-government by the . . . physicians." Delphey invoked American individualism to describe physician autonomy when he declared that compulsory health insurance "will revolutionize the practice of medicine so that the physician will professionally cease to be an individualist and will be but a cog in a great medical machine." Dr. William Cunningham agreed, writing in "A Bolshevik Bolus" that health insurance would reduce the physician "to a condition of practical serfdom by sweeping away his professional independence."[88] Health insurance, these opponents implied, would threaten physicians' American individualism by threatening their autonomy.[89]

THE PRICE OF QUALITY

Physician opponents also argued that compulsory health insurance would lower the quality of medical care. But arguments about quality were inseparable from those about economics and professional autonomy. Lower the physicians' income, opponents warned, and the standard of medical care would also fall. The connection between price and quality may seem indisputable — the high cost of American medical care today is frequently linked to its superior quality, the "best in the world." But the tie between cost and expert care has not been universal or automatic. Commercialism, or too great a regard for remuneration and private gain, had long been perceived by the medical profession as a threat to the service ethic of physicians and to the purity of the physician-patient relationship. Quality of care, then, could even have an inverse relationship to the physician's concern with his fees. In the early twentieth century, many Americans still did not assume that fee-for-service medicine was much better than free care. Since so many highly trained urban physicians put in time at free outpatient dispensaries, there was little reason for patients to imagine that the ministrations of a private doctor would be superior.[90] At the same time that they fought compulsory health insurance, physicians had to make a concerted effort to convince the public that high-quality medicine had a price. The crux of their argument was that any efforts to limit or control physicians' incomes and autonomy through measures such as compulsory health insurance would be paid for in the form of inferior medical care.

In drafting the health insurance bill, the AALL had been more concerned with access to medical care than with its quality. Medical treatment would improve under health insurance, the AALL thought, mainly because there would be more of it, since people would no longer fail to call a doctor because of financial constraints. Quality was not unconnected to cost in reformers' minds, in that they thought a physician with a regular income would be more secure than one who depended on fee-for-service, and thus would be less likely to exploit patients or to provide low-income patients with inferior care. Crucially, however, the health insurance proposal treated quality as a function of economic and medical efficiency rather than of high fees paid to physicians. The solution to the uneven quality of medical care was not to pay more money to individual doctors but to distribute the total cost of health care through insurance.

Faced with the argument that health insurance would improve medical care and delivery, medical opponents of health insurance moved to strengthen the tie between quality medicine and physicians' ability to set their own fees. They contended that physicians would not be able to do their jobs properly under a system of health insurance, because only doctors receiving a substantial income could provide effective medical care. "You know that unless the physician is adequately compensated, so that he may have proper housing, proper clothing and proper feeding, he is not in condition to do good work," Dr. Eden Delphey argued at a New York Assembly hearing on health insurance. Because health insurance "will LIMIT [doctors'] earning capacity," insisted Dr. John J. A. O'Reilly, it followed that the plan would also "LIMIT their capacity for usefulness to the Public." Even the president of the American Medical Association, Charles H. Mayo, told members "to beware of 'anything which reduced the income of the physician,' since a lowered income 'will limit his training, equipment and efficiency, and in the end will react on the people.' "[91] Other practitioners warned that government interference with doctors' independence would imperil the advancement of medical research. Dr. John P. Davin declared that "[a]ll the great discoveries in medicine have resulted from individual effort. There is no initiative in bureaucratic medicine."[92] Compulsory insurance would destroy the superiority of American medical science, according to an upstate New York surgeon: "Bring on your Health Insurance and what incentive will a young man have to spend his time in research work? You will strike a body blow at the very foundation of medicine."[93]

The effort by American physicians who opposed health insurance to link fees and autonomy with quality was complicated by the testimony of some of their European counterparts who practiced under a health insurance system. British doctors' experience with the National Insurance Act was leading to an opposite conclusion about the relationship between cost and quality:

the elimination of private fee payments could pave the way to better medical treatment. "It is my firm belief that the abolition of the 'medical fee' has improved the relations between doctor and patient and made intercourse easier and pleasanter," a British doctor wrote from County Durham to the New York Academy of Medicine. "It is now the patient's fault entirely if he puts off seeking the doctor's advice — he cannot urge his 'inability to pay the fee' in excuse for any delay."[94] A Sheffield physician agreed that medical care had improved under the British National Insurance Act because "the conscientious doctor has been able to give proper attention to serious cases without the stigma of trying to run up a big bill."[95]

These physicians thought that replacing fee-for-service medicine with a regular income based on capitation led to superior medical care, since doctors could make more visits without worrying about the patient's ability to pay. Some American physicians were reaching similar conclusions, including Dr. C. E. McDermid, the industrial physician with the Utah Fuel Company, which ran a medical care plan for its workers. McDermid wrote to John B. Andrews, "I think that the greatest pleasure of my professional life among my patients is that I can make one or a dozen calls a day with no thought on the patient's part that I am making additional calls for anything but observation and study of the case. . . . I can hold that person's respect more effectually for he knows the more I do the less I make." A New York industrial physician agreed that because "the relationship between industrial worker and company physician . . . is entirely free from the element of money, . . . the conditions are ideal for giving the employee the best possible service."[96]

Opponents countered that physicians would provide less treatment under health insurance because they would no longer have a financial incentive. Physicians would do their best work when promised fee-for-service payment; any other method of compensation would encourage doctors to rush through their visits and offer slapdash treatment. A doctor from Buffalo predicted that health insurance would only "make matters worse by furnishing a heartless, overworked, 15-cent-a-call contract physician."[97] This doctor's comment melded the rumors about low fees with arguments about the relationship of payment to medical quality.

The AALL listened carefully to physicians' complaints. Although the reformers were infuriated by the false rumors, they took seriously doctors' concerns about autonomy and fees. By 1920, the bill had changed dramatically in response to physician demands. After a series of meetings with doctors in early 1919, the AALL changed the medical provisions of the bill to allow more autonomy for the medical profession under health insurance. Instead of local panels, the 1919 bill created statewide panels, allowing greater freedom for doctors and more patient choice, and assured that a physician representative would not just sit on the health insurance commission but would be its head. After doctors put further pressure on health insurance sponsor Senator Frederick Davenport, Davenport amended the bill to allow complete control of fee setting by physicians: as noted above, fee schedules under this plan would be proposed by the county medical societies, the same doctors who formed the backbone of physician opposition.[98] With doctors controlling the health insurance commission and their own fee schedules, reformers hardly could do more to placate them.

But these changes in the bill did not end physician opposition to health insurance. Ronald Numbers writes, "[A]s physicians won more and more concessions, they grew increasingly less inclined to compromise."[99] Physicians' organized opposition to health insurance actually *increased* after 1919 — not because the legislation was no longer inevitable, but because it seemed even more likely to pass after the bill's success in the New York Senate. Even though health insurance died in an assembly committee in April of 1919, its earlier victory in the senate made opponents fear the bill had a better chance of passage in 1920. This led physicians to renewed organization, as they created doctors' "professional guilds" throughout upstate New York and joined with insurance companies and manufacturers in the anti–health insurance New York League for Americanism (see Chapter 8).[100]

The AALL had made a fatal error in leaving medical organizations out of its original bill. By doing so it allowed doctors to dictate endless changes in the legislation while leaving the field wide open for the spread of destructive rumors among the profession's rank and file. The AALL mobilized doctors to participate in refining the bill, but its overtures also led to the rise of a powerful organized opposition that was critical to the proposal's defeat. The organizational and rhetorical power of the county medical societies forced pro–health insurance medical leaders to reverse their positions. Samuel Kopetzky, under whose leadership the Medical Society of the State of New York had endorsed health insurance in 1916, backed away from his support after the tide of opposition rose, but this did not protect him from removal as committee chair because of pressure from the county societies.[101] Frederick Green of the AMA, initially among the strongest medical supporters of health insurance, also withdrew his endorsement in 1917. Denying he had ever been in favor of health insurance, Green admitted that he no longer believed most physicians supported its principles.[102] As an AMA leader, Green's switch was a political response to the demands of his organization's rank and file, the fiercely anti–health insurance county and state medical societies.

By the time the health insurance campaign reached its apex in 1919, the medical profession was amassed in opposition. Effective organization and mobilization at the county level meant that New York physicians were no longer, in the words of Dr. John O'Reilly, "insignificant atoms beneath the notice of politicians."[103] But, even though the stage had been set for the growing political power of the medical profession, doctors alone could not defeat health insurance. Dr. William Cunningham remarked of the 1916 and 1917 assembly battles, "If the doctors had been left to themselves they would have been swamped." The failure of the AALL's bill, Cunningham believed, was due not just to "the obstinacy of the [doctors'] resistance" but also to "the fortunate support of the labor unions (non-socialistic) and the big insurance companies."[104] Only in partnership with other interest groups would physicians prevail against health insurance.

5

Moneyed Interests

EMPLOYERS AND INSURANCE
COMPANIES AGAINST COMPULSORY
HEALTH INSURANCE

In November of 1915, the headline of the New York employer's journal *The Monitor* warned, " 'Health Insurance for Workers' is the Shrapnel in First Gun Fired by Social Welfare Folk." The journal advised its readers to begin "girding our loins," for "[i]f a certain percentage of workmen will kill time, loaf, lay-off and otherwise interfere with the production of a plant merely to pander to their own laziness, what might not happen if they could put their loafing on a scientific basis and draw pay for doing it?"[1] *The Monitor*'s military metaphor was an apt one for the fierce battle that business would wage against compulsory health insurance. Many employers agreed with insurance executive Frederick Hoffman that "compulsory health insurance is perhaps the most serious menace to the manufacturing interests of America at the present time."[2]

The campaign for compulsory health insurance brought businessmen together in a remarkable consensus. New York employers, both large and small, resoundingly rejected the inclusion of health insurance in the new regulatory state. Economic interest played the key role in industry's opposition to the legislation. As one factory owner put it, "average manufacturers" opposed compulsory health insurance because "when it comes to paying the bill we are generally called upon to pay it." The American Association for Labor Legislation's bill would require employers to meet two-fifths of the cost of health insurance. Unlike workmen's compensation, which many big employers supported because it would protect them against large legal settlements for workplace injuries, health insurance offered no obvious financial return on business's investment in the premiums.[3]

The compulsory health insurance campaign brought to light a commonality of interest between manufacturing and insurance sectors. The commercial insurance industry occupies a unique and little-examined place in the debate over social policy during the Progressive Era.[4] Seemingly more of a white-collar business than an exploitative industry, the insurance industry was still perceived as holding sway over the lives of workers through its control of the hugely successful industrial insurance market, which sold inexpensive life insurance to wage earners. Like employers, insurance companies had a major financial stake in the defeat of compulsory health insurance. Not only would the legislation compete directly with the most lucrative parts of the insurance business, but the AALL's proposal also would systematically exclude profit-making insurers from participating in the health insurance plan.

It was far more obvious that health insurance would mean an economic loss for employers and insurance companies than it was for physicians. But the opposition of employers and insurers to health insurance cannot be explained solely by economic self-interest. Like physicians, businessmen made little distinction between economic questions and issues of autonomy and power. To be free to make profits, employers had to retain control over vital aspects of the workplace, a control that in Progressive Era New York was already being threatened by organized labor, reformers, and government. Insurers, too, fought to retain control over the extent, type, and cost of insurance they offered, especially as their industry came under increasing public scrutiny and government regulation. Their successful fight against health insurance helped industrialists and insurers place significant limits on state involvement in business activity and insurance provision.[5] And for some employers, the quest for control meant that even increasing private benefits for workers at their own expense would be preferable to accepting government-run health insurance — and indeed would be a means of opposing such a system.

The Progressive mood of distrust of unabashed profiteering made it difficult for industrialists and insurance executives to oppose compulsory health insurance publicly on the grounds of economics. The health insurance campaign forced business leaders to express their economic interests in more palatable ways. Whether by emphasizing the superiority of private employee benefits, the dangers of worker abuse of compulsory health insurance, or the loss of jobs that being forced to pay premiums would entail, both employers and insurance companies in opposing health insurance sought to construct their self-interest as the public interest.

NEW YORK EMPLOYERS ORGANIZE

Employers channeled their burgeoning anger at health insurance proposals into powerful and efficient organization. Despite the complaints of business that "the workingmen have organized . . . for the furtherance of their aims, but the employing interests have sadly failed to fulfill their duty and to grasp their opportunities,"[6] New York was in fact a bustling center of business cooperation. The National Civic Federation, which promoted cooperation between businessmen and conservative labor leaders, was headquartered in New York City, and the Associated Manufacturers and Merchants, the state branch of the National Association of Manufacturers, was vigorously active upstate. The National Industrial Conference Board counted dozens of New York manufacturers and business associations among its members. All three organizations threw their resources into the fight against compulsory health insurance in New York State.

The NCF sponsored the 1914 report attacking European health insurance, and its Social Insurance Department continued to oppose compulsory insurance throughout the decade. (The NCF's activities will be described in more detail in Chapter 6.) The diverse membership of the NICB, founded in 1916, included both anti-union and reform-minded manufacturers.[7] The Associated Manufacturers and Merchants of New York State was a product of the 1915 amalgamation of the New York State Manufacturers Association and the Associated Industries of New York State. Its 748 member companies united to fight labor legislation. Unlike the NCF and the NICB, which worked to support reforms beneficial to their members, the AMM saw its purpose as almost entirely obstructive, and made no apologies for its opposition to practically all forms of labor legislation. "[E]ven if no constructive work were done by the Association it would have a man's job on its hands attempting to hold off obnoxious, impractical and wholly unnecessary legislation," the AMM declared. Albany, according to the AMM, was in the thrall of "organized Labor, [and] the united force of Social Welfare Organizations," whose uplift schemes were a threat to the rights of employers. With such influences exerting power over public opinion, asserted the AMM, "is it any wonder that New York has been the experimental station for every theorist and uplifter in the country?"[8] AMM members, most of whom were upstate employers, felt particularly aggrieved by "the dissimilarity of conditions between New York City and 'up-state' and the refusal of New York legislative agents to recognize that 'up-staters' had any rights."[9]

The AMM's most public and visible spokesman was Mark Daly of Syracuse.[10] In addition to his tireless work upstate, Daly represented the AMM in the

Representatives of the Associated Manufacturers and Merchants of New York State. Mark Daly is second from left (*The Monitor* 3 [January 1917]; photograph reproduced by permission of M. E. Grenander Department of Special Collections and Archives, University at Albany, State University of New York).

NCF, regularly attending NCF Executive Committee meetings in New York City where he was treated as an authority on compulsory health insurance. Despite their dissimilarities, all three New York employers' associations collaborated closely on the health insurance issue. The NICB's health insurance expert, Margaret Loomis Stecker, joined the NCF's Social Insurance Committee to aid in its "active propaganda work" against the bill. To complete the circle, the AMM became a NICB member in 1918.[11]

Like the NCF, the NICB expended a great deal of energy on research and statistical studies that it hoped would refute arguments for a health insurance system. It created a well-financed committee on health insurance, charged with formulating "definite plans of how to deal by legislation or otherwise with the growing sentiment in favor of an organized method by which to take care of sick persons who cannot take care of themselves." Another committee was formed to compile statistics on worker absenteeism, in the hope that the findings would contradict reformers' claims that sickness was a major problem for workers. Not surprisingly, the conference board's absenteeism study concluded, "[E]stimates heretofore accepted of time lost on account of sickness are considerably higher than would seem to be warranted by the facts."[12]

The NCF also worked to deflate estimates of worker illness. Aware that most sickness studies provided fuel for health insurance demands, the NCF's Gertrude Easley suggested that the federation avoid discussions of sickness statistics altogether; instead, "it would be better to say that the extent of sickness is unknown." [13] The AMM conducted its own study of upstate firms and found only 3.2 percent of absences due to illness. Reported Mark Daly, "[T]he number absent for personal reasons, such as fishing, papering the spare room, and so on, is . . . 3.9 percent, greater than the percentage absent for illness." [14] The AMM's figures, argued Daly, indicated that reformers had grossly overestimated the amount of wage loss due to illness. Irene Sylvester Chubb of the AALL responded wryly to these studies of absenteeism: "I think perhaps they forgot that prohibition was going into effect July 1st because they intimated that the real cause of absence was the workers' misconduct." [15]

While the NICB and the NCF sought to discredit the Progressives with statistical weaponry, the AMM took a more direct approach. The former two organizations, especially the NCF, strongly wished to avoid aggravating class conflict by making forthright rhetorical attacks on workers; their public pronouncements approved of labor organization and sought to ameliorate public distrust of corporate greed. Members of the AMM, however, made no attempt to tone down their aggressive antiworker language. "Under this delectable [health insurance] bill," the AMM journal *The Monitor* warned New York employers, "any worker in YOUR plant may be seized with cramps in the stomach and for twenty-six (26) weeks thereafter he will draw two-thirds of his pay as he comfortably sucks on his pipe and reads the newspapers at home. . . . Who pays? You do, as usual." *The Monitor* also liked to refer to health insurance as "scientific loafing." [16] In the pages of the same journal, realtor Henry W. Berg deemed the health insurance bill "as insane as anything that emanated from the wildest asylum in this country." [17] The AMM's unrestrained rhetoric was a counterpoint to the more temperate tactics of the other employer groups.

Business's main objection to compulsory health insurance was that it would result in mounting costs for industry. Frederick Hoffman warned the Pennsylvania State Manufacturers Association in 1918 that "the probable cost of such insurance to industry would not be less, and it might be as much as three times as high, as the aggregate amount paid by manufacturing interests for taxation." Even though workers would be required to pay for two-fifths of the insurance costs through wage deductions, and the state would kick in another fifth, Hoffman predicted that the burden would increasingly shift to industry: "The demand would unquestionably be made for an increase in wages proportionate to the deductions imposed." [18] Despite the AALL's repeated assurances that the premiums would only cost employers about 1.5 percent of their wage bill, [19] employers continued to believe that health insurance payments would add to the growing burden on company funds imposed by the cascade of Progressive legislation. "The manufacturer today has all he can stand," fumed one New York employer, "with national and state income taxes, real estate tax, insurance of all kinds, etc. besides all the expense he is put to by labor laws and having inspector after inspector call to go over this that and the other thing."[20] A company president in Massachusetts claimed that his business had been practically ruined by the imposition of minimum wages, and health insurance would be the last straw. Livid at the prospect of yet another costly reform, he blamed the AALL for his hardships: "[I]t is such people as you who are making these troubles," he wrote to John B. Andrews.[21]

But to fixate upon the employer's financial burden under health insurance was seen as an unwise political choice in a time of widespread distrust of manufacturer profiteering and sensitivity to the uneven distribution of wealth in the nation. As Metropolitan Life Insurance Company president Haley Fiske warned stockholders in 1911, "The sentiment of the world is against the exploitation of wage earners for enormous profits."[22] While employers talked among themselves about the economic drain that health insurance would impose on company profits, their public pronouncements emphasized the proposal's costs to the worker, the consumer, and the public.

The threat of job loss was a potent weapon wielded by employers. Mark Daly of New York's AMM warned that if health insurance were passed, "the public won't buy, the employer won't manufacture, and the man won't have a job."[23] Another business owner wrote to John B. Andrews that the employer, "as you are very well aware, adds the expense of this insurance to the cost of his product."[24] According to these manufacturers, their opposition to health insurance was not a matter of self-interest but of employers' ability to provide products and jobs that benefited all of society. Arguments about federalism, or competition between states, rested on similar grounds. New York employers warned that a health insurance law would force them to relocate their businesses to states without such burdens. If health insurance passed, declared William McConnell of the New York Board of Trade, manufacturers "will find it convenient to move away where they can transact business without these constant inflictions."[25]

WHO IS RESPONSIBLE FOR WORKERS' HEALTH?

To employers of industrial labor, compulsory health insurance meant more than added costs. Health insurance threatened to greatly expand employers' responsibility for workers' health. Requiring employers to cover their workers for medical costs and lost wages during any type of illness would go well beyond workmen's compensation laws, which had neatly and narrowly defined the employer's responsibilities to encompass only injuries that were clearly job related.

Compulsory health insurance was especially menacing to employers' autonomy because of the peculiar place of health in the origins of the American welfare state. The effect of industrial labor on the health and stamina of workers was widely discussed throughout the Progressive Era, and reformers successfully used arguments about the protection of workers' health to justify state intervention in the workplace. The Supreme Court case *Muller v. Oregon*, which upheld maximum-hours laws based partly on their positive impact on women workers' health, and the rapid spread of workmen's compensation laws signaled to employers that reformers' emphasis on health was likely to lead to the adoption of still more legislation.[26] Progressive reformers used new medical understanding of the relationship between health and environment to argue that employers should take far greater responsibility for their workers' health. According to the AALL, the workplace itself, aside from being a source of dangerous injuries, was a hotbed of sickness threatening the health and stamina of American labor. Industrial physician Alice Hamilton thought that requiring employer contributions to a health insurance fund "will serve to call [the employer's] attention to the cost of sickness and will be a strong incentive to more care in conducting his industry and more attention to sanitary methods and precautions." The chronic fatigue resulting from long working hours, reformers argued, was a major cause of disease and as such should be the responsibility of employers.[27]

The AALL tried to persuade manufacturers that taking more responsibility for workers' health would be in their own interest as an aid to industrial efficiency. Once again, John B. Andrews greatly underestimated the resistance his organization would encounter. His misplaced optimism was expressed in a 1916 circular letter to supporters, which reassured them that employer opposition to health insurance "is not nearly as strong as it was to Workmen's Compensation five years ago, many employers declaring that they first feared Workmen's Compensation would put them out of business but that they have since found in practice that it is a good thing for them as well as for their employees."[28] Senator Frederick Davenport also believed that reasonable employers could not fail to see the advantages of a system of compulsory health insurance. Protecting workers' health would not only enhance their efficiency, it would also build their loyalty to the employer. Davenport proclaimed, "The measure proposed in this state . . . lays the foundation in the simplest human affairs for the more intimate cooperation of labor and capital in industry." Such cooperation, according to Davenport, was essential to stem the threat of labor unrest; in the health insurance plan "lies the greatest protection that the employing class has against impetuous radicalism."[29]

A few Progressive-minded employers did actually respond to these arguments and join the health insurance cause. The head of an engineering enterprise agreed with Davenport that health insurance's greatest appeal lay in its
potential to increase workers' morale and appreciation of their employers:
"The workers want health insurance and I believe that we can afford to give it
to them in view of the *esprit de corps* which we may expect to gain."[30] Others
emphasized that poor health threatened worker productivity and thus manufacturer profits. The owner of the Reinhard Manufacturing Co., "manufacturers of high grade ribbons," wrote to New York State senators on behalf of the
AALL, "Health insurance will set up a protection to the stamina of our working population which will be worth many times what it may cost."[31] At a 1919
hearing in Albany, a manufacturer named Henry Alexander testified, "[T]he
overhead charges of keeping the worker who is only 40 percent productive because of sickness on the job are more than the cost of sending him home on
company time to get proper medical care."[32]

These same few manufacturers appeared repeatedly at hearings on health
insurance and were quoted in AALL propaganda, and their support helps account for the AALL's unwarranted optimism regarding business. However,
their words were drowned out by the chorus of opposition from New York's
employer organizations. Employer representatives especially resisted the increased responsibility for their workers' health implicit in the health insurance
legislation. They insisted that workers should be responsible for their own sickness. Frederick M. Hitchcock of the AMM conceded that industry might be held
accountable for specifically occupational sickness, "yet such diseases constitute but a small fraction of the total number of the ills of industrial workers."[33]
The duty of the employer need not extend beyond "establishing safe and sanitary work places with ample light and ventilation," according to M. W. Alexander of the NICB, but since workers' health "is as much, or even to a larger extent, dependent upon their mode of living during the longer period when they
are not at work, than during their working time, the primary duty of conserving the health of the workers must rest primarily upon themselves and society
and not upon the employer."[34] Acknowledging the employer's responsibility
to provide a safe workplace did not extend, and in fact clearly delineated the
limits of, responsibility for workers' health.

Employers insisted that workers' illnesses and injuries were caused not by
working conditions but by irresponsibility or laziness, by workers' unsanitary
home lives or intemperate social lives, so that for the state to compel business
to pay for them was particularly unjust. Certain modes of living practiced by
workers, employers argued, were the primary cause of ill health and could be

avoided by simple self-restraint. "There are many causes of sickness which are beyond the control of manufacturers, such as alcoholism, feeble-mindedness, venereal diseases, etc.," claimed the AMM's Hitchcock. "It is not fair, in our opinion, to make the employer pay for sickness of employees which has been contracted either through intemperate or licentious living." [35]

Even if workers did not engage in health-destroying immoral behavior, employers claimed that working-class home life itself posed a threat of illness for which they should not be held responsible. AMM leader Mark Daly declared that New York employers who offered an eight-hour workday "are not willing to compensate for sickness which may be contracted during the other sixteen hours of the day in unclean homes and elsewhere." [36] Employers adopted sanitarianism — the concept that disease was related to cleanliness — to their own ends. "You know as well as I do, who has been an employer of labor for forty years," a company president wrote to Frederick Davenport, "that these people do not and cannot take care of themselves as you and I do. They do not live as they should and they are exposed to . . . unsanitary rooms, halls, houses, etc." Employers should not have to pay for the health protection of those who could not or would not take care of themselves, proclaimed this executive; and as for the health insurance proposal, "it is a crime for any such bill to be proposed." [37]

Another objection employers raised to the health insurance plan was that it would unjustly reward irresponsible workers who failed to provide for themselves, and were thereby undeserving of their employer's help. In a letter to the AALL's John B. Andrews denouncing the health insurance proposal, a brush manufacturer pronounced himself appalled by the "idea of caring for everybody in this world, whether they have been thrifty or not." [38] Because workers would be compelled to pay for part of their health insurance premiums, the thriftless employee would burden not only his employer but also his fellow workers. The NCF complained, "No distinction is made in the bill between workmen. The dissolute, lazy and incompetent workman is grouped with the industrious, careful and temperate workman. The latter pays for the vices of the former." [39]

If health insurance were to reward the careless worker, employers reasoned, it would inspire similar behavior among all covered employees. The owner of the New York Mills Corporation contended that "this law would [encourage] indifference, lack of initiative and lack of responsibility and loyalty to employer. It would also tend to dishonesty on the part of an employee to obtain coveted benefits." [40] In the eyes of New York employers, workers were predisposed to an endless variety of habits and behaviors — dirtiness, intemperance, immorality, laziness — that made them unfit to participate in a system of compulsory health insurance and undeserving of their employers' contributions.

SICKNESS FEIGNED OR FANCIED:
THE QUESTION OF MALINGERING

Workers' tendency to dishonesty and fraud, according to manufacturers, would make a health insurance system inoperable. Employers' most frequent argument against compulsory health insurance was that their workers would take advantage of the cash benefits by malingering, or simulating illness. They claimed that the incidence of malingering in Britain had increased dramatically since the passage of the National Insurance Act in 1911, and that workmen's compensation laws were leading to similar behavior among American workers. "The inevitable tendency of many workers under compulsory health insurance is to feign illness," announced the NICB, which "weaken[s] the moral character of workers." The AMM argued of the health insurance plan that "there is no effective check provided in the measure against malingering," which would dramatically increase among employees "who will seek to secure two-thirds wages . . . [for] feigned or fancied sickness disability." [41]

The AALL had tried to prepare for the charges of malingering by setting the cash benefits of its proposal at two-thirds of regular wages, an amount that the reformers argued was not high enough to foster simulated illness. Frederick Davenport assured one critic that prevention of malingering was built into the New York plan, because "the amount of the sick benefit [is] so small that it will not pay to shirk." [42] Also, reformers emphasized that the participation of physicians in the administration of the benefits would guarantee expert medical supervision of the insured, which was the surest way to prevent malingering. But the AALL did not question its opponents' assumption that malingering would be a serious challenge to a health insurance system.

Malingering was first reported in medical journals by military physicians who faced the challenge of diagnosing false illness among soldiers trying to avoid duty. According to the medical journal *Military Surgeon*, the word "malingering" is "derived from [the Latin] 'malus,' meaning bad, evil or base; and 'aeger,' signifying indisposition, sickness or illness." [43] But the topic came to the attention of the wider medical profession during the first decades of the twentieth century with the spread of workmen's compensation and private sickness benefit systems, and especially the creation of state health insurance systems in Europe. According to one medical journal, "It has been the rule, following the introduction of industrial insurance in a country, to find reports of a great amount of malingering." Estimates of false illness under European health insurance ranged from a high of 25–36 percent of the insured in some parts of Germany to a low of 8 percent in one study of British health insurance. [44]

Malingering became a much discussed topic in U.S. medical journals after the introduction of workmen's compensation in 1911. The most common kind of faking under compensation insurance was that of invisible injuries, particularly back pain. Some participants in workmen's compensation realized that their financial reward would increase depending on the severity of their pain. One worker was distressed that he only received $1,000 for an accident and wished he had complained more loudly to the compensation board, because a friend of his with a similar injury had "talked [them] up and was given $3,000." Some malingerers went further than just exaggerating an injury. A physician recorded cases of workers using hot pokers to create blistering and then pretending they had been burned on the job. One laborer appeared in the physician's office with severe bruises that, upon examination, were found to be caused by human bites. (The doctor did not specify who did the biting.) [45] A more sophisticated—if still painful—method of malingering was practiced by a soldier who bit his tongue and spit blood into his urine sample while the doctor's back was turned.[46]

These and other reports fueled employers' claims that workers would see health insurance coverage as an opportunity for rampant fraud. "The majority of labor today, will do as little as they possibly can," argued one employer.[47] An upstate New York factory owner denounced the health insurance bill because he was certain that workers would take every possible chance to take paid time off. His opinion was based on his personal experience with workers, he insisted: One day at his factory he decided not to deduct the pay of a man absent because of illness. The sick worker "told another man what he got; the following week there were more absentees in the factory than ever before and . . . practically every man . . . got a day's absence claiming illness." [48]

Employers saw the sickness benefits themselves—the appealing idea of being paid in cash for staying at home—as the major temptation to malingering. But workers who faked or exaggerated illness or injury under existing benefit systems had motivations that were more complex than the simple desire for unearned income. Workers enrolled in benefit schemes sometimes used sick pay as a kind of unemployment insurance, or even as unofficial strike benefits. The president of a New York City fraternal society told a researcher that "during slack season, and especially during time of strike, the sick benefit payments went up sometimes as much as 20 per cent." On one of his frequent study tours abroad, Frederick Hoffman found that "in Germany, during periods of unemployment, there is invariably a rapid rise in the curve of sickness[;] . . . fraudulent claims are made for sick benefits as a means of tiding over the pecuniary needs of prolonged periods of unemployment." [49] One doctor even observed that some employees saw worker's compensation benefits as a kind of retirement pension. He wrote, "Unfortunately human nature seeks rest as the sun of life sinks. . . . At about 50 years of age, a man . . . begins to feel that society owes him a rest and a pension and exaggerates [his disability] accordingly." [50]

Decades before the federal government acknowledged, through the Social Security Act, that wage earners might indeed deserve some help during unemployment or retirement, some workers used sickness and accident benefits to create their own, informal system of social insurance. Similarly, in a time of extremely long and mostly unregulated hours of labor, malingering could be a method for workers to win some leisure away from the workplace—a way to gain more control over their time. The same doctor noted that his malingering patients used their time off work to "sit around and talk or read . . . and do the chores." [51] Workers would exploit sickness as an excuse to prolong the weekend. The Metropolitan Life Insurance Company, which had its own health benefit plan, reported, "Rarely do we find [the employee's] incapacity terminating on . . . the last 4 days of the week. Almost invariably he returns to duty on Monday morning." [52] Workers deceived their bosses by using sick days for rest or recreation, but deception was not their goal so much as claiming some time off in the face of employer resistance to limitations on working hours. To employers who accused workers of malingering, a New York labor leader responded angrily, "The workman is not a machine guaranteed to grind out so many days work a year; he is an American citizen and is entitled to a few days' leisure." [53]

In some cases "malingering" could not even be called fraud or exaggeration but simply the attempt of workers to participate in medical diagnosis—in other words, to define their own pain or sickness, whether in agreement with their doctor's opinion or not. In a study of malingering, one doctor found that physicians and patients often had "different conception[s] as to what constitutes a complete healing." Frequently, there was a "difference between the time in which a patient may be discharged by the doctor and the time in which he would be able to do heavy manual labor." [54] Workers might "malinger" because they did not feel capable of returning to work, in essence demanding a diagnosis based on their own judgment of their health and well-being, rather than their physician's perception.

These accounts of the complex motives behind malingering received little attention compared to the employers' portrayal of the excessive fraud that they said would occur under a health insurance system. The image of the deceptive and lazy worker dominated the discussion, drowning out any attempts to reframe the debate away from the question of malingering and toward the actual problem of sickness among working people. But a few reformers did try. Lillian Wald, the famous nurse and settlement house worker, told assemblymen at the

1917 Albany hearing on health insurance that her years of experience among New York's working poor had convinced her that " 'the real malingering is the malingering of health rather than the malingering of sickness,' that is, the fear of stopping work to secure . . . needed medical attention when the loss of even a week's wages might mean destitution." [55] Others argued in a similar vein that the statistic so often invoked by opponents — that the number of sick days per worker increased under a health insurance system — was an indication not of malingering but of workers' ability to take the sick days they truly needed, rather than continuing to work no matter how ill they were.[56] In fact, many charity workers testified that the tendency to work during illness was so common that it contributed to a total breakdown of health for many workers, and to their eventual disability and destitution.[57]

But Wald's phrase "the malingering of health" was not adopted by the reformers as a weapon in the health insurance campaign. Few were as outspoken as she in their criticism of the malingering argument, or as explicit as hospital administrator and health insurance advocate John Lapp, who contended that "[t]he extent of malingering is exaggerated for political effect." [58] Instead, the supporters of health insurance emphasized how their plan, by keeping payments low and providing expert supervision, would efficiently curtail the inherent and inevitable tendency of workers to malinger.

Employers' emphasis on malingering was an extremely effective rhetorical strategy, for the opponents of health insurance could appear to be condemning only the possibility of fraud, rather than opposing the benefits themselves. The threat of malingering, which opponents said was a mark of workers' deceptiveness, was thus used to mask the interests of the enemies of health insurance who opposed the plan because it threatened their autonomy and their profits.

THE PROMISE OF EMPLOYER BENEFITS

In their studies inspired by the health insurance campaign, no subject received more attention from manufacturers' groups than the question of employer-sponsored health plans. As the AALL's bill came closer to passage in 1919, employers increasingly saw company insurance plans and health clinics as an effective way of obstructing the movement for compulsory health insurance.

Beginning around 1915, some large employers in major industrial centers had begun providing their workers with private benefits. Life insurance plans were the most common, but a few firms also offered sick pay. A representative of the American Telephone and Telegraph Corporation, which was one of the first companies in the nation to offer life insurance and pensions to its employees, echoed Progressive reasoning when he explained to a meeting of the NCF, "As we see it, the men and women who give their working lives to furnishing telephone service are fairly entitled, as a part of their conditions of employment, to know that they will not face destitution in sickness or in old age." [59] Employers also had financial incentives for creating private benefits. The NICB noted that factory health clinics would "materially improve the health conditions of the working force and, therefore, their productivity, and materially reduce [the employer's] own financial liability in connection with industrial accidents." [60]

Discussion of employer insurance and health plans reached a fever pitch during the campaign for health insurance. This was a direct reaction to the threat of the plan's success. An insurance executive admonished employers in 1918 to take out group insurance plans for their workers, for "if [they] do not . . . do this voluntarily, it is more than likely that ere long the State will compel them to do so." A Buffalo manufacturer wrote, "I feel quite certain that employers would be willing to pay quite a little more for insurance . . . this is because they are firm in their belief that the state and the nation fail when it comes to the management of a business." Both the NICB's 1919 study of factory health plans and its later, extensive survey of mutual aid societies were launched in response to the threat of compulsory health insurance. The NCF amassed voluminous material on employer health plans and in 1917 held an all-day meeting where employers discussed their experiences with workplace-based medical care. [61]

Employers met the challenge of compulsory health insurance, in part, by successfully advocating the growth of private benefits for workers. As historian Andrea Tone argues, "Employers eager to check and repel the tide of government regulation proffered welfare capitalism as an alternative to welfare statism." [62] The discussions inspired by the health insurance campaign laid the foundation for a heyday of welfare capitalism in the following decade. Both group insurance plans and medical services offered by employers increased dramatically following the defeat of health insurance; by 1926, the Bureau of Labor Statistics reported that more than four hundred large companies provided medical care for their employees. [63] In the long run health insurance would come to be seen as a burden on employers, especially as medical costs increased dramatically. However, employers' opposition to compulsory health insurance gave them a critical and long-lasting victory: private health plans today are still voluntary on the part of the employer, not a right of workers guaranteed by the state.

COMMERCIAL INSURANCE COMPANIES AND
COMPULSORY HEALTH INSURANCE

The U.S. insurance industry saw the compulsory health insurance campaign as a direct attack on its very existence. "If we have one duty to perform greater than another," declared an executive of the Travelers Insurance Company in 1917, "it is to turn the tide of public opinion against all kinds of federal and state insurance schemes."[64] Private insurers grimly envisioned the eventual disappearance of the entire commercial insurance industry were the AALL's plan successful. The National Fraternal Congress resolved that the adoption of compulsory health insurance would "bring about the result that all forms of insurance—life, casualty, fire and every other form—shall be carried solely by the government."[65] The Insurance Federation of New York lamented of the compulsory health insurance plan, "This is only the entering wedge; if once a foothold is obtained it will mean attempts to have such State Insurance of all kinds including Fire." The federation made sure that insurance agents would see compulsory health insurance as a threat to their very jobs: "It would mean the end of all Insurance Companies and Agents and to you personally the complete wrecking of the business and connections you have spent a lifetime in building and the loss of your bread and butter."[66]

The hysteria was not entirely unjustified. During the first two decades of the twentieth century, companies had achieved great success with industrial insurance, that is, individual life insurance policies sold to workers by agents who collected the premiums on monthly door-to-door visits. Industrial insurance did not cover illness; its appeal to workers lay in the modest funeral benefit it paid out upon the death of the policyholder.[67] The compulsory health insurance bill included a death benefit, which the AALL thought was "the most urgently felt insurance need of the classes subject to this act"[68] and which would render industrial insurance superfluous. As one insurance executive angrily told Andrews, commercial policies "provide a very large part of the insurance protection contemplated by the Health Insurance Bill . . . including funeral benefits."[69] Frederick Hoffman was equally alarmed, informing his employers at Prudential, "We, of course, cannot compete with Compulsory Insurance, including a death benefit of, say $100."[70] Since compulsory health insurance targeted low-income workers, who were the primary purchasers of industrial policies, its passage would likely wipe out private industrial insurance. Complained the insurance executive, "[A] very large proportion of the workers [holding industrial insurance policies] are earning less than $100 per month," the income limit specified by the AALL's bill.[71]

Insurance enterprises perceived themselves as even more vulnerable to state intervention than other businesses because of the widespread public distrust of their industry. During the depression of the 1890s, reports of extravagant salaries paid to insurance executives and high commissions to agents made insurance companies among the most vilified of businesses. The muckraking press carried frequent stories of insurers refusing to pay out just claims to their policyholders, and New York State's Armstrong Investigation in 1905 exposed the undue influence of insurance companies on the state legislature.[72] Even after the Armstrong Investigation brought about much-needed reforms, the industry's public image remained one of the worst of all businesses. Organized labor, especially, was suspicious of the industrial insurance industry, which it accused of preying on workers' fears and economic insecurity to its own profit. James Holland of the New York State Federation of Labor noted that "profit-making insurance companies" offered only "the most expensive form" of industrial insurance to workers, and he praised the New York workmen's compensation law for undercutting the power of private insurance companies in the state.[73] Reform rhetoric lambasting commercial insurance was reflected in a letter from John B. Andrews to a New York State senator praising her "championship of the cause of poor and ignorant men and women who are annually swindled by insurance companies." The League of Women Voters frowned upon industrial insurance companies that did "a fat business in collecting the weekly dimes of wage earners for burial insurance."[74]

Insurance executives were acutely sensitive to the public perception that their companies made unreasonable earnings. Haley Fiske, president of Metropolitan Life, told a New York audience, "People will look at our marble building on 23rd St. and that tower, which I hope you will agree with me is a noble specimen of architecture, and they say, look at the profits of industrial insurance."[75] Lee Frankel, director of Metropolitan's Welfare Division, took offense at a speech depicting his industry as the beneficiary of worker hardship, responding, "I am not here as the representative of the 'horrible example' held up to you this evening, an industrial insurance company which charges excessive rates for burial insurance."[76] Insurance companies were already on the defensive when the New York health insurance bill was proposed.

The exclusion of commercial insurance companies from participation in the system was one of the AALL's original standards for compulsory health insurance. This proved a popular tenet of the New York plan. Sidney Webb wrote from England that one of the worst features of his country's National Insurance Act was its failure to prohibit the participation of private insurance companies, which Webb referred to as "non-democratic bodies."[77] The International Fur Workers' Union praised the New York bill for its "complete exclusion of private insurance companies from the opportunity to make profits out of the sickness and misery of wage-earners." [78] Reformers took advantage of the insurance industry's negative image to promote their plan for health insurance. The AALL's J. P. Chamberlain argued that compulsory health insurance could offer workers protection that the private insurance industry "is confessedly unable to provide, or for which it is able to provide only partially and at an enormous ration of expense." [79] European state-run health insurance was more economically efficient than the commercial insurance industry in the United States, according to Olga Halsey. "The famous Leipzig sick fund [in Germany] spends less than 10 percent of its premium income on the administration," she noted, "whereas industrial health insurance companies in this country are spending from 35 to 60 percent on administration costs." [80]

Insurance company executives knew that with their industry's public image so poor their opposition to compulsory health insurance would be interpreted instantly as brazen self-interest. AALL supporter Rufus M. Potts, the insurance commissioner of Illinois, confirmed the industry's fears when he announced, "The howl about [health] insurance interfering with private business comes from extravagantly paid men who would be supplanted by government officials at moderate salaries." [81] Even employers' organizations contrasted their own opposition to health insurance with that of insurance companies. The NICB noted that insurers' dislike of the plan stemmed "from a selfish commercial standpoint," as opposed to the supposedly disinterested stance of manufacturers. [82]

In this hostile atmosphere, the insurance industry at first proceeded cautiously with its campaign against health insurance proposals. Prudential and the Metropolitan, the two largest industrial insurers, sent representatives to social insurance conferences and on research delegations to Europe but maintained a low profile during the first years of the health insurance battle. Beginning in 1915, Prudential charged Frederick Hoffman with the task of fighting compulsory health insurance proposals. As Hoffman said in 1920, the activity that "has drawn most heavily upon my time and strength in recent years . . . [has been] our *Health Insurance* investigations, and my participation in public meetings opposed to the propaganda." A man with extraordinary connections, Hoffman acted as Prudential's unofficial lobbyist against health insurance. On one 1916 trip to Washington, he met with such influential figures as members of the Children's Bureau, AFL president Samuel Gompers, and the U.S. surgeon general. [83] Prudential spared no expense in its efforts against health insurance, even sending Hoffman on a European research trip in 1919, complete with a full-time private secretary. [84]

Hoffman's correspondence with his employers at Prudential reflect his understanding that the health insurance proposal posed an economic threat to his industry but at the same time required him to downplay insurance companies' self-interest. There was no doubt, Hoffman warned his employers, that reformers' schemes for health insurance were "a menace to our interests" and "will imperil our future." [85] But he still cautioned against associating with any of the more aggressive trade federations that lobbied for insurance interests. One such association, the Insurance Federation of New York, had begun its fight against compulsory health insurance in 1916, calling for "concerted action on the part of all insurance men" to defeat the legislation.[86] Hoffman was approached by the federation's officers, but he told his boss, Forrest Dryden, that he was "apprehensive regarding too close an affiliation on the part of life insurance companies with the Insurance Federation," calling the group a "militant political organization neither always discreet in its activities nor generally successful in its results." Similarly, Hoffman balked at the idea of cooperating with the president of the Insurance Economics Society, a Detroit-based lobbying group that played a major role in the defeat of health insurance in California, "since, as I explained to him, his activities are in defense of the business which he represents, whereas [Prudential's] activities are limited entirely to scientific discussions of statistical and insurance data, etc." [87]

But Hoffman's claims that Prudential was simply a detached observer in the health insurance battle were spurious. His private correspondence with Prudential president Dryden veered between emphasizing health insurance's threat to the economic interests of insurance companies and insisting that Prudential held only a disinterested stake in the health insurance debate. Hoffman sounded wounded when Prudential was accused of self-interest, complaining to the AALL's Irving Fisher, "You are entirely in error when you assume that Industrial Life insurance companies, as such, are opposed to compulsory insurance on the ground of a possible conflict of interests." [88] Hoffman worked to mask Prudential's stake in the outcome of the health insurance battle. When he offered to share the findings of his European studies on health insurance with the NCF, Hoffman "did not go into details, for it seemed to me best not to overemphasize our interest in this matter." Reporting to Dryden on a speech he made denouncing health insurance, Hoffman noted, "As has been usual in all such cases, I left the Prudential and insurance out of the discussion entirely." [89]

Hoffman's behind-the-scenes work culminated in his influence on the health insurance commissions of Connecticut, Illinois, and Wisconsin. Although he was never an actual member of the commissions, Hoffman participated in their meetings "in [an] advisory capacity." Hoffman was nationally known for his published works on health insurance, and commission members probably saw him as an expert, not a lobbyist for the insurance industry. But Hoffman's work on the state commissions boldly crossed the line from impartial scientific study to the direct shaping of policy. His pressure on the commissions, he reported in 1918, "is bearing fruit. All of these Commissions will unquestionably report against any form of Social Insurance," which indeed they did. But Hoffman still insisted on Prudential's neutral role in the debate, referring to "the absolute impartiality of our cooperation" with the state commissions.[90]

Prudential had made a sound investment when it chose Frederick Hoffman as its spokesman against compulsory health insurance. His agitation was tireless, his influence widespread. Reporting on his progress, Hoffman told Dryden that Prudential's considerable expenditures on his efforts were paying off, "yielding results commensurate with the expense incurred."[91] Hoffman's studies of European social insurance were read and cited extensively; his participation in state health insurance commissions resulted in reports favorable to Prudential's interests. However, the health insurance bill's progress in New York in 1919 so alarmed Hoffman that he decided to move out from behind the scenes and advocate a more visible and active role for the insurance industry in the health insurance debate.

Despite his initial distrust of militant insurance industry mouthpieces like the Insurance Federation, Hoffman changed his tune by 1919, deciding that such organizations could be key players in anti–health insurance agitation: "Of late my views have somewhat changed regarding the Insurance Federation, for, after all, it may prove to be the only organization able to carry on a really effective public campaign, educational or otherwise, to oppose the rising tide of socialism and paternalism."[92] Hoffman's preferred technique—employing statistics and studies to discredit reformers' claims—was to be supplemented by vigorous political activity on the part of insurance companies.

This activity culminated in the creation of a front organization run by insurance companies solely to fight health insurance proposals in New York State. In the summer of 1919, Carleton D. Babcock, head of the Insurance Economics Society, arrived in Syracuse to open the office of an organization known as the New York League for Americanism. Babcock, a former journalist, was fresh from the health insurance battle in California, where he had run the successful campaign on behalf of private insurers to defeat the health insurance referendum in 1918. (He was responsible for the famous pamphlet titled "Made in Germany—Do You Want It in California?") While in the employ of the insurance industry as the head of its lobbying organization, the Insurance Economics Society, the blustery Babcock was one of the activists Hoffman initially condemned as an overly audacious defender of insurance interests. In the NYLA, however, the insurance industry found a highly effective voice. Concealing the fact that the league was actually a branch of the Insurance Economics Society,

Babcock painted himself as the champion of patriotism, not private insurers, in the Red Scare year of 1919. Amply funded by the insurance industry, and later by employers too, the NYLA became the umbrella organization for business groups to fight health insurance under the banner of patriotism.[93]

THE GENESIS OF COMMERCIAL HEALTH INSURANCE

Most insurance industry opposition to compulsory health insurance was provoked by the threat to the life insurance business; commercial companies had little experience with health insurance itself. The compulsory health insurance movement led the industry to recognize that it might develop its own health insurance plans, which would bolster the argument that state-run insurance was unnecessary. "The question of Health insurance is a mighty big one and is being discussed over all this country," said a Metropolitan Life Insurance Company executive in 1917. "This form of insurance is bound to come sooner or later—either compulsory or voluntary,"[94] and insurance companies began taking steps to ensure that voluntary, commercial health insurance would prevail.

Health insurance was an expensive and risky venture for commercial companies, and as a result such policies were rarely offered.[95] It took the movement for compulsory health insurance to galvanize the insurance industry's previously tentative forays into commercial health and disability plans. The AALL considered innovations in private health policies as blatant attempts by insurance companies to "capture as much as possible of the [health] business for their own financial profit."[96] Insurance interests, however, were at least as concerned with halting the move toward state-run insurance as they were with the money-making potential of private plans. Frederick Hoffman suggested to Prudential higher-ups in 1916, "It would seem entirely feasible to introduce into Industrial insurance a provision for medical attendance," emphasizing not the possibilities for financial gain of such an enterprise but that "[a]ll the essential arguments in favor of compulsory health insurance would be met by such an innovation."[97]

The commercial insurance industry explicitly connected the expansion of the private insurance market to a political strategy for the defeat of reform proposals. An agent of the Aetna Life Insurance Company warned physicians that the AALL's plan would be "force[d] . . . through this Legislature . . . UNLESS, in the meantime, THE OCCASION FOR COMPULSORY HEALTH INSURANCE IS REMOVED." The "best and only way" to accomplish this, continued the Aetna representative, was "by employers furnishing to their employees Group Disability Insurance administered (as under the Aetna plan) with the sole view of providing a satisfactory substitute for wages during disability." Aetna's group disability plan, the agent concluded, "can aid materially in the movement to SUPPRESS THE DEMAND FOR COMPULSORY HEALTH INSURANCE."[98]

The movement for compulsory health insurance, which intended in part to curb the power of commercial insurance companies in American life, instead became a catalyst for insurance industry involvement in health protection. Branching into health, group life, and disability insurance would allow insurance companies to accomplish two goals: to capture an area of insurance for which the demand seemed to be increasing, and to check the encroachment of government into the insurance business. In most cases, these motives were inseparable. In an address to the 1917 annual meeting of the Travelers Insurance Company, insurance executive Hiram J. Messenger proclaimed, "Health insurance is engaging the interest of all our legislators, and we should be in a position to meet their fantastic socialistic state Health insurance ideas by offering a good brand of sickness protection such as we know can be profitably written in a very much larger volume." The wide public interest in compulsory health insurance, and the threat of its passage in New York State, Messenger warned, meant that "[t]he time to start action on this matter is NOW."[99] And companies took action. Prudential started its group life insurance division in 1916, one year after the AALL announced its health insurance proposal, and began selling group health insurance in 1925, five years after its defeat. According to historian Jennifer Klein, the Equitable added disability benefits to its life insurance policies in 1917 as a direct response to the AALL's campaign. The Metropolitan sold its first individual health policy in 1921 and, alongside other large companies, began to market group disability insurance policies with increasing success throughout the 1920s.[100] As with employers, insurance company reaction to the threat of compulsory health insurance was clearly one of the factors that spurred the growth of welfare capitalism in the twenties.

New York labor leader James Lynch made an uncannily accurate prediction when he announced that if the movement for compulsory insurance failed, health insurance would "be instituted by the employers of this country in association with the private insurance carriers."[101] The expansion of private group insurance for workers would benefit both employers and insurance companies. Large employers willing to spend money on private plans could increase worker security and reduce labor unrest, while smaller firms would not be required to purchase the insurance. Crucially, employer-run plans could be reduced or eliminated in times of economic downturn. In the expansion of private benefits, insurers saw a chance to meet the demand for health insurance that the Progressives' campaign had uncovered. By offering to industry group plans that included disability insurance, as they increasingly did during the 1920s, commercial insurance companies tapped a potentially limitless source of new profit. For both employers and insurers, the desired outcome of private insurance plans was not just to thwart labor unrest or increase profits but to block the expansion of the welfare state. The triumph of private over compulsory insurance meant that employers and insurance companies could retain or increase their control of areas of influence threatened by government interference.

Clearly, an alliance of insurance companies and business owners opposed to compulsory health insurance would be a powerful one. But such an alliance was not automatic. Employers were reluctant to wholeheartedly embrace the insurance industry, particularly because of the poor public image of commercial insurance. Despite their close collaboration, the manufacturer-dominated National Civic Federation tried to keep its relationship with Frederick Hoffman hidden from public scrutiny. The NCF's Gertrude Easley noted that "it would probably be of no benefit to us to have [Hoffman] represent us as a committee of one in any way, because of the feeling against the insurance companies. He feels a bit offended, I think." [102] Although his feelings may have been hurt by the snubbing, Hoffman acknowledged that one benefit of Prudential's work with the NCF was the perception of the latter organization as more disinterested than the insurance industry. The NCF, Hoffman told his superior, had done a superb job of disseminating information on health insurance "representing our point of view, which if issued directly by the [insurance] companies, would not have had the same far-reaching effect." [103] Despite the occasional awkwardness of their association, insurance executives participated actively in the work of the NCF, whose committees included not only Hoffman but Haley Fiske and Lee Frankel of the Metropolitan as well. An outright alliance between insurance companies and New York manufacturers finally emerged with the creation of the NYLA in 1919. Shortly after setting up shop in Syracuse, the insurance company–sponsored league was joined by Mark Daly's AMM, which provided Babcock with still more funds. The Prudential Insurance Company donated copies of Frederick Hoffman's health insurance reports to Daly, which he apparently distributed to all AMM members.[104] The foundation for insurance company–manufacturer cooperation in the health insurance battle had been laid.

The campaign for health insurance aroused the opposition of an extraordinarily diverse collection of business enterprises, bringing them together in unprecedented unanimity. The employer divisiveness that preceded the acceptance of workmen's compensation was nowhere in evidence during the health insurance campaign. Manufacturers determined that they had nothing to gain financially from health insurance, and much to lose in the proposal's expansion of employer responsibility for the health and income maintenance of workers. Insurance companies rallied against the threat of compulsory health insurance to their domination of the industrial insurance market. Both employers and insurers seized on the campaign for health insurance as an opportunity to halt the surge of Progressive legislation and to limit state intrusion into their business affairs.

But to oppose health insurance on these grounds would invite charges of shameless profiteering and self-interest and weaken business's ability to influence the debate. Insurers and manufacturers instead adopted a variety of rhetorical strategies to downplay or mask their economic stake in the health insurance battle. Employers' public pronouncements emphasized the cost of health insurance to the consumer, through higher prices, and to workers, through the threat of job loss and the moral danger of malingering. Commercial insurers were even more careful to camouflage their financial stake in the health insurance question by confining their opposition to behind-the-scenes work, by portraying their interest in health insurance as solely "scientific," and, finally, by creating a front organization, the New York League for Americanism, that claimed to champion not insurance companies but patriotic values.

6

The House of
Labor Divided

Organized labor in the United States has been a principal supporter of universal health insurance since the 1930s.[1] In the Progressive Era, however, the mainstream labor movement embodied in the American Federation of Labor forcefully opposed compulsory health insurance. AFL president Samuel Gompers called the AALL's social insurance proposals "a menace to . . . [the] rights, welfare, and . . . liberty" of American workers. The American Association for Labor Legislation's health insurance plan, according to its opponents, was destined to fail because it was resisted not only by the designated providers of health insurance — doctors and employers — but also by its potential beneficiaries, the workers themselves.[2]

But on closer examination, the story is more complicated. Samuel Gompers's distaste for social insurance was far from universal in the ranks of organized labor. As one labor leader declared in 1919, "Misleading statements have recently been circulated in New York State in an attempt to make it appear that organized labor is opposed to a health insurance law. Quite the contrary is true."[3] In defiance of the official AFL position, local trade union leaders in New York threw their support behind the AALL's proposal, and in 1919 the New York State Federation of Labor became a co-sponsor of the health insurance bill.

The question of whether "labor" approved of compulsory health insurance was a contentious one. Both the reformers and the forces of opposition sought to claim the allegiance of organized labor to their side. Business groups printed pamphlets featuring Gompers's attacks on the AALL and eagerly recruited conservative labor leaders to the anti–health insurance cause. Reformers amassed testimony in favor of health insurance from trade unionists and enlisted labor representatives to champion the legislation at state assembly hearings. Both sides claimed to speak for the true interests of labor.

But labor was too divided against itself to present a unified voice or interest. The AFL leadership sought to protect craft unionism from the meddling of reformers and government, while local unionists wanted health insurance to protect industrial workers and the unorganized. This led to a debate between the national AFL on the one hand and state-level leaders, industrial unions, and women organizers on the other that raised sharp disagreements over the relationship of workers to the state. As the dispute grew more contentious, the AFL's attempt to block health insurance drew it startlingly close to business interests—so close that Samuel Gompers would enlist the help of a prominent commercial insurance executive in his quest to rebut his fellow unionists' support for compulsory health insurance.

Samuel Gompers's relationship with the AALL had already soured by the time of the health insurance campaign. Gompers had earlier been an honorary vice president of the AALL, but he resigned angrily in 1915 because of its support for a bill he considered antilabor.[4] After his resignation, Gompers continued to publicly oppose the AALL's activities. In 1916, the labor leader published his unforgettable attack on health insurance, "Labor vs. Its Barnacles," in the AFL journal *American Federationist*. Of health insurance, Gompers wrote, "Compulsory sickness insurance for workers is based upon the theory that they are unable to look after their own interests and the state must interpose its authority. . . . There is something in the very suggestion . . . that is repugnant to free-born citizens. Because it is at variance with our concepts of voluntary institutions and freedom for individuals, Labor questions its wisdom." Gompers judged legislation by its perceived effect on his vision of a labor movement built on craft unionism. Compulsory health insurance would undermine trade union power, Gompers argued, by replacing union-run benefit schemes with a state-administered system.[5] In his view, workers could best secure their health through strong unions that would win higher wages and provide benefits for their members. Gompers's antipathy to the health insurance bill stemmed from "his anxiety that the labor movement shall be the all-in-all of the workers," explained a union leader to John B. Andrews.[6]

Health insurance would undermine not only workers' unions, according to Gompers, but also their individual liberties as Americans. The AFL leader's fierce reaction to the proposal sprang from his strongly held conception of the "independence" of the American worker.[7] Government interference in any aspect of workers' lives was suspect, but in the case of medical care it represented a direct threat to the privacy of workers' home lives and even of their bodies. Gompers cautioned that the AALL's plan was "especially serious" because "it has to do with such intimate matters as health. When once a political agent is authorized to take care of the health of citizens, there is no limit to the scope of his activities or his right to interfere in all of the relations of life." The AFL leader predicted that health insurance would sanction the invasion of workers' privacy by government doctors, who would employ compulsory physical examinations to screen out unfit laborers. Even workers' own homes "would not be sacred from intrusions," wrote Gompers.[8] The AALL's insistence that compulsory examinations were not required under health insurance was not enough to dissuade Gompers from his belief that the legislation would mean state intrusion into the intimate realms of health and home.

The AALL's hope for the support of trade unionists received another blow in 1916 when James Holland, president of the NYSFL, announced his opposition to the New York health insurance bill. Although he claimed to approve the principle of health insurance, Holland feared that private insurance companies would profit from the plan, and also that workers would be denied free choice of doctors.[9] Holland was particularly incensed by the bill's requirement that workers pay for part of the costs of health insurance, declaring that reformers "have no right to tell me where to pay my money; I do not think a law compelling me to pay it would be constitutional." In a direct jab at the AALL, Holland told a hearing at Albany, "The people most interested in this bill were never consulted, [namely] the labor people of the State. . . . This was drafted, and then given to us to eat, and we refuse to eat it."[10]

The rebuff from both Gompers and the NYSFL caused much consternation at the AALL office. Olga Halsey wrote to James Holland, informing him that "[t]hose in favor of health insurance legislation cannot but regret your opposition," particularly since the hated private insurance interests had gleefully pounced upon Holland's criticisms as evidence of labor's rejection of compulsory health insurance. "I have noticed that some of the insurance journals are out in headlines saying 'Labor interests against Mills Bill,'" Halsey told Holland.[11] Reformer Mary Van Kleeck agreed that Holland's pronouncements made it seem "as though our trade union friends were playing into the hands of their enemies."[12]

The AALL scrambled to defend itself from accusations that it had failed to confer with labor in drafting the health insurance bill. "The records of our office show that consultation with labor has not been omitted," Halsey told Holland. "Thus as soon as the tentative draft was ready for distribution in December, copies were sent, urging cooperation, to the State Federation, to the leading city centrals in the country, and to all the city centrals in New York a week later."[13] Halsey could not deny that labor's advice was solicited only *after* the proposal had been drafted. John Andrews admitted that trade unionists had not been closely involved in the AALL's deliberations on health insurance but claimed he had been unable to find labor leaders who could attend regular meetings.[14] The reformers found themselves suffering for their failure to see labor as an equal partner in their campaign.

The combined attacks from Gompers and Holland forced the AALL to stop taking labor's support for granted. The reformers began rallying trade unionists to their cause. Early in 1916, Andrews wrote letters explaining the health insurance bill to dozens of union leaders around the country, seeking their endorsement. Although belated, the AALL's direct-mail campaign was fruitful, gathering a large volume of responses from union leaders in favor of health insurance. From the president of the Granite Cutters, Andrews heard, "To wage earners health insurance is next in importance to compensation for industrial accidents."[15] William Green of the United Mine Workers disagreed with Gompers's contention that workers should and could take care of themselves. "The care of those among the workers who are ill, incapacitated, or . . . no longer able to earn a livelihood, will not be voluntarily assumed," argued Green. "Therefore . . . in the interest of the public welfare, compulsory legislation . . . seems to be the only feasible plan."[16] (Had Green become AFL president in 1916 instead of in 1925, the AFL's response to compulsory health insurance would have been dramatically different. Green would devote much of his time in office to fighting for national health insurance legislation.[17]) In another letter to the AALL, the Central Labor Union of White Plains endorsed health insurance on the grounds that "we believe this measure to be fully justified by the self-respect such a bill would instill, and the burden it would remove from our local charities."[18] And the secretary of the American Wire Weavers' Protective Association wrote to Andrews that the average worker "will stay on and work when he is physically unable to do justice to his work, or his employer" because his family would suffer from the lost wages. "[F]or that reason," he concluded, "I think that the Health Insurance legislation is one of the best things ever done for the workers of this State."[19]

These letters made clear that Gompers's view was not shared by all union leaders. And in fact, New York State's most powerful labor men were starting to move away from the AFL's position toward an explicit endorsement of health insurance. Although both James Holland and labor commissioner James Lynch spoke for the opposition at the 1917 Senate Judiciary Committee hearing on the Mills Bill, they were already sounding less hostile toward compulsory health insurance. "Our opposition was not to the principle of the Mills bill," explained Holland, "but because we could not endorse the method of compulsory money contributions by wage earners . . . and could not secure a clear conception of how its many intricate details would develop in actual practice."[20] Both Holland and Lynch expressed their support for the creation of a commission to investigate health insurance. And by 1918, the NYSFL had thrown its full support behind the health insurance proposal.

The state's labor leaders changed their minds about health insurance in part because of the AALL's newfound concern for labor's opinion. Lynch felt that the AALL had "changed its policy entirely" when it came to conferring with trade unionists; since 1916, he said, the reformers had sought the advice of labor in all their undertakings.[21] The AALL addressed the objections raised by James Holland by assuring him that health insurance guaranteed free choice of physician and no mandatory physical exam, and that private insurance companies would be banned from the proposed system.[22] Holland also reversed himself on the issue of wage deductions, and he came to see the worker contribution as an essential means to ensure representation for labor in the system's governance. The NYSFL held a conference on health insurance early in 1918, at which labor representatives carefully studied the AALL's proposal. The meeting ended with a charge to the federation's executive council to promote the compulsory health insurance plan.[23]

At the NYSFL's 1918 convention in Rochester, union delegates seemed convinced that the health insurance bill could be shaped in the interest of labor. A member of the executive council commented, "[A] social insurance bill will be introduced sooner or later, whether we like it or not, and the question is whether that bill should be one that we have framed or whether it should be one that the employer may frame."[24] Labor leaders were alarmed by the opposition of employer and commercial insurance interests to health insurance. Critics of the AALL, argued James Lynch, were playing into the hands of "profiteering employers [who] desire to throttle health insurance." Responding to a description of German health insurance as an attempt to crush the socialist movement, a delegate elicited laughter when he remarked, "I don't think [health insurance] is a mask to stave off Socialism, because I am under the opinion that Socialism will come anyhow." Other delegates made emotional appeals on behalf of health insurance with descriptions of workers plunged into poverty by exorbitant medical costs when sickness struck their families.[25] The assembled delegates enthusiastically applauded these speeches, and their favorable sentiments were confirmed when the convention endorsed compulsory health insurance by a vote of 270 to 1.[26]

Like Holland, James Lynch dramatically reversed his position and became a staunch supporter of health insurance. Lynch, a printer and sometime Irish nationalist, won the presidency of the International Typographical Union in 1900 (he worked alongside Gompers in the printers' eight-hour strike of 1905). In 1914, he left the union to become New York's commissioner of labor.[27] As commissioner, Lynch made a name for himself as a champion of labor reform and regulation. His initial criticism of the AALL's compulsory health insurance proposal stemmed not from a principled dislike of labor legislation but from his resentment at the reformers' failure to consult labor while formulating the bill—including (or especially) himself. But thanks to the AALL's belated lobbying, Lynch struck up a close working relationship with Andrews and quickly threw his weight behind the health insurance plan. Well known throughout the state and highly respected by his former union colleagues, Lynch convinced the Typographical Union to pass a resolution in favor of health insurance at their 1918 convention, and he regularly praised health insurance in the union's journal. He argued that compulsory contributions would be a tiny fraction of workers' pay, and, besides, unlike for workers compensation, employers should not be responsible for the entire burden of workers' illnesses. Lynch reassured the typographers that insured employees would not be required to undergo a physical exam and that they would have free choice of physicians. Gompers did not speak for all organized labor, said Lynch: "We propose to make up our own minds on the subject. And we think we are intelligent enough to do that."[28]

State labor leaders boldly aired their differences with Gompers. John Mitchell, head of the New York Industrial Commission and former leader of the United Mine Workers, informed a New York newspaper, "Whereas the utterances of Mr. Gompers . . . represent individual opinion only, over forty state and national federations of labor are on record in favor of health insurance."[29] Lynch's and Mitchell's defiance of Gompers reflected a long-standing rift between the national AFL and state labor groups on questions of legislation. Scholars have described how local labor leaders regularly ignored the directives of the national AFL by supporting social insurance and other reform measures.[30] Unlike the national AFL, state federations of labor were voluntary organizations created explicitly to pursue legislation favorable to workers and so were far more open to new proposals for state action. Also, state-level organizations were more concerned with the needs of unorganized workers than was the AFL and hence supported the broad worker protections offered by labor legislation.[31]

The state federation was not the only labor renegade on the health insurance issue. New York's women labor leaders also made up their minds independently of Samuel Gompers. The Women's Trade Union League and the International Ladies' Garment Workers' Union joined the health insurance campaign after the AALL added maternity benefits to its proposal in 1916. Labor leaders like Rose Schneiderman and Pauline Newman saw the maternity benefits, which provided maternity care and sick pay to insured women, as an essential element of protection for women workers.[32] The WTUL had been founded in 1903 to organize female industrial workers. Its members, an alliance of middle- and working-class women, struggled to redress the AFL's sorry neglect of women workers, who were viewed by male labor leaders as "at worst, unorganizable and, at best, temporary members of the workforce."[33] The WTUL championed both unionization and protective legislation for women. The ILGWU was an AFL affiliate with an all-male leadership, but its members were primarily immigrant women. The ILGWU's status as an industrial union differentiated it from most AFL unions, as did its support for labor legislation. Also, the ILGWU had long been concerned with the health of its members, having established its own Union Health Clinic in 1913.

ILGWU organizer Pauline Newman became one of the health insurance bill's most ardent and effective supporters. Newman, a young Lithuanian-Jewish immigrant, had worked in New York City's sweatshops since the age of ten. At fifteen, she joined the Socialist Party, and in 1910 she was hired as an organizer for the ILGWU.[34] She was also an active member of the WTUL. Although only in her twenties, Newman was an experienced and passionate public speaker. At the March 1916 Albany hearing on the health insurance bill, Newman declared that her union endorsed health insurance because "it is about time that society . . . take the responsibility of protecting the health of the workers." If it would not, would the state let workers "die and suffer and become a burden?" Government, said Newman, should protect "the health of its people, instead of protecting business."[35]

Although Newman's socialism and her fiery outspokenness were in distinct contrast to the AALL's ideology and lobbying methods, John B. Andrews was quick to see the effectiveness of her style and acclaimed Newman as health insurance's most impressive labor spokesperson. He told John R. Commons that Newman had "made the best labor speech at our hearing."[36] Another observer described Newman as an extraordinarily powerful advocate of the legislation, reporting after Newman's speech on health insurance in Philadelphia, "The Academy of Music was literally packed and everybody was breathless while she spoke."[37] When Newman returned to Albany in 1917 to testify for health insurance, she acknowledged the AFL's position, saying, "I am sorry some of my friends in the labor movement have different views on the subject," but she predicted that in "a few years" they would come to agree with her on the importance of health insurance to workers.[38]

Newman's defiance of the AFL throws into sharp relief the gendered assumptions behind Samuel Gompers's view of health insurance. Gompers condemned social insurance by invoking a definition of American labor that rested on republican notions of masculinity and independence. Compulsory health insurance was objectionable to Gompers because it threatened privacy, autonomy, and independence—qualities associated with the AFL's "muscular fraternity of skilled male workers,"[39] not with women. Since women, even working women, were by definition dependent, they could not be defined as true workers in Gompers's sense. This ideology was at the heart of the American Federation of Labor's support of protective legislation for women workers, even as it opposed similar measures for men: women's independence was not threatened by state intervention because womanhood was synonymous with dependency.[40]

Pauline Newman directly challenged these notions of dependence and independence. Gompers's picture of the "independent" American worker eliminated not only working women, she said, but most working men as well. "They claim that labor can take care of itself," said Newman in a speech on health insurance. But, she continued, only three million out of about thirty million wage earners in the United States belonged to the AFL, "which means that a very small minority may be in a position to care for itself, while the great mass of unorganized workers are not in any position to look after their own sickness and their own problems." It was not enough for organized workers to protect themselves while the unorganized went without protection. "That is why [the ILGWU] is in favor of health insurance and social insurance," declared Newman. "We can take care of ourselves, but who are we? A mere hundred and fifty thousand."[41]

In her speeches, Newman tried to shatter the myth of the independent working man by insisting that not for just women but for most wage-earning people complete self-reliance was an unreachable goal. Assistance from the state was therefore a matter of justice for all workers. Her devotion to women and the unorganized (two categories that often were synonymous) led Newman to see social legislation not as a threat to workers' autonomy but as the surest means to improve conditions for the greatest number.

Newman also held a very different view of the state than that of the AFL leader. Gompers strongly felt that the state was inimical to workers' interests. His distaste for state activism arose, quite understandably, from years of experience with government repression of trade unions. Gompers distrusted state involvement in workers' lives because of the long history of judicial attacks on labor by the American state.[42] Perhaps because Newman came of age at a time when government, especially in New York, was beginning to address the inequities of industrial society (and also because of her socialist ideology), she had great hopes for the ability of an activist state to improve workers' lives. "[H]ealth insurance is neither more nor less than a step toward social responsibility," said Newman. "It will make the people realize they are not separate and apart from the state." In Newman's view, government involvement was not an attempt to repress the labor movement but a matter of justice. As Newman told the New York Senate Judiciary Committee at its 1917 hearing on health insurance, "I do not call [state action] paternalism, because I am looking forward to the time when the state will come to the conclusion that it owes something to its working men and women."[43]

By 1918, the AFL was clearly facing major challenges to its stance on health insurance from the NYSFL, the WTUL, the ILGWU, and numerous union locals. At the 1918 AFL convention in St. Paul, labor's split over health insurance emerged as delegates put forward opposing resolutions. Representatives of the ILGWU introduced a resolution that went even beyond the AALL's bill by calling for "the adoption by the Government of a comprehensive national system of Social Insurance." It was never brought to a vote. Instead, the convention passed a resolution instructing the AFL Executive Committee to investigate the question of health insurance. The committee quickly produced a report that "by unanimous vote concluded in favor of voluntary health insurance and against compulsory health insurance."[44] This may have been the official AFL position, but it would not go unchallenged. Instead, it inspired vigorous discussion within the labor movement over the possible impact of compulsory health insurance on unions and on the health and welfare of workers.

LABOR DEBATES HEALTH INSURANCE

While labor supporters and opponents of health insurance did not always fall into easily delineated categories, some generalizations are still possible. Supporters tended to include state labor federations, women-dominated trade unions, industrial unions, and unions whose members suffered a high rate of on-the-job disease and mortality. Those who opposed compulsory health insurance included labor leaders with close relationships to Samuel Gompers, unions that strongly adhered to the bread-and-butter unionism of the AFL, and unions with their own welfare benefit schemes (although there were some extremely important exceptions to this last rule). The debate between supporters and opponents revealed a great diversity of voices within American labor on the questions of health insurance and state intervention in workers' lives.

Opponents of health insurance from the labor movement argued that the AALL's plan would undermine the ability of unions to organize and attract more members. First, compulsory health insurance would weaken union recruiting by replacing labor-controlled benefits with a state-run system. Much of the union opposition to health insurance "came from a feeling that . . . the elimination of their special funds for this purpose also meant that it would eliminate an organizing feature that was particularly attractive." More broadly, government intervention in the workplace would subsume trade union activity. Anti–health insurance unionists insisted that "organized labor will secure all desired improvements in working conditions by the strength and pressure of their organization" rather than by making demands upon the state.[45]

Ironically, in their attempts to provoke opposition to health insurance, business leaders argued that the plan would actually *increase* the power of labor unions. Insurance executive Frederick Hoffman warned that pro–health insurance labor leaders in New York saw in the proposal "far-reaching possibilities of increasing the power and prestige of organized labor." Indeed, European trade unionists, Hoffman reported, "look upon [compulsory health insurance] as a valuable source of increased power, particularly in the direction of a more effective organization." Incensed that labor would be represented on the health insurance commission proposed by the AALL's bill, Mark A. Daly told the members of New York's Associated Manufacturers and Merchants that compulsory health insurance "would permit James M. Lynch, John Mitchell, or any other leader of labor, to drive into the unions every worker in the State, male and female, in spite of the personal desires of the workers themselves. It is nothing more or less than the State of New York acting as organizer for the New York State Federation of Labor."[46] Compulsory health insurance, these business leaders thought, would strengthen labor by giving it a permanent voice in state government.

Labor supporters did not go as far as business leaders in proclaiming the advantages of health insurance to union organizing. (Perhaps, had they done so, the AALL might have won the support of more conservative trade unionists.) Instead they emphasized the measure's benefits to unorganized workers. Health insurance, argued James Lynch, "is especially important to the very large number of wage-earners in this state who have not yet organized themselves." Because they lacked access to union benefit funds or were too poorly paid to afford joining private benefit societies, unorganized workers had nothing to lose with the establishment of a health insurance system, and much to gain. The NYSFL's concern for unorganized workers contrasted sharply with the AFL's neglect. At a meeting of the NYSFL, one delegate echoed Pauline Newman by pointing out that unionized, well-paid workers might not have much interest in health insurance, but "we must not lose sight of the fact that there are hundreds and thousands of men that will come under the provision of this bill who have no voice at all here, and we ought to consider those men in our deliberation."[47]

Labor opponents of health insurance argued that the proposal was a direct threat to the sickness funds administered by trade unions. One New York unionist told the NYSFL that his union had its own sickness benefits, and thus he "did not feel at liberty to vote for a bill which may interfere with that organization." If workers were required to pay premiums for state health insurance, they would have nothing left over to maintain their union benefit societies, which would most likely collapse.[48]

But other labor leaders reasoned that existing union sickness benefit schemes were not worth preserving. J. G. Skemp of the Painters' Brotherhood noted that "the sick benefit provided by many trades unions is inadequate in amount and is paid for too short a period," and, unlike the compulsory health insurance fund, which would require state and employer contributions, "the entire amount [of the union benefit fund] comes from the earnings of the workman."[49] Another reason union benefits were inferior to compulsory health insurance, according to supporters, was that labor unions simply did not have the resources to guarantee them. The president of the Tunnel and Subway Constructors' International Union said that his union had provided sickness benefits until "it was determined that such a large number of its members suffered from stone-cutters consumption" that the fund would be depleted. As a result, the union eliminated the benefits.[50] Other trade unionists pointed out that union benefit funds rarely provided medical care, a pillar of the compulsory health insurance proposal in New York. Most important, the union sickness plans touted by health insurance opponents covered only a small number of workers. Even the delegate to the NYSFL who rejected the compulsory proposal because his own union provided sick pay conceded, "I realize that all organizations haven't got these benefits."[51]

Some labor leaders argued that compulsory health insurance was superior to union benefits as a matter of principle, because society as a whole should be responsible for the costs of sickness. The United Mine Workers' William Green wrote that "the burden of taking care of workers who are ill . . . is altogether too great to be borne" by trade union benefit funds. Green also thought it unjust that "the working people themselves bear this financial burden" without assistance from employers and the state.[52] The Typographical Union agreed, declaring in 1917 that the "necessity of American workers to provide their own benefits is a gross injustice."[53] The Typographical Union was a determined supporter of compulsory health insurance even though it already had one of the most successful union benefit programs in the country, which provided life insurance and tuberculosis care to its members. These benefits were undoubtedly a major incentive for union membership. Since the Mine Workers, the ILGWU, and the Typographers had far more extensive benefits than most American unions, there was clearly no automatic correlation between a union's provision of benefits and its opposition to compulsory health insurance.[54]

While labor opponents of compulsory health insurance wanted to defend trade union benefit schemes, much of their distaste for the reformers' plan stemmed from their negative experience with employer-run benefits (see Chapter 1). Any system such as compulsory health insurance that involved employer contributions and governance aroused suspicion, particularly because employer plans were seen as a means for reducing labor turnover by forcing workers to stay in their jobs in order to collect the benefits. Compulsory health insurance, opponents argued, would have the same effect: "In plain English, the workers under this scheme are chained to their jobs," the AFL's Grant Hamilton announced.[55]

John R. Commons, founder of the AALL, countered that compulsory insurance would end forever the tendency of benefit schemes to reduce workers' freedom to move from job to job. While private insurance tied the laborer to a particular employer, "[u]niversal insurance will liberate him. . . . It prevents the workman's dread of sickness and death from being used to tie him to his job." The WTUL agreed, declaring that "universal application of health insurance by the obligatory method" would guarantee that "labor is safeguarded in its freedom to move about in accordance with its needs without suffering loss of benefits."[56] While opponents' fears about being tied to jobs were wholly understandable in light of labor's experience with employer-controlled welfare schemes, the AALL's bill did partly address this concern. Because most employers in New York State would be required to provide coverage, changing jobs within the state would not mean losing benefits.

The idea of compulsory wage deductions to pay for health insurance premiums was a central feature of the AALL's health insurance plan, not only for reasons of financing but as a matter of principle. In a much-repeated argument, supporters of health insurance insisted that their plan would remove all elements of charity because workers paid their share of the premiums. Those who condemned health insurance as charity were mistaken, said the secretary of the Pipe Caulkers and Tappers Union, "because the worker contributes just as much as the employer," adding that it would be "equally just to say that the employer receives charity, because the worker contributes."[57] Workers' payments into a health insurance system would guarantee both their right to democratically participate in running the system and their freedom from pauperization and paternalism.

But the worker contribution raised the hackles of many labor leaders. A delegate to the NYSFL angrily declared, "I want to know if my organization is going to be made to pay twenty-four cents a week, because if we are, we are going to see that means are taken to tack that twenty-four cents onto the wage scale." The question of wage deductions deeply divided labor and gave rise to confusion over which type of health insurance financing would be most beneficial to workers. Many unionists seemed to agree with the delegate who thought that "health insurance may be all right, but I object to the worker having to pay for it," and they suggested that the state and the employer bear the entire burden of the premiums.[58] But others took the opposite approach, supporting worker contributions on the grounds that they would give labor more control and responsibility in the administration of health insurance.

Labor's bickering over the details of the health insurance bill reflected deeper disagreements about health care and the relationship of workers to the state. No one could deny the importance of workers' health or the economic devastation caused by time lost to sickness, but neither could trade unionists agree on the best method for addressing the problem of illness among working people and whether the state should be involved.

The provision of medical care made health insurance different from other types of social insurance that were intended solely for income maintenance. Although health insurance supporters in the labor movement agreed on the importance of maintaining workers' incomes, what appealed to them most about the AALL's plan was its promise to reduce ill health among workers. That labor supporters spoke more frequently about the health benefits of the legislation than the financial ones reflects how large the threat of illness and disability loomed among their constituencies. Since so much poor health was caused by conditions in the workplace, health insurance would force employers to provide a more sanitary environment. Not only would sanitation improve, but the conditions of work, too, would be adjusted to ensure workers' health. The *Union Labor Journal* informed its readers, "[W]e imagine [health insurance] will have the effect of reducing the excessive working hours yet customary in some employments" that were detrimental to workers' health.[59] The leader of the Pennsylvania State Federation of Labor put it more bluntly: "If the employers are held responsible for the health of their employees, it will remove the incentive to wreck their health in the mad rush for profits."[60]

Workers in industries with very high health risks saw a particular advantage in compulsory health insurance. The Fur Workers' Union passed a resolution strongly in favor of the AALL's bill in part because "the trade of fur workers is constantly menaced by dust, chemicals, poisons, and dangerous disease germs, rendering workers therein specially susceptible to tuberculosis and other trade maladies," making health costs a major concern of the union's members.[61] The ILGWU, the most active union supporter of health insurance, had long worked to address its mostly immigrant members' high rate of tuberculosis. Other unions in the dangerous or unhealthy trades that supported compulsory health insurance included the United Mine Workers, the International Brotherhood of Foundry Employees, the Tunnel and Subway Constructors' Union, and unions of steam engineers, textile workers, and paper mill workers.[62]

Illness was a threat to workers' economic as well as physical well-being not just because they lost wages but because of the cost of medical care. One New York trade unionist said that his fellow union members "have stated to me many times, 'Why should I save money? The moment I get about a hundred dollars together, the wife gets sick, the baby gets sick, or somebody else, and it's all wiped out.' . . . That is the bugbear of a wage-earner's life — sickness in his family."[63] A member of the Typographical Union wrote that he and many of his fellow workers "never lay off or visit a physician when feeling slightly and sometimes very ill, for the reason that we fear the doctor's bill and the fear of enforced idleness without pay."[64] Delegate Curtis of the NYSFL attacked the high fees of physicians, calling the medical care available to working people in New York City "atrocious . . . the treatment they receive and the amount they are charged by the doctors who treat them, would make your head swim." The class-conscious Curtis argued that health insurance would force high-priced physicians to care for workers: "Why shouldn't we regulate the doctors under health insurance so that the workingman would be entitled to the same treatment as the millionaire is?"[65]

Labor opponents of health insurance, while agreeing that workers' health needed improvement, insisted that workers could provide for themselves through their unions. At an earlier AFL convention, one orator expressed this view by declaring that workplace conditions and workers' health would improve "[i]n the same degree that the trade union movement becomes powerful." Strong unions would improve workers' health, Gompers's associate Grant Hamilton agreed, through "this great sanitary measure — increase of wages."[66] Embracing the AFL's wage-based unionism, labor opponents of health insurance argued that economic improvements guaranteed by unions, not compulsory health insurance, would ensure the health of their members. Although they acknowledged the importance of health to workers, labor opponents of health insurance tried to move the debate away from the question of health care and back to economic issues that fell squarely within the realm of traditional trade union activity. The AFL's Social Insurance Committee, which issued the report unfavorable to compulsory health insurance, criticized the AALL's contention that sickness was the major cause of poverty. Instead, the committee argued powerfully, "poverty with its many other hardships, in addition to sickness, is the result of economic injustice, and the removal of this injustice is one of the great tasks of the American Labor movement."[67] To AFL leaders, their opponents' emphasis on workers' helplessness in the face of sickness undermined the attempts of the labor movement to foster independence, self-determination, and higher wages through unions.

The debate over health insurance raised an even more contentious issue that divided labor opinion: the role of the state. Samuel Gompers's distrust of government had stiffened in long years of battling state repression of the labor movement. His supporter Grant Hamilton rejected the increased role for the state demanded by health insurance legislation, pointing out that federal and state governments "have been made the instruments of oppression under the guise of benefiting the workers."[68] The state was perceived as a negative force not just because it repressed unions, but because its intervention created un-American dependency and unmanliness. Warren Stone of the Locomotive Brotherhood, another associate of Gompers, put it contemptuously: "I do not believe in a government that tucks you in bed at night." Health insurance was particularly suspect to labor leaders wary of the state because of its involvement in the highly personal and private area of medical care. Echoing Gompers's concern that health insurance would lead to the invasion of workers' homes, the AFL's Hugh Frayne remarked that if the AALL's bill passed, "I suppose the next step will be to see that we are properly mated."[69]

With distrust of government so widespread in the AFL, trade union advocates of health insurance had to justify their support by arguing, as did Pauline Newman, that the state could be a benevolent force in the lives of workers.[70] Government, commented James Lynch, could act as a check on the power of employers to provide or take away benefits at will; workers under compulsory health insurance "will not then be at the mercy of the rapacity, or greed, or kindness, or charity of the employer. The state . . . will see that full and even justice is accorded."[71] State-controlled benefits at least offered some measure of accountability, unlike benefits controlled either by employers or by commercial insurance companies. Delegate Schneider told the 1918 convention of the NYSFL, "I would rather throw my little lot, my few dollars that I insure my family with, into the state, than to continue to throw it into private casualty [insurance] companies."[72]

The resolution in favor of compulsory health insurance put forward by the ILGWU at the 1918 AFL convention included language portraying the state as an instrument to better the conditions of its citizens, especially in matters of health. "It is generally recognized," the garment workers' union resolved, "that it is the supreme duty of the Nation to maintain and uplift the physical and economic standards of its citizens and to care for such of its workers as become physically unable to earn a livelihood."[73] This statement reflected some wishful thinking on the part of the ILGWU, because its definition of the state's role, far from being "generally recognized," was hotly contested. Which view of the state and which response to compulsory health insurance would prevail as the "voice of labor" would depend more on political strategy than on rhetorical persuasion.

THE AMERICAN FEDERATION OF LABOR AND THE NATIONAL CIVIC FEDERATION

The AFL's alliance with the influential NCF played a crucial role in the public depiction of Gompers as the true voice of labor, and eventually in the defeat of compulsory health insurance. The NCF, which brought together prominent businessmen and conservative labor leaders, was one of the most vocal opponents of the New York health insurance proposal. The NCF saw in Samuel Gompers the key to its attack on compulsory health insurance. Gompers, in turn, willingly enlisted the NCF's support in his battle with the NYSFL over health insurance, expressing a sense of brotherhood with the business-oriented leaders of the NCF that he seemed to lack with local unionists.

Chicago journalist Ralph Easley had founded the NCF in 1901 to promote conciliation in labor disputes. Easley, a "man of restless energy," demonstrated a remarkable ability to bring together labor leaders and the "masters of capital" in pursuit of industrial peace. Easley recruited prominent industrialists like Andrew Carnegie, Mark Hanna, and Cyrus McCormick to his cause, as well as the AFL's Samuel Gompers and John Mitchell. By 1905, when the NCF created a welfare department to study employer welfare programs and labor legislation, the organization claimed several hundred members, mostly large employers and craft unions. The NCF became an important force behind the creation of workmen's compensation legislation, and it worked closely with the AFL for the passage of compensation laws which, it argued, would benefit both workers and employers.[74] Left-wing labor leaders, industrial unionists, and the socialist movement, however, strongly distrusted the NCF, arguing that associating with men like Hanna was simple collaboration with the enemies of labor. Gompers, forced to defend his participation in the NCF, insisted that he did so while retaining his independence, and that only through meeting employers "face to face" could labor present and win its demands. Gompers was also convinced that working with the NCF would provide the labor movement with legitimacy and public acceptance.[75]

For Gompers, membership in the NCF included a strong personal relationship with Ralph Easley. The AFL leader was a frequent guest at the Easleys' country home in Connecticut, and a letter from Gompers's secretary to Ralph Easley points to the close relationship between the two men. "Mr. Gompers always enjoys his little visits to your farm," she wrote. "Your companionship and friendship have never failed him and whenever he has been with you on a trip or has hidden himself away at your home on the farm, he has always returned feeling rested and happy."[76]

Their friendship rested on ideological affinity. Gompers and Easley agreed on a definition of the American worker that precluded the increased role for the state represented by health insurance. Dear to the hearts of both Gompers and Easley was the image of the independent, manly laborer, who was naturally hostile to government intervention. As Easley told the AALL's Olga Halsey, "[T]he American workingman does not desire to be regulated in his personal affairs."[77] In 1917 the avuncular Easley married the NCF's secretary, an ardently conservative woman named Gertrude Beeks, who handled much of the organization's correspondence and strongly influenced its policies. That year also marked Ralph Easley's shift to the right following the Bolshevik revolution. The NCF leader feared that class relations in the United States might undergo a similar breakdown, and he devoted the rest of his life to the fight against socialism.[78] Easley's growing political conservatism paralleled Gompers's, especially when it came to compulsory health insurance.

The AFL had been involved in the NCF's attack on health insurance from the beginning. The committee that produced the NCF's negative 1914 study of European social insurance (described in Chapter 3) was chaired by the AFL's J. W. Sullivan, "the personal representative of Mr. Gompers," who, according to Frederick Hoffman, was "very friendly toward legitimate business undertakings."[79] After Gompers made his famous "Barnacles" speech, the NCF printed thousands of copies for distribution in its campaign against health insurance.[80]

Confident of the labor stamp of approval conferred by its close association with Gompers, the NCF was unpleasantly surprised by the contrary position of state-level trade unionists. When the NYSFL took up the cause of health insurance in 1918, the NCF was dismayed and immediately complained to Gompers about his rebellious subordinates. Gertrude Beeks Easley wrote to Gompers informing him that James Lynch had announced his approval of health insurance; she thought that "the matter [should] be brought to your attention immediately," since she regarded it as "very serious."[81] The NYSFL's reversal infuriated the Easleys, not least because it conveyed the impression that the AFL's opposition to health insurance had been superseded. In 1919 Gertrude Easley told Gompers, "The great, big cry is 'Labor wants it.' This, of course, is due to the Holland-Lynch combination in the state federation of labor."[82]

Paralleling their opponents' criticisms of the blind followers of Gompers, the anti–health insurance forces argued that James Lynch led a similarly sheeplike flock of supporters into endorsement of health insurance. J. W. Sullivan reflected the AFL's elitism when he tried to explain local unionists' support of health insurance. "The State Federation of Labor is made up of men having lesser positions in the labor world, and less educated in trade union matters," Sullivan told a NCF meeting. "They usually follow one leader in the state, saying, 'Jim says it is a good thing; let it go.'" Gertrude Easley remarked indignantly that the NYSFL had "gone for" the health insurance bill "under James Lynch's guidance." The only explanation for the NYSFL's near-unanimous vote in favor of the legislation, Easley thought, was that Lynch had deliberately misled the members, painting a rosy picture of health insurance that "deceived the rank and file."[83]

The NYSFL's leaders practiced deception, according to the NCF, and their motivations for supporting health insurance were rooted in greed and self-interest. The NCF's P. T. Sherman told Gertrude Easley, "[A]s you and I know well enough, [labor's] principal motive is the desire for public office and to build up a machine under the State Industrial commission."[84] Gertrude Easley agreed that the health insurance proposal would be a windfall for James Lynch because he headed the New York Industrial Commission, which would administer the benefits under the AALL's plan. Lynch supported health insurance, she sneered, "probably because it will give him a big job and give him a chance to fill one thousand jobs under such a plan."[85]

The American Federation of Labor's cooperation was central to the NCF's attack on health insurance. AFL leaders Hugh Frayne, J. W. Sullivan, Sara Conboy, and Matthew Woll — all close associates of Gompers — regularly attended NCF meetings in New York and helped the organization produce anti–health insurance propaganda. Woll, Frayne, and Conboy were also members of the AFL's Social Insurance Committee and authors of the 1918 AFL resolution against compulsory health insurance — but, because of rank-and file distrust of the NCF, their participation in the NCF was not publicized at AFL conventions.[86]

J. W. Sullivan, a former typographer, was the AFL member who participated most actively in the NCF. As a member of the NCF's Committee on Foreign Inquiry, he had visited Great Britain in 1914 and helped produce the influential negative report on foreign social insurance. He was well-traveled and spoke several foreign languages. He was also known for his fiery temper and outbursts at NCF meetings.[87] Like Gompers, Sullivan saw his role as defending the organized working class against the debilitating effects of government intervention. Although the unskilled or immigrant worker might benefit from health insurance, Sullivan believed, labor union members would reject it as a violation of manhood and independence. Again echoing Gompers, Sullivan promoted a race-specific definition of American labor.[88] He told a meeting of the NCF, "[I]n this country, there are three classifications of labor: 1) those able to organize; mostly Americans or near-Americans; 2) the vast class of migratory men of lesser skill, made up largely of foreigners; and 3) Colored people." Sullivan estimated that 50 percent of workers in the United States "hardly make a living," while the other 50 percent—apparently the native-born workers who were organized or "able to organize"—would reject "any interference from any governmental agency—poking their noses into our affairs."[89]

Sara Conboy, who represented the United Textile Workers of America on the AFL Executive Committee, was quoted by the NCF almost as often as was Gompers. Conboy's statements, and her participation in NCF activities, were central to the NCF's attempt to weaken and discredit the labor coalition in favor of health insurance. In pamphlets and press releases, which described her as "the foremost woman labor leader" in the state, Conboy defied local trade unionists who "think that I ought to feel bound by the stand of the New York State Federation of Labor in favor of health insurance."[90]

But many of Sara Conboy's pronouncements were actually written by the NCF before Conboy attached her name to them. NCF records include a "Memorandum of Suggestions for Answer(s) by Mrs. Conboy," an outline for a Conboy speech attacking the NYSFL apparently written by Gertrude Easley, and a draft of an NCF press release featuring several quotations from Gertrude Easley that, in its final version, were attributed to Sara Conboy. This was a case of the NCF literally putting words in labor's mouth. Conboy's collaboration with the NCF occasionally made her uneasy; at one point she told Gertrude Easley that she "wants it quite clear that it is not going to be indicated in any way that she is backing the employers." However, Conboy allowed the notorious Carleton D. Babcock, insurance representative and leader of the New York League for Americanism, to quote from her speeches in his anti–health insurance material.[91]

As this misleading use of Conboy's name shows, in the health insurance battle the NCF's relationship with the AFL sometimes went beyond collaboration to manipulation. The AFL's final resolution on health insurance at its 1920 convention may have been influenced by pressure from the NCF. In May of 1920, Gertrude Easley wrote to AFL vice president Matthew Woll, "It will be nothing short of a tragedy, really, if the A.F. of L. comes out at its annual convention with a divided report [on health insurance]. . . . It would help immensely if the Executive Council of the American Federation of Labor would take a position for further inquiry rather than to report showing part of the committee in favor of the proposition."[92] As the NCF hoped, the convention passed a resolution placing the question of health insurance on the back burner for further study.[93]

The fate of that AFL resolution was shaped once again by the NCF. Although it was a blow to the AALL's proposal, the AFL resolution was not a strongly worded assault on the concept of health insurance; indeed, it admitted that the executive council had been "unable to reach a unanimous agreement on the subject."[94] Since Gompers had published his first attacks in 1916, the AFL had been forced to recognize the widespread support for health insurance among its membership. In order to ensure a negative report, Gompers decided to turn over the AFL's study to an avowed enemy of health insurance, none other than NCF member and Prudential vice president Frederick Hoffman. According to Hoffman, in November of 1920 Gompers requested a meeting with him "for the purpose of discussing the health insurance situation." At this meeting, Gompers asked the insurance executive to write the AFL's report. Gompers told Hoffman that the health insurance investigation voted by the AFL would be too technical and complicated to be carried out by the labor organization. Hoffman reported to the Prudential, "[Gompers] said he felt that he could not do better than to ask me to prepare for him a report covering essential details *from the labor point of view*, suitable for presentation to the [AFL]. . . . I said that I would be very glad indeed to prepare for Mr. Gompers a statement of my own conclusions, supplemented, of course, by references and exhibits clearly disclosing the absolute impartiality of my investigations. . . . I was gratified to have him assure me of this absolute personal confidence in the impartiality of our findings."[95]

In his opposition to compulsory health insurance, Gompers went well beyond his controversial association with the NCF to ally with a business element detested by organized labor: the commercial insurance industry. Indeed, he was willing to allow an insurance executive to represent the "labor point of view." And Hoffman's anti–health insurance views, of course, would reflect only those of one sector of the labor movement. Hoffman was fully aware of these implications. He told his employers at the Prudential Insurance Company that "the opportunity" of writing the AFL's study "should not be missed."[96] Although the study would never take place because the health insurance bill was defeated, Gompers's proposal to Hoffman was an astonishing example of the AFL's behind-the-scenes collaboration with business interests on the health insurance question, and of Gompers's willingness to use the "enemies of labor" to block a piece of legislation supported by many trade unionists.[97]

Some in the labor movement thought that Gompers's collusion with capi-

tal's representatives had gone too far. Left-wing trade unionists and socialists had always been critical of AFL participation in the NCF, culminating in
Morris Hillquit's well-publicized attack: "[The NCF] takes nothing from capital, it gives nothing to labor, and does it all with such an appearance of bound-
less generosity, that some of the more guileless diplomats in the labor movement are actually overwhelmed by it."[98] AFL vice president William Green was
angered that Gompers enlisted his crony J. W. Sullivan of the NCF to investigate health insurance in 1919, writing, "I resent the selection of men to do
important work of this kind in such a haphazard and unsatisfactory manner."[99]
"Frankly, it seems to us to be wholly inconsistent for you to be a member of
the NCF when that Federation is attacking in a most vicious way the friends
of organized labor," a member of the AFL's Social Service Committee wrote to
Gompers in 1921. "So far as I can see, the National Civic Federation has fallen
into the hands of a few capitalists and is now nothing more nor less than the
apologist of Wall Street."[100] Cooperation with the NCF, however, was central
to Gompers's efforts to legitimize the AFL, to fight socialism and radicalism
within its ranks, to block state encroachment into workers' lives, and to promote his vision of unionism as the official voice of American labor.[101]

The efforts of the NYSFL and local trade unionists on behalf of health insurance, and of the AFL against it, unearthed deep divisions in the labor movement over the relationship of workers to the state. State assistance in the form
of health insurance was anathema to the AFL's ideal of the independent and
self-reliant American laboring man. The leaders of the NYSFL and ILGWU, on
the other hand, thought the citizenship of workers would be enhanced, not
weakened, by state intervention.

The roots of the conflict between Gompers and local trade unionists lay,
at least partly, in their differing relationships to the state and its institutions. Their ideology was closely related to experience. Gompers's antistatism
emerged from years battling state repression of the labor movement. New York
State labor leaders, while not naive about state power, had very different local
experiences with government efforts to improve working conditions. With the
proliferation of state industrial commissions and factory investigation boards
during the Progressive Era, some trade unionists were actually becoming part
of the state apparatus. In this sense, the NCF's repeated accusation that New
York labor leaders were seeking to increase their own political power through
the establishment of a health insurance commission was not an exaggeration.
James Lynch, for example, who had risen from the presidency of the Typographical Union to the statewide office of commissioner of labor, was as much
a politician as a trade unionist. His work in the administration of New York's

workmen's compensation law had given him not only the ability to oversee a complex bureaucracy but also an awareness of the limitations of labor legislation and hope for its expansion. In fighting for health insurance, Lynch may have been simply pursuing his own enrichment, as the NCF claimed, but such an objective was not incompatible with the loftier goal of improving the health and security of New York's workers. Lynch's experience in Albany had led him to develop an optimistic assessment of what the state could do, both for himself and for labor.

Also, local labor organizations displayed considerable concern for women and the unorganized, groups generally ignored by Gompers and the AFL. These different constituencies led to different conceptions of citizenship. Female, immigrant, and unorganized workers lacked the "independence," in the AFL's view, inherent in masculinity, native birth, or union membership. So, like Pauline Newman, they were open to the possibility that their citizenship could be enhanced by government programs such as health insurance, rather than seeing state involvement as a threat to their supposed self-reliance.

But in the end, the AFL view of labor and the state triumphed in the battle over health insurance. Scholars have attributed the overshadowing of the state labor federations' political vision to their structural weakness; they had scant administrative capacity and only a tiny number of votes at AFL conventions.[102] Even more significant, however, was the ideological and political dominance of the AFL's vision. Samuel Gompers was widely accepted as the spokesman for all of labor, a status reinforced by business groups and the press. Local union leaders had to struggle to present alternative views. And the AFL's alliance with the National Civic Federation gave it direct access to the kind of political influence that counted in the battle over health insurance—influence over state legislators (see Chapter 8).

The AFL reigned as the representative for "labor," narrowly defined as workers who were male, native born, and organized. Business approved of this definition and encouraged its hegemony by allying with its representatives against labor groups that did not fit the mold. The official AFL rationale for opposing health insurance struck a chord with the manufacturers, insurance companies, and physicians who denounced health insurance as un-American and paternalistic. Business interests found the AFL's insistence on working-class self-help congenial, and they eagerly used the AFL's opposition to portray health insurance as an assault on workers' independence. To Samuel Gompers, intent on strengthening unions in the face of government resistance, the state was a force far more sinister than the businessmen and insurance executives who agreed with him that American workers did not want compulsory health insurance.

7

Insuring Maternity

WOMEN'S POLITICS AND
THE CAMPAIGN FOR
HEALTH INSURANCE

The New York compulsory health insurance bill was one of the rare proposals before the New Deal that aspired to assist male breadwinners *and* to offer protection for mothers. Unlike protective labor legislation and other reforms aimed at women only, the American Association for Labor Legislation's model bill for health insurance covered workers of both sexes. And the legislation was unique in that it entitled women to protection both as workers and as mothers. Since insured women could continue receiving part of their wages when they left work to give birth, the maternity benefits of the health insurance bill acknowledged women's work outside the home and the importance of their income to the household. Many women supported the health insurance plan because of its protections for mothers, but some also thought that it would improve the status of women as workers. By 1919 New York's powerful women's reform movement adopted health insurance as part of its legislative campaign for the protection of working women.

Despite the vigor and visibility of this women's coalition, the campaign for health insurance divided women nearly as much as it unified them. Some women reformers angrily rejected the central premise of maternity benefits—that women could be both mothers and workers at the same time. In the name of protecting both motherhood and the wages of single women, prominent reformer Florence Kelley persuaded the AALL to eliminate maternity benefits from its 1916 bill. This unleashed a storm of debate over maternity benefits that ended in their restoration to the bill a year later. Then, in 1919, activist women tried to use the new power of the vote to win a slate of protective labor reforms, including the AALL's health insurance program. They nearly succeeded, but the campaign gave rise to new divisions among women when a group of women workers and professionals suddenly denounced labor legislation as a threat to their jobs. Although organized women were crucial supporters of the health insurance bill and helped bring it close to passage, the campaign also brought to light serious ideological and experiential differences among women that had long-term implications for women's politics and for the welfare state.

THE BATTLE OVER MATERNITY BENEFITS

During her years in London, the AALL's Olga Halsey had been deeply impressed by the British National Insurance Act's provisions for women. British women workers were entitled to a cash benefit and medical care when they left work to bear a child, and even the non-wage-earning wives of insured men received maternity care. As "a woman who has watched the maternity benefit of the great British National Insurance Act at work in one of the most poverty-stricken districts of London,"[1] Halsey worked to ensure that maternity benefits would be a centerpiece of the American proposal. The AALL's model bill included benefits that would provide, for both working women and the wives of male workers, "medical care for two weeks before and four weeks after birth," and for insured women workers, "the regular cash benefit [for sickness] also."[2]

Childbirth forced women to lose wages and to require medical attendance, consequences it shared with illnesses covered by health insurance. But maternity benefits, treated as a separate category in the AALL's model bill, held special meaning because they addressed simultaneously the needs of women, the health of children, and the "protection of the race." Also, both cash and medical benefits for maternity raised volatile questions about the propriety of women's wage work.

The fear of dying in childbirth haunted women of all classes. According to historian Molly Ladd-Taylor, "Between 1900 and 1930 . . . approximately sixty white and over one hundred nonwhite women died for every ten thousand live births" in the United States.[3] Reformers thought that working women, their bodies weakened by wage labor, were especially vulnerable. Also, unlike their wealthier counterparts, working-class women lacked access to prenatal care and to medical attendance during childbirth. "Proper care during the period of pregnancy and confinement is so expensive," noted a New York charity worker, "that working women and wives of working men usually go without the medical and nursing care, which is so essential in prevent[ing] the maternal deaths now so shockingly frequent."[4] James Lynch told a convention of the New York State Federation of Labor, to great applause, that if health insurance "did nothing but care . . . for the women of this country who go down into the Valley of the Shadow of Death in order that we may be born, that alone would justify the . . . bill." [5]

Reformers also hoped that medical care as part of a maternity benefit would mean more women attended by physicians and nurses, rather than midwives, because midwifery was not a covered service in the AALL's bill. Said Olga Halsey, "In this country where fully forty percent of births are by midwives . . . steps should be taken to assure that women receive more careful attention than many now receive." [6] Halsey reflected the (erroneous) belief common among elites that midwife-attended births were a major cause of high maternal and infant mortality rates, and that women, generally immigrants, who insisted on a midwife clung stubbornly to the outmoded customs of their homelands. In this view, maternity benefits that reduced the use of midwives would not only save lives; they would help Americanize those immigrant families that depended most heavily on traditional birthing practices. [7]

Infant mortality, too, would drop with the introduction of maternity benefits, reformers thought. The New York Maternity Center announced in 1918 that "over 12,000 babies under one year died last year in New York City." High infant mortality rates were a nationwide concern; in 1910, the infant mortality rate in the few states that kept such statistics was 124 per 1,000 live births; for most states it was likely higher. [8] The improved medical attendance promised by maternity benefits would save the lives of babies as well as their mothers. For the AALL, this promise stemmed less from the sentimental impulses behind "child-saving" than from the "scientific" goal of conserving the nation's labor power. When John B. Andrews announced that "[a] maternity benefit is an effort to make some provision for future working men," he expressed the AALL's concern with the production and reproduction of a healthy labor force — something possible only with healthy mothers. [9] Reformers saw maternity benefits as part of a program of racial preservation; Olga Halsey said that current conditions left childbearing women without medical and economic support, hence "debasing the race stock." [10]

Even noninsured women facing confinement would receive medical care if their husbands participated in the health insurance scheme. Again, this was intended as protection for working men, since the costs of childbirth were a burden on the entire family's budget. A Brooklyn woman who wrote to the Children's Bureau in 1918 exhibited all the needs that maternity benefits for dependent wives intended to address. "My babies come fast and where I am going to meet the Doctors bills I cannot see. I have a daughter one year old this Jan. And we have had little else but Doctors bill[s] in the past 3 years," wrote Mrs. W. S. Doctors' bills were not her only problem; this woman could not even afford a set of bed clothing for her confinement "without going into debt. I have a very good husband," she assured the Children's Bureau, "but he has such poor health."[11] Had her husband been covered by the AALL's health insurance plan, Mrs. W. S., who was not herself a wage worker, would have received free medical care, possibly leaving enough money to pay for bed sheets from her husband's wages. Her husband's illnesses would have been covered as well, so the family would not have suffered his frequent wage losses.

Women who did work for wages needed more than medical care for childbirth. Just like male workers, they needed income protection. Certainly, there was a maternity-protection aspect to the cash payments; Halsey pointed out that "the provision of the cash benefit . . . will enable the mother and child to have extra nourishing food" when they most needed it.[12] But cash maternity benefits were unique in their implication that women's wages were essential to household income and hence deserving of protection. Wages for women remained notoriously low in part because of the entrenched assumption that men, not women, were solely responsible for family support.[13] The health insurance proposal, by offering cash benefits for maternity, distinctly recognized the importance of women's income to the family. In New York, as in a few other states, women were already *prohibited* from working for four weeks after giving birth, but the laws provided no compensation for lost wages. Such laws blatantly denied that women's wages needed protecting; their result was a kind of enforced unemployment that affected women exclusively.[14] The AALL agreed that women should take time off work to have their children, but also that men should take time off when they were sick, and that the lost wages of both men and women should be compensated.

For all these reasons, the AALL assumed that New York's women's groups would be enthusiastic about the maternity benefits of compulsory health insurance. But when its draft bill was published in 1915, the cash maternity provision was immediately attacked. To the AALL's surprise, the critic was Florence Kelley of the National Consumers' League, champion of protective legislation and one of the nation's most well-known social activists. Her name was practically synonymous with industrial reform. Kelley, the daughter of a wealthy Philadelphia politician, had studied social science (and socialism, with Friedrich Engels) in Europe before joining Jane Addams at Hull House. She was a high-profile crusader against child labor, and as general secretary of the NCL she led campaigns to improve working conditions for women in industry. At the time of the health insurance campaign, Kelley lived at the Henry Street Settlement in New York City while agitating for a women's minimum wage.[15]

Kelley's criticisms sent Andrews and his colleagues reeling. Although she declared in favor of the principle of compulsory health insurance, Kelley presented the AALL with a memorandum explaining two strong objections to cash maternity benefits. First, poorly paid single women would be taxed for a benefit they didn't need; second, the benefit would force pregnant women into the workforce. The AALL's proposed maternity cash payment for working women, Kelley declared, constituted "Discrimination against Self-Respecting Unmarried Women" who would be forced to pay "for the cash premiums to lighten the burdens of husbands who send their wives out as wage-earners. Offering a cash bonus amounts to saying to the wage-earning husband: 'Send your wife into a mill, factory, or sweatshop, and the public and the single woman in her factory will send you a present for your next baby.' "[16]

What can account for this fighter for working women so quickly denying women's right to this form of support during childbirth? Kelley's opposition to maternity benefits is partly explained by her most passionate commitment: to raise the appallingly low wages of single women workers. The wages of all women were low because of the persistence of the male breadwinner ideal, which refused to acknowledge that many women had to support themselves or their families without a man's help. When employers underpaid married women ostensibly because they had their husbands' support, single women were forced to accept the same wages.[17] Kelley angrily told the AALL, "For three quarters of a century in Europe it has been increasingly recognized that no other influence is such a drag upon wages as the presence in an industry of married women."[18] The goal of Florence Kelley's minimum-wage campaign was to raise the wages of single women who had no husbands to support them. Married women in factories thwarted this aim, Kelley believed. The AALL's maternity benefits would encourage married women to work, depress wages for all women, and force single women to pay for benefits they themselves did not need. (Kelley implied that single women never bore children.) Kelley's anger on this point may also be explained by her resentment at Andrews and the AALL, who had refused to support her minimum-wage campaign[19] — and possibly by her feeling that the AALL was treading on her territory.

But defense of single women's wages was not the only impetus behind Kelley's antipathy toward cash maternity benefits. She also expressed more familiar maternalist and race-preservationist opposition to married women's work on the grounds of protecting future generations. "In families where the mother works for wages," Kelley insisted, "the children suffer, if they do not die outright." Because of the danger to children, Kelley opposed "any law which provides for recognition by the state, of the practice of sending child-bearing wives out of the home into industry."[20] Both Kelley and the AALL wanted to safeguard the health of mothers and babies, the AALL by providing maternity benefits, Kelley by keeping mothers out of the workforce altogether.[21]

But large numbers of married women *did* work, a fact of which Kelley was obviously aware. To attack maternity benefits was to deny these women equal rights with men under compulsory health insurance. To avoid this quandary, Kelley pointed a finger at their husbands. Cash maternity benefits were not for women, she said, but "for men who send their wives out to earn wages."[22] And these husbands were not of a type deserving of assistance. Kelley sent the AALL a description of "Men Whose Wives Notoriously Work for Wages." They fell into three categories: the first consisted of alcoholics, the insane, and victims of venereal and other diseases; the second, "Negroes"; and the third, "the unskilled, unorganized aliens." The particular makeup of these groups, Kelley argued, made offering them maternity benefits a dangerous proposition. Encouraging the reproduction of the first category was patently "undesirable . . . from the point of view of eugenics." As for the "Negroes" whose wives worked for wages, "It is doubtful whether the great mass of white taxpayers will care to subsidize [them]." Finally, giving the poorest aliens a cash maternity benefit "is an actual bribe to increased immigration of the kind of men who make their wives and children work." She offered no evidence for her statements but called them "the facts of common knowledge."[23] In her opposition to cash benefits for maternity, Kelley invoked a racial definition of the deserving family. While the AALL argued that maternity benefits would aid assimilation and protect future generations, Kelley insisted that the benefits would subsidize the survival of the undesirable "racial" custom of working mothers.

Olga Halsey, the AALL's greatest champion of maternity benefits, immediately drafted a rebuttal to Kelley's arguments. Halsey argued that omitting maternity benefits would constitute discrimination against childbearing women and that the employment of married women in industry, "altho[ugh] undesirable, ought not to be ignored."[24] Halsey and a committee of AALL members met with Kelley to explain their position, but the NCL secretary apparently remained unconvinced. Finally, the AALL's Social Insurance Committee met on January 3, 1916, to deal with Kelley's opposition. Although Halsey and Isaac Rubinow continued to argue for the retention of maternity benefits, Lillian Wald (who lived with Florence Kelley at Henry Street) moved to eliminate them. The committee then voted to eliminate the cash maternity benefit from the New York bill, although the principle of the benefits would remain in the AALL's model bill.[25] The AALL leadership's later rationales for the decision seem a bit weak. "A majority of the members of our committee voted to eliminate the maternity benefit," Andrews wrote a Women's Trade Union League leader, "not because they were convinced by the arguments presented against this feature — but in order to avoid disagreeable controversy at the beginning of the educational work for the bill in New York State."[26]

Kelley's opposition was so effective because of her prestige as a reformer and her influence among women's groups. The Social Insurance Committee thought that by responding to her they were responding to the concerns of organized women. But it quickly became evident that the women's network that Kelley supposedly represented was by no means united on the question of maternity benefits.

The strongest challenge to Kelley came from Pauline Newman, the Jewish immigrant trade unionist. Just as she had defied Samuel Gompers's position on health insurance, Pauline Newman spoke out passionately against Florence Kelley's arguments that had led to the elimination of maternity benefits. As Newman herself put it, "[T]o be the fighter, is more natural to me, than to be the diplomat."[27] Newman and Kelley had not always been at odds. Alongside her commitment to the unionization of female wage earners through her work with the ILGWU, Newman thought it essential to work with the middle- and upper-class leaders of the NCL and the WTUL on behalf of protective legislation for women workers. But class, ethnic, and ideological differences occasionally led to clashes between labor women and their "affluent women allies." According to her biographer Annelise Orleck, Newman had earlier fought the attempts of the New York WTUL's native-born Protestant secretary to reduce the influence of Jewish women in the organization. This incident heightened Newman's sensitivity to racial slights and her perception that cross-class alliances, while necessary, were fraught with difficulty and did not always express a shared "sisterhood" among women.[28]

Although they shared many goals — especially that of a minimum wage for women — the controversy over maternity benefits brought Newman into direct conflict with Florence Kelley. In 1916, as Newman emerged as a major spokesperson for the AALL's health insurance bill, she never made a speech without calling for the reinstatement of maternity benefits. In doing so, she explicitly attacked Kelley's objections to the benefits. Newman, who was unmarried herself, disagreed with Kelley's assertion that single working women would resent contributing to maternity insurance. "Most of the unmarried girls who will contribute their share to the maternity insurance fund may some day be beneficiaries themselves of that fund," commented Newman. "One might as well object to paying taxes for health insurance in general on the ground that one has never been sick and does not expect to be." Speaking to the American Nurses' Association, Newman declared, "I would be more than willing to give up more than 1.5 per cent from my own wages, knowing it would go to some woman that she might rest for a few weeks before, and a few weeks after, confinement."[29]

Newman fervently attacked the centerpiece of Kelley's argument: the idea that men would send their wives to work to receive maternity benefits. "These persons [opposing maternity benefit] seem to have little conception of the psychology of the workingmen or women," said Newman caustically. "Married wage-earning women are forced to enter industry regardless of whether they will be taken care of during the period of childbirth. It is the struggle for existence that does, and will, drive married women into industry, not maternity benefit."[30]

Kelley's insistence that reformers must not enshrine married women's work in law also came under Newman's fire. She particularly objected to the claim that "the married working woman is not an American tradition. . . . What is the use of using lovely phrases when they express a fancy and not a fact?"[31] The fact, insisted Newman, was that married women did form a significant portion of the workforce, and their numbers showed no signs of diminishing.[32] Married women's labor might not be the ideal, but it was the reality, and Newman wanted to protect it immediately rather than just hope for its elimination in the future.

When Newman testified at the 1916 Albany hearing on behalf of the AALL's health insurance bill, she demanded the restoration of cash maternity benefits. She invoked her experience as a worker and organizer as the basis for her expertise on maternity benefits and health insurance. Irritated with both Kelley and the AALL, Newman took a stab at privileged reformers: "Some of us are too busy acting in the industrial world to have time to be onlookers of the show." The maternity benefit clause, "the most important one," Newman told the Judiciary Committee, had been left out of the health insurance bill "for very illogical reasons": that married women would be lured into industry, and that underpaid single women would be unfairly taxed for maternity benefits. But the benefits were so small, Newman argued, that they "could not convince or induce any married woman to go into industry." As for single women: "The girls I am representing are in favor of paying a small amount to pay for this, as their share." Eliminating maternity benefits would not relieve the low pay of single women, declared Newman; only a legislated minimum wage would do so. On the wage question, Newman was once again in exact agreement with Kelley—except she went even further in demanding gender-neutral wage laws. "It is about time that you enact some legislation to correct the underpaying of *human beings*, whether girls, men or women," she told the assemblymen.[33]

Both Pauline Newman and Florence Kelley illustrate Kathryn Sklar's important argument that maternalism, or the protection of mothers and children, was not the sole concern of women Progressives; rather, "[w]ork (and its obverse—unemployment) set the framework within which they viewed social problems and posed solutions."[34] Yet Newman and Kelley held distinctly different ideas about women and work. For Kelley, women had the right to work and deserved workplace protections, but only while they were single and childless. She saw work and motherhood as mutually exclusive, at least for the Americanized. Newman, on the other hand, along with her counterparts in the women's trade union movement, thought that "work should not preclude motherhood"[35] and that protecting mothers already in the workplace outweighed the goal of keeping others out.

Kelley and Newman agreed on the importance of raising wages, but the wage question also illustrates a crucial difference in their visions of protective legislation and the welfare state. Kelley's reform crusade on behalf of women was wage based. In this, her orientation was similar to the American Federation of Labor's. Even though Kelley sought to raise wages through legislation and the AFL looked to increase them through collective bargaining, both saw wage hikes as their central mission and viewed most welfare programs and benefits (whether provided by the state or the employer) as a substitute for, and hence a threat to, higher wages.

Newman, on the other hand, envisioned remedying wage fluctuations with a system of state benefits to which workers would always be entitled. She was highly critical of the AFL's obsession with wages. "There is something narrow, something wrong with our movement in the States," Newman told a convention of Canadian trade unionists in 1919. "Is it because it still clings to the old idea of getting higher wages and allowing the corporations to take it back in the higher prices of the necessities of life?"[36] She thought that higher wages should be a long-term goal of the labor movement, but not at the expense of demanding more immediate benefits for workers. Those reformers who argued that "the true solution is the adequate wage," said Newman, "fail to realize that . . . the attainment of an adequate wage is too remote to stand in the way of the maternity benefit, which is the due of the working mother and the wife of the workingman."[37]

Unlike so many of her contemporaries, Newman did not see reform as a zero-sum game, in which benefits were traded for wages, or workers' independence and dignity were traded for assistance from the state. While Kelley opposed maternity benefits as "wage subsidies," Newman saw no contradiction between her fight for maternity and health insurance and a minimum wage, or between worker organization and state assistance. She maintained her lifetime commitment to union organizing alongside her work for protective legislation and workplace benefits. The famous rallying cry of the garment workers' strikes—workers wanted bread but roses too—carried over into Newman's vision of the welfare state. Workers should have bread but also roses, higher wages but also state-supported benefits, unions but also protective legislation, work but also motherhood.

The AALL was delighted with Newman's defense of maternity benefits. Despite their rapid surrender, the AALL staff were unhappy with the deletion of the cash payments, and Olga Halsey, especially, hoped that "with better informed opinion it may be possible to restore, later, maternity benefits."[38] With this in mind, Andrews and Halsey wrote to dozens of women reformers around the country and in Europe, asking for their opinion on maternity pay, and whether Florence Kelley's warnings should be heeded. Newman had based her passionate advocacy of maternity insurance on her own experience as a worker and on her broad vision of the possibilities for reform. The AALL, of course, relied on quite different sources of inspiration: statistics and expertise. They would try to refute Kelley not with rhetoric and ideology but with facts.

The British women contacted by the AALL all disagreed with Kelley's position. They reported that the maternity benefits of the National Insurance Act had not appreciably increased the number of married working women in Britain. The modest payment of thirty shillings, wrote Mary Macarthur of the British Women's Trade Union League, "has not induced married women to take up temporary employment." Sophy Sanger of the International Labour Association was bewildered by Kelley's concerns, telling Andrews, "I cannot quite follow your difficulty in connection with the Maternity Insurance . . . this is a purely theoretic objection, taking no account of the real motives leading married women to go out to work."[39] Mrs. M. R. Smith, secretary of the Women's Friendly Society of Scotland, informed Andrews that rumors did abound of married women taking "an occasional day's work when they are aware of the fact that Maternity Benefit will have to be claimed at a not far distant period." However, in her own opinion, "it has not been the case that women have entered employment merely in order to obtain the benefits of the Act."[40]

The British experience seemed to contradict Kelley's fears of pregnant women pouring into the workforce to obtain maternity benefits. But what of the uniquely American "racial" diversity that Kelley thought contributed to married women's employment among immigrant groups? Mary Conyngton of the U.S. Bureau of Labor Statistics told the AALL that her agency had made several studies that "seemed to indicate that the work of married women was on the whole a matter of economic necessity rather than of racial tendency." She even found that the percentage of American-born working women who were married (10 percent) was greater than that of women workers as a whole

(8 percent). The industry with the largest number of married women workers was Southern textiles, "composed exclusively of native-born white Americans of native stock." [41]

Conyngton's statistics seemed to decisively contradict Kelley's racial arguments. Indeed, no one contacted by the AALL echoed Kelley's eugenic concerns. But several prominent American women strongly agreed with her position that maternity benefits might depress wages. Mary Van Kleeck, one of New York's most renowned experts on working women, feared that the benefits might "appear to be first cousin to the discredited principle of relief in aid of wages, which surely has been proved to be wholly unsound." Alice Henry of the WTUL was herself in favor of maternity benefits but acknowledged that "the fear that the pension may act as a degrading subsidy to the man's wages, and hence tend to lower wages in the open market" might lead some reformers to oppose maternity benefits.[42] Both Van Kleeck and Frances Perkins of the NCL "did not see why industry should bear the cost of maternity insurance" since health insurance was intended to distribute the cost of sickness among those responsible for it, and employers were not responsible for maternity.

All of these reformers assured the AALL that their opposition to cash assistance did not preclude support for medical maternity benefits. Van Kleeck informed Andrews that she strongly favored medical care "for both mother and child." While Ella Crandall of the National Organization for Public Health Nursing did "not believe that the cash benefits are particularly desirable," she was still "extremely sorry to find that the maternity insurance has been eliminated from the bill because . . . we do believe strongly that the nursing benefits to the mothers are a great social advantage." (Crandall seemed to think that medical benefits had also been eliminated, which was not the case.) [43]

The position of these American reformers on maternity benefits was quite distinct from that of their British counterparts. No one, it seemed, was opposed to medical care for mothers and babies, but cash benefits were a different matter. Some reformers wanted to protect single women's wages and married women's health, but not married women's right to work. So, even as they distanced themselves from the excesses of Kelley's position, these women concurred with her main argument: that married women's wages should not be protected by maternity benefits.

Even so, by the end of 1916 the AALL concluded that it had been too hasty in yielding to "the violent opposition of Florence Kelley." There seemed to be enough sentiment in favor of maternity benefits to justify putting them back in a revised health insurance bill.[44] When the legislation was reintroduced in New York in 1917, the cash maternity benefit was included once again. An AALL press release announced that its bill was "more advanced" than the previous year's, mainly because of the addition of maternity benefits.[45] The highly publi-cized reinstatement of maternity aid brought the AALL support from women's groups that had previously been indifferent to the health insurance measure. Any opposition to cash benefits was silenced. The Babies Welfare Association of New York noted that the maternity benefit "is at present commanding the attention of practically every charity organization in this city." Julia Lathrop, the influential head of the federal Children's Bureau, declared, "The protection of maternity is a public question which cannot longer be evaded. No system of health insurance is complete which ignores maternity insurance." Public health nurses, settlement house workers, and women's trade union leaders came for-ward to announce their advocacy of health insurance. Even the NCL eventually endorsed the measure.[46]

With this new support from women's groups, the tone of the health in-surance campaign was transformed. The AALL continued to emphasize the economic and medical rationality of health insurance, but both the AALL and women reformers also courted public sympathy by amassing examples of the hardships faced by childbearing women and their families. Settlement workers and others with direct experience in working with the poor described women who would work up to a few days or even hours before giving birth to avoid losing wages. New York researchers reported that "pregnancy is a frequently recurring factor in causing dependence among families near the poverty line." [47]

Both male and female health insurance advocates couched their defense of maternity benefits in the language of protection for mothers and babies that scholars now call maternalism. Still reeling from Kelley's attacks, insurance proponents emphasized that rather than forcing wives into the workplace, ma-ternity benefits would insure that a woman could spend the first weeks of her baby's life at home. "The cash benefit provided for mothers who must work," stated an AALL press release, "will enable many who might otherwise be com-pelled to return at once to the factory, to remain away from work and to nurse the child during the first few weeks of life." [48]

Many reformers embraced the AALL's argument about the importance of maternity benefits to race preservation. Medical and financial assistance for maternity was necessary not only to protect the health of working women but also to safeguard future generations. Frail and overworked mothers led to inferior babies and a weakened national stock; in the words of the Health Insurance Commission of Pennsylvania, "Upon the health of the woman in industry depends . . . the welfare of the race and the vigor of our future citizen-ship." [49] U.S. entry into World War I intensified arguments for race protection. Reformers lamented the notoriously wretched physical condition of draftees and traced the "tragedy of this lost asset of national health" not only to poverty and bad nourishment but to "the employment of mothers outside the homes and the overwork of mothers."[50] Rest for the mother "immediately before and after child-birth when she cannot and ought not to work," wrote Mrs. F. A. Halsey of the Harlem Council of Women (and Olga Halsey's mother), "will, we believe, save the lives of mothers and babies, and give the state a stronger citizenship in years to come."[51]

Champions of health insurance drew upon the language of maternalism to argue that their legislation would protect babies, protect mothers, and protect the race. But the intent of the maternity benefits, as we have seen, was not exclusively maternalist. Although few spoke of it as explicitly as Pauline Newman, cash maternity benefits still acknowledged women's dual role as worker and mother and recognized the importance of women's wages to the family. John B. Andrews confronted the tension between the protection of motherhood and the rights of women as workers when he argued that maternity benefits were necessary to counteract the effects of protective legislation. "In New York and Massachusetts and two other states," Andrews wrote to trade union leader Alice Henry, "we already prohibit the industrial employment of women two weeks before and four weeks after delivery. Not to provide some maternity benefit for this period of a forced lack of income and just at the time when the working mother needs financial assistance the most, is to me an absurdity." Irene Andrews agreed: "It is only a matter of justice," she said, "that a working mother who is prohibited by the state from earning wages at this most critical time of her life should be compensated by the state for the loss of her meager income."[52] Ironically, women needed maternity insurance in order to protect themselves from other, *maternalist* legislation.

By acknowledging the detrimental effect of childbearing on women's earning power, the coverage of maternity as an insurable sickness in the health insurance bill would put women workers on more equal footing with men. The California Health Insurance Commission recommended treating maternity as a sickness and allowing insured women to receive cash benefits during confinement; by doing so it recognized the importance of women's wages to the maintenance of the family. Maternity was similar to sickness not only because it required medical assistance, said the commission's report, but "also because it results in temporary incapacity or disability to perform remunerative labor." The AALL's Irene Sylvester remarked that, in comparison to gender-specific protective legislation, "Obviously, health insurance protects both men and women equally."[53]

The reformers who supported medical care for insured mothers but who disliked cash maternity benefits were implicitly asking for the health insurance bill to discriminate against women. To separate maternity from other illnesses meant that a condition that affected women only—childbirth—would be the sole excluded condition under health insurance. However, few reformers besides Newman publicly emphasized the egalitarian aspect of health insurance. They thought it safer and more expedient to use maternalist or eugenic arguments rather than risk accusations of promoting married women's work outside the home.

HEALTH INSURANCE AND THE WOMEN'S VOTE

New York women's organizations entered the postwar political fray in 1918 with a dramatically new bargaining chip: the vote. Lillian Wald memorably expressed the energy and excitement of New York's newly enfranchised women when she told Jane Addams, "We are nearly bursting over our citizenship.... I had no idea I could thrill over the right to vote."[54] In the form of the Women's Joint Legislative Conference (WJLC), New York women reformers took up the cause of health insurance as part of a slate of bills intended to protect women workers. By 1919, health insurance became inextricably tied to a women's reform program.

The WJLC of New York was formed in 1918 as a coalition of the WTUL, the Woman Suffrage Party, the state and city Consumers' Leagues, and the Young Women's Christian Association; in other words, all the most prominent New York women's reform groups. The AALL's Irene Sylvester Chubb was also an active member.[55] According to the WTUL's Maud Schwarz, the conference was created "for the purpose of getting all these organizations to combine their forces on a legislative program."[56] The WJLC was spearheaded by the WTUL, whose leaders, both middle-class and working-class women, saw woman suffrage as a tool for securing protective legislation.[57] New York would be a test case of the ability of newly enfranchised women to advocate legislation for improving conditions for women workers. The WJLC's "Women's Legislative Program," also known as the "women's welfare bills," consisted of six measures: the AALL's health insurance bill, now co-sponsored by Progressive Republican senator Frederick Davenport; a minimum wage for women; the eight-hour day for women; and three bills limiting hours and banning night work for women in office, elevator, and transportation work.[58]

Women's sponsorship of health insurance was a triumph for the AALL, for its bill was now harnessed to a dazzling and effective political strategy, honed during the long years of the suffrage struggle. The WJLC would rely on attention-getting suffrage and labor tactics to lobby for its legislative program. The AALL's efforts at the first three public hearings on the health insurance bill

Greene, in New York (N. Y.) Telegram

"A woman's work is never done." A cartoon depicting the Women's Joint Legislative Conference agenda, tying health insurance to the women's postwar reform program (*American Labor Legislation Review* 8 [December 1918]; photograph courtesy of The University Library, University of Illinois at Chicago).

had consisted entirely of expert testimony. But in March of 1919, trainloads of women workers headed to the Albany hearings to demand support for the women's welfare bills. For the first time, calls for health insurance echoed in the streets. Young women strikers from local textile mills, "together with the delegations from New York City and upstate, formed in parade at the station and marched up the hill to the Capitol before the hearing." [59] The visibility of the women at Albany attracted extensive attention from New York newspapers. Among the working women attending the hearings was Mollie Specter, a garment worker. "I think the legislature ought to pass the health insurance bill," she told the New York *Globe*, "because it would keep people from having to take charity, like they do now, when they're sick. . . . Now, I know girls and men who go back to work long before they are really able, just because they do not want to be the objects of charity." [60]

The chamber of the New York Assembly "was packed to the doors" on the morning of March 5, 1919, with a crowd estimated at two thousand. [61] A WJLC pamphlet later reported of the hearings, "Many said they were the most impressive ever held at Albany." The hundreds of women were joined by "about 300 State Federation of Labor men [who] crowded the Assembly Room to display their support. . . . Both Senators and Assemblymen said that never before in the history of the legislature had there been so popular a demand for any measures as for these." [62] Organized labor and women, not the AALL, created this agitation and brought unprecedented attention to the reform program. The visible political activity shunned by the AALL would bring the health insurance bill closer to passage than ever before.

Thanks to the women's pressure, a majority of senators pledged to support the legislative program. A victory for health insurance and the other bills seemed imminent. But the measures also had to be approved by the assembly Rules Committee, headed by Republican speaker Thaddeus Sweet, an upstate manufacturer representing Oswego. Sweet prided himself on his ability to stall Progressive legislation in his committee and avoid an assembly vote. In a statement to the New York press, the ferociously anti-Bolshevik Sweet called the women's legislative program an example of "the sentiment which has poured into this country and which is trying to create Soviet government here." [63]

The WJLC began to target Sweet directly, warning that any Republicans who colluded in keeping the welfare bills in committee would suffer from the power of the women's vote. The New York *World* reported on April 1 that Mrs. Norman Whitehouse, chair of the state Suffrage Party and of the WJLC, had launched a campaign of "direct methods" to force passage of the labor bills. "Mrs. Whitehouse Scolds Senators," headlined the *World*; "Threatens retaliation at polls if they fail." Mrs. James Lees Laidlaw, another Suffrage Party chair, declared that women voters would question the leadership of the "men who show the wanton disregard for public welfare, the utter ignorance of social problems, that are being shown by these so-called leaders in Albany." She exulted in women's newly won political influence: "We know that we now have power in our hands. It is for us to use it uncompromisingly."[64] When Sweet bragged that the welfare bills would die in the Rules Committee, an "angry" delegation of women invaded his office to demand passage of their "pets," reported the papers. The WJLC called a mass meeting at New York City's Cooper Union on April 3 to "protest machine politics in the Legislature and the attempt on the part of its leaders to prevent discussion and action" on the health insurance and other welfare bills.[65]

The gendered language of the headlines, describing the WJLC's lobbying as "scolding" and their bills as "pets," aimed to domesticate women's political participation. But press images of ladies harassing hapless legislators also reflected fear and resentment of women's newfound power. Male leaders in Albany did not even try to hide their indignation. Speaker Sweet justified his refusal to bow to the women's pressure by telling the press that "[n]o self-respecting man . . . would stand for that kind of intimidation."[66] The upstate employers' journal *The Monitor* complained, "In the history of Albany there never has been more annoying or unfair lobbying than that which has been done by the women. They have presumed upon their sex to take advantage of the chivalry of the legislators." *The Monitor* deemed women's threats of voter retaliation "silly."[67] And reaction to the women's strategy went beyond trivialization to take on a darker tone. Mark Daly, lobbyist against health insurance for the AMM of New York, invoked the threat of male violence to keep women in their place. He compared giving women the vote with pampering a high-strung horse. If the horse still refused to behave, remarked Daly, "we'd get a rawhide quirt and hire the best horseman we knew and then scientifically and firmly lick the hell right out of him."[68]

Even without literally taking up a whip, Sweet and some of his fellow assembly members were determined to punish the WJLC. Asked why he refused to let the welfare bills out of his committee, Sweet's "excuse was that the legislators, in a proportion of three to one, had asked him to prevent the bills reaching the floor, where they might have to vote for the measures under pressure from women."[69] Sweet acknowledged the power of women's lobbying but trumped it with his own power to block their legislation.

While the bills sat in the assembly Rules Committee, the senate passed all the WJLC measures on April 10, thanks to the defection of several Progressive Republicans from the party ranks (see Chapter 8). But, despite the victory in the senate, Sweet would not budge in his refusal to let the health insurance,

Courtesy New York Women's Joint Legislative Conference.

"Protected." This WJLC cartoon, by depicting the male breadwinner as the recipient of benefits, downplays the gender equity of the health insurance proposal. (*American Labor Legislation Review* [1919]; photograph courtesy of The University Library, University of Illinois at Chicago).

minimum-wage, and eight-hour bills out of committee, where they died when the assembly session ended on April 17. (Sweet did, however, allow the elevator and transportation bills onto the assembly floor, where they passed.) Furious WTUL leader Maud Schwarz said that the defeat "has demonstrated to us that the Republican Party was this time responsible for the failure of our bills, and if we do not do everything in our power to defeat them, we may just as well [not] have a vote."[70]

The WJLC and the AALL prepared for a renewed effort. The centerpiece of the reformers' strategy was the defeat of Speaker Sweet and thus an attack on the cumbersome legislative process that made it so difficult to pass Progressive measures. Women were "sour on Sweet," announced suffragist Harriet Laidlaw. Public anger at Sweet's defeat of the bills, reform leaders argued, could be channeled into an overhaul of the New York political system. As a WJLC pamphlet put it, the women's legislative program, despite its failure, could be "the means of unearthing vicious machine control and autocratic methods" in the New York legislature.[71] Without such systemic change, no victory for labor legislation—or for newly enfranchised women—was possible.

THE WOMEN AGAINST THE WELFARE BILLS

Although the united energies of women had succeeded in bringing the welfare bills as far as they did, it was divisions among women that helped frustrate their progress in late 1919. The WJLC decided to run a woman candidate, Democrat Marion Dickerman, against Speaker Sweet in the state elections. Dickerman had just returned from nursing soldiers in Europe, and the WJLC hoped to play on the patriotic image of the war nurse to win women's support for her campaign and for their legislative program.[72] But the WJLC and Dickerman were chagrined to find a group known as the Women's League for Equal Opportunity (LEO) vigorously supporting Speaker Sweet for reelection. To the WJLC's horror, no sooner had the assembly campaign begun than Sweet blanketed upstate New York with leaflets proclaiming, "The Real Women Workers Voiced Their Approval of Speaker Sweet's Course in Regard to the Welfare Bills." Who were these women workers demanding an end to "coddling" labor legislation? And what could account for their support of Sweet?

The LEO had been formed in New York City in 1915 by women printers, a small group that opposed protective labor legislation as a threat to their jobs.[73] Printers, who were more highly skilled and better paid than the vast majority of female workers, also needed to work at night and so were particularly incensed by night-work bans. Some business and professional women, whose jobs were not under threat but who opposed protective legislation on equal rights principles, also joined the LEO.[74] And LEO membership burgeoned in 1919 thanks to the success of the WJLC's elevator and transportation bills, which limited night work and mandated a nine-hour day for women in those industries. Management used the new laws as justification for dismissing women workers; every one of the Brooklyn Rapid Transit Company's female employees lost her job in 1919.[75] Although it was widely understood that employers had planned to discharge women anyway after the war because of union pressure, the blame fell on the reformers who had supported protective legislation. "These ladies [of the WJLC]," mocked LEO member Amy Wren, "can, every one of them, go out to-morrow morning and get the newspaper and read it about six o'clock. When is the newspaper printed? At night. But it is printed without the women. They are no longer there. They were all fired out of a job."[76]

Thaddeus Sweet, the very same politician who had so resented pressure from voting women, tried to harness the power of the women's vote to his advantage when it came time for reelection. Sweet saw in the League for Equal Opportunity a chance to portray himself as a champion of women workers by opposing the WJLC's minimum-wage and eight-hour bills. His campaign literature displayed the slogan: "Thaddeus C. Sweet stands for Truth — Not Falsehood. Americanism — Not Bolshevism. Working Women's Interest — Not 'Uplifters' Unwise Schemes."[77] The LEO became heavily involved in the political campaign in Speaker Sweet's home county of Oswego, which was run almost entirely on the argument that protective legislation imperiled the rights of women workers. These women's alignment with the most reactionary politician in New York might be partly explained by the strong antisocialist ideology of some LEO leaders (particularly printers Ada Wolff and Ella Sherwin). But more important was the genuine sense of grievance most LEO members felt against legislation that limited their job opportunities — grievances so strong that they were willing, even eager, to work with the notorious Sweet against the women's welfare bills.[78]

The league's challenge to the WJLC foreshadowed later disputes among women's groups over protective legislation and the Equal Rights Amendment. Protective labor laws, LEO members announced to upstate voters, robbed women of their rights as citizens and workers by treating them like children. The LEO's Ada Wolff made an explicit attack on maternalist rhetoric in her denunciation of the WJLC program: "Not one of these bills was wanted, or asked for, by the women whose livelihoods were concerned; they were 'mothered' by wealthy women who have never worked for their daily bread." How could women exercise their newfound political power, asked the LEO, if they were subject to different laws than men? One Sweet campaign poster featured a statement from the LEO complaining that "having attained our heart's desire

Poster for Thaddeus Sweet's 1919 New York Assembly campaign (Marion Dickerman Collection, Franklin D. Roosevelt Library).

[suffrage] in this State, some of our former suffrage workers are coercing our lawmakers into passing legislation forever classing woman the citizen with, and limiting her opportunities to those of children." [79]

Women from the LEO traveled from New York City to the Oswego area throughout the autumn to campaign for Sweet. At a rally in Marion Dickerman's hometown of Fulton, an audience consisting largely of working women heard LEO speakers denounce the "meddlesome" legislation. The speakers praised "the grand, heroic stand that Speaker Sweet took in killing the 'welfare' bills." Printer Margaret Kerr-Firth of the LEO told the audience of the "immense tax on the laboring class by the compulsory health insurance bill" and called WTUL leader Rose Schneiderman "socialistic" and a "fraud." Margaret Murray, a former transit worker who had lost her job because of night work restrictions, described the women reformers of the WJLC as "butterflies of fashion, with more money than brains." Using strongly feminist language, Murray said that the real intent of protective legislation was "to force the women back into the slavery of their own kitchens, where there is no limit to hours and the minimum wage is demonstrated with a starvation stipend."[80]

Sweet's campaign workers circulated a petition against the welfare bills among women in upstate mills and factories. Soon Sweet was able to produce a petition opposing protective laws signed by, he claimed, 12,000 women workers. In response, Marion Dickerman claimed that her campaign had gathered 100,000 signatures in favor of the bills, and she accused Sweet of coercing women into signing his petition: "Mr. Sweet well knows that the signatures were obtained inside the factories at the demand of the employers."[81] Dickerman and the WJLC came up with examples of workers ordered to sign Sweet's petition by their employers, but in some cases a different sort of persuasion was used. One woman textile worker told a Dickerman campaigner, "They told me [health insurance] would come out of my pay, and I signed because I didn't want to support some dago's wife every time she had a baby."[82] Florence Kelley might have been dismayed—but should not have been surprised—to find her racial arguments against maternity insurance proving effective against the entire slate of women's welfare bills.

Dickerman campaigners were startled and distressed to find themselves fighting other women. The WJLC quickly tried to unmask the LEO as a tiny group unable to speak for the needs of most women workers. In her campaign speeches, Marion Dickerman claimed that the LEO had only 1,500 members, while "the Women's Trade Union League had 70,000 and the New York State Federation [of Labor] 800,000 members who represented the true desires of New York's working people for labor legislation."[83] Just as the LEO had accused supporters of protective legislation of being privileged women who believed falsely that they could speak for the working class, the WJLC argued that LEO members were not really workers either: "Why should an organization composed chiefly of highly paid professional or semi-professional women, some of whom have worked themselves out of the wage-earning group, devote itself to defeating the efforts of the wage-earners to gain by legislation such leisure and compensation as the more favored self-supporting women already enjoy?"[84]

The accusation that the LEO's members already possessed advantages they denied to other women was echoed by Pauline Newman. She had missed all the action in Albany while organizing garment workers in Philadelphia, but upon her return Newman quickly attacked the LEO. She pointed out that the women printers in the LEO were members of the International Typographical Union, which "has spent three million dollars in order to establish the eight hour day in [the printing] trade. From this one would think that members of such a union would help to establish the eight hour day by legislation for those who have no union. But some people will think of themselves only, and never mind the under dog." Newman also accused the LEO of playing into the hands of employers opposed to the welfare bills: "You and your associates are doing the same work as that of the exploiters of labor." According to Newman, LEO leader Ada Woolf's arguments against the welfare bills sounded like they represented those of "the master class. A type like Mrs. Woolf will always be with us, until she will be kicked out from the labor movement and placed where she rightfully belongs — on the other side." [85]

Undeniable class and occupational differences distinguished the WJLC from the LEO. Although members of both groups represented a wide spectrum of income levels, the WJLC was dedicated to the needs of unskilled factory women, while the LEO spoke mainly for professional and skilled workers. One LEO member described herself as an "independent executive" and "concert manager," and Amy Wren, an outspoken LEO leader, was president of the Brooklyn Woman's Bar Association. But the LEO could not be dismissed as simply a club for privileged women. Stella Jackson, an elevator operator and LEO member, testified that the ban on night work for women would force her to return to dead-end domestic labor, a life she dreaded. [86]

Cases like Stella Jackson's made it extraordinarily difficult for the WJLC to discredit the argument that protective legislation was discrimination against women. The challenge from the LEO threw the women of the WJLC into a frenzy, first because they had expected unanimous support from women based on gender, and second because they were unprepared to defend themselves against charges of violating women's newly won citizenship by treating women differently from male workers. Perhaps if they had emphasized the egalitarian provisions of the health insurance bill as well as the restrictions of the hours and wage proposals, they might have been able to meet the LEO's accusations more effectively. But by the time the feud between the women erupted, the WJLC had decided to drop health insurance from its welfare slate.

Marion Dickerman, who had agreed to run for office on extremely short notice, decided not to fight for health insurance because she did not have time to study the complexities of the bill. [87] The leaders of the WJLC agreed to put health insurance on the back burner, in part because of opposition within their own ranks. Just as Dickerman's campaign went into full swing, some League of Women Voters members threatened to withdraw from the WJLC if it continued to support health insurance.[88] To make matters worse, when some of the New York City WJLC members tried to drum up support for the welfare bills among the women's clubs of upstate New York, they found unexpected opposition to health insurance. The Consumers' League of Buffalo refused to support the health insurance measure, and a leader of the New York State Federation of Women's Clubs told legislators that her organization opposed the bill, despite its official endorsement.[89]

These women who refused to support health insurance were at the same time willing to work for the minimum-wage and eight-hour proposals. Maternalism certainly played a role in their position: they were comfortable with legislation that protected women based on their maternal and domestic roles but drew the line at a program for both sexes. But their opposition to health insurance did not rest solely in gender ideology. WJLC leader Vira Whitehouse, after lecturing to upstate women's clubs, realized that the "women are all intensely interested, quite heated up in fact, but torn between our views and those of their doctor- or manufacturer-husbands."[90] John B. Andrews wryly noted that the Buffalo Consumers' League, which had refused to endorse health insurance, was "officered by the wives of physicians."[91] The philanthropic urges of elite and middle-class women could be tempered by class allegiances — especially in the case of health insurance, which would directly affect the income of doctors and the profits of employers, and hence their wives' economic status.

Having dropped health insurance from her platform, Marion Dickerman had to base her campaign on the idea of protection for women only, leaving her with little defense against the equal rights rhetoric of the LEO. And Sweet made political hay from Dickerman's choice, deriding her for indecision while continuing to attack her campaigners for their original support of health insurance.[92]

Still, the WJLC's campaign succeeded in winning some votes away from Sweet, but in the end Marion Dickerman lost the election and Sweet retained his seat as Speaker of the assembly, where he continued to obstruct welfare proposals and spearheaded the expulsion of Socialist representatives (see Chapter 8).[93] The WJLC's hope for a united bloc of women voters in favor of protective legislation was dashed by the challenge of the League for Equal Opportunity. Although the LEO probably did not turn a large number of voters (if any) against the women's legislative program, its rhetoric enabled antiwelfare politicians like Sweet to exploit divisions among women and use them to attack reformers and their proposals. Sweet's reelection marked a turning point in New York postsuffrage politics. Just the previous year, women voters and a protective legislation slate had successfully defeated three antilabor New York State legislators.[94] But the same strategy backfired in 1919 as Sweet identified and manipulated women's ambivalence about gender-specific legislation to his advantage. Protective legislation advocates now realized that the women's vote did not automatically belong to them.

With Sweet back in his seat of power, the women's legislative program again died in committee in 1920. The WJLC gave up the fight for health insurance and maternity benefits; throughout the 1920s, its member groups would continue to fight for protective legislation, but for women only. The ideas of the League for Equal Opportunity would take the form of the campaign for an Equal Rights Amendment that would divide the women's movement for years. The promise of the "women's welfare bills," which, by aligning health insurance and protective legislation, hinted that the health of male as well as female workers required protection, had vanished.

The campaign for health insurance highlights both the power of organized women and the absence of an entirely unified vision among them. Most women reformers and labor leaders supported the concept of health insurance and medical maternity benefits, and without their support the bill would never have come so close to success. But the campaign also disclosed a myriad of differences that impeded women's unity. Maternity benefits raised the contentious question of whether families with working mothers deserved support. Florence Kelley and some of her allies opposed cash maternity benefits on the grounds of protecting single women's wages and discouraging the undesirable "racial" practice of sending wives out to work. In contrast, Pauline Newman and the women of the AALL saw cash benefits for maternity as the centerpiece of health insurance, essential for protecting women's wages as well as the health of mothers and babies. And the rivalry of the WJLC and the LEO exposed a rift between women who advocated restrictions on women's work and those who demanded equal rights rather than protection. This rift quickly shattered the dream of women's postsuffrage political unity.[95]

The defeat of health insurance had long-term consequences for American women. Both cash and medical maternity benefits vanished from the reform agenda, and with them any attempt to recognize working mothers in legislation. Women activists turned their attention back to protective laws that would restrict women's work, preserving, in the words of Alice Kessler-Harris, "the paradoxical situation in which the idea of motherhood became the object of protection in the workplace, while women who became mothers derived no job [or wage] protection at all."[96] Progressive women also threw their energies into the new federal Sheppard-Towner Maternity and Infancy Act, which funded visiting nurses and health education for childbearing women. Thanks to a vigorous campaign led by the Children's Bureau and Florence Kelley, the bill passed in 1921. But successful as Sheppard-Towner was in reducing maternal and infant mortality, it represented a quite different path for maternity protection than did compulsory health insurance, one that did not move the nation further toward recognition or support of working mothers.[97] Although Irene Andrews and Irene Sylvester of the AALL had championed including cash maternity benefits in Sheppard-Towner, the act made no such provision.[98] Children's Bureau head Julia Lathrop backed away from her earlier support for maternity benefits, testifying before Congress that increasing men's wages would preclude the need for an "endow[ment] of motherhood" in the United States.[99] Unlike compulsory health insurance, Sheppard-Towner tried to protect mothers and babies without protecting women's incomes. By the end of the twentieth century, American women would still not have a right to maternity pay.

8

The Politics of Defeat

The progress of the health insurance bill in the New York legislative sessions of 1919 and 1920 was tortuous and dramatic. Aside from the spectacle provided by the political activity of newly enfranchised women voters, the postwar debate over compulsory health insurance took place against the backdrop of fierce conflict within the state Republican Party and the frenzy of the Red Scare. With New York's Republicans already riven by disputes between old-guard conservatives and the followers of Theodore Roosevelt, the 1919 health insurance proposal generated a highly public breakdown of party unity. The American Association for Labor Legislation's bill was introduced jointly in 1919 by Republican senator Frederick M. Davenport and Democratic assemblyman and minority leader Charles D. Donohue. The Republican Party controlled the legislature, as it had for decades, but its leadership could not contain the nine members rebellious enough to side with the Democrats in favor of the health insurance and women's welfare bills.[1]

The fate of health insurance was sealed by the convergence of economic and political power with the ideological force of the Red Scare. The bill had, of course, faced charges of un-Americanism since its inception. But in the volatile atmosphere of the Red Scare, accusations that health insurance was a gateway to Bolshevism reached a fever pitch. Opponents still tarred the bill with the brush of Prussianism, but their rhetoric displayed a new emphasis on the socialistic features of compulsory health insurance and its threat to the American economic system. In the words of the Associated Manufacturers and Merchants of New York State, the proposal was "a vicious attempt to ruin and disorganize business." Speaker Thaddeus Sweet called health insurance "legislation so confiscatory and burdensome that business and industry will be abandoned." Another assemblyman warned that the AALL's bill represented Soviet-style "state regulation of personal matters."[2]

Opponents' attacks on the Bolshevik nature of health insurance became more impassioned as they grew increasingly alarmed at the progress of the bill. A great blow to opponents came on January 1, 1919, when Al Smith, the newly elected Democratic governor of New York, declared his support for health insurance in his inaugural address. Shortly afterward, a distressed Frederick Hoffman told his superiors at the Prudential that "the outlook [is], in many respects, very serious, on account of [Smith's] endorsement of health insurance."[3]

The legislation seemed even more likely to pass because of its bipartisan sponsorship. The 1919 health insurance bill was co-sponsored by Frederick Davenport, one of the most respected members of the New York Senate and a major figure in the Progressive wing of the Republican Party that had been so important to the election of Al Smith.[4] After an early career as a Methodist minister and college professor, Davenport had been elected to the New York Senate in 1908. He was the Progressive Party candidate for lieutenant governor of New York in 1912 and for governor in 1914. A "quintessential progressive," throughout his career he denounced the disproportionate influence of big business in American life. Davenport recalled that when he first ran for state senate in 1908, "I think the first general speech I made was on the growing power of corporations in politics in this country."[5] His campaign literature informed voters, "I am against rule by great corporations and powerful financial interests. I am against putting the shrewd servants of powerful and designing corporations in public office." Davenport was dedicated to reforming a corrupt Republican Party, and his repeated denunciations of the "political guerrillas" of the "Republican machine" that dominated Albany made him some enemies among his party colleagues.[6]

Davenport, however, was careful not to appear soft on socialism. He condemned Bolshevik influence as eagerly as the most conservative Republicans but argued that the best bulwark against this threat to the United States was the adoption of labor and welfare legislation to improve the living standards of American workers. He saw himself as part of a Progressive "movement of the liberal capitalists of our time" whose intent in supporting social legislation was "to destroy radicalism at its roots." It was the opponents of labor legislation, Davenport argued, who provoked worker discontent; referring to the AMM's anti–health insurance propaganda, he said angrily, "[T]hese are the fellows that create Bolshevism."[7]

Without a doubt, Davenport was the politician whose commitment to compulsory health insurance was the most tireless and steadfast. He worked closely with the AALL to refine the 1919 version of the bill, and over the course of the year he made countless speeches in support of health insurance. Davenport drew laughter from a labor audience by remarking that he had "talked on

Frederick Davenport (Theodore Roosevelt Collection, Harvard College Library).

this subject [health insurance] so many hours in the Senate" that he had lost track of time.[8] His dedication to compulsory health insurance made him a target of attacks from business and the medical profession. An upstate physician warned him, "[Y]ou have lost many good friends" by supporting health insurance; he and his fellow doctors hoped that Davenport would "stop look and listen with this foolish legislation; and not kill your political usefulness."[9] Davenport's anti-Bolshevik rhetoric did not shield him from Red Scare accusations of radicalism. In a characteristic outburst, Gertrude Easley of the National Civic Federation told Samuel Gompers, "As far as I can judge, Senator Davenport is a socialist himself or inclined in that direction."[10]

But Davenport's devotion to the cause of health insurance brought striking results. Aided by the Women's Joint Legislative Conference (see Chapter 7), he was able to persuade several of his Republican colleagues to join with him in support of the compulsory health insurance bill. At the end of March 1919, nine Republicans defied the party leadership by announcing their support for health insurance and the other welfare measures. The New York press quickly filled with stories on the "insurgent Senators" and "Republican malcontents" who were leading a "Senate Uprising" against the party status quo. The response to the insurgency was testimony of public discontent with the Republicans' complacent control of the legislature. An editorial in the New York *World* expressed satisfaction that the "revolt of the Republican Senators will further advertise the folly of a majority leadership which, charged by power with responsibility, wastes time and money and does nothing." [11]

In his speech before the senate on April 10, 1919, immediately before the vote on health insurance, Davenport asked his fellow Progressive Republicans to join him in resisting his party's conservative bent. The outcome of the vote would be a test of the party's ability to adapt to changing social conditions. "[I]f the Republican party is not wise enough," he admonished his colleagues, "to see in time that it not only must be absolutely fair and just to the property interests of this State, but also absolutely fair and just to the great body of industrial workers of this State, then there is no future for the Republican Party in the State of New York or in any other of our great industrial commonwealths." [12] The nine insurgent Republicans joined twenty-one Democrats in voting for passage of the Davenport-Donohue compulsory health insurance bill. With the defection of nine party members, the conservative Republican leadership was able to muster only twenty votes against health insurance, and the bill passed in the New York Senate on April 10. It was the first time that any legislative body in the United States approved compulsory health insurance. Never before had health insurance supporters come so close to victory.

As the debate on the bill moved to the assembly, opponents were thrown into a panic. A delegation of "big manufacturers and business men" descended upon Albany and flooded the assembly with "threatening" telegrams, asking Republican leaders for reassurance that the party had not deserted their interests. They were comforted by Speaker Thaddeus Sweet, who pledged that he would never let the welfare bills out of his assembly Rules Committee. In addition to decrying the "scolding" of women reformers, Sweet called the senate Republican insurgents "Bolsheviki" and noted that twenty assembly Republicans would have to defy him in order to bring the welfare bills to a vote. He was confident that such a defection was impossible. [13]

John B. Andrews once dismissed Thaddeus Sweet as "a little paper manufacturer," [14] but the Speaker was in fact one of the most powerful politicians in New York State. After twenty years as a prosperous businessman — he ran the Sweet Brothers Paper Company in upstate Phoenix, New York — Thaddeus Sweet successfully campaigned for an assembly seat in 1910. In 1914, he was elected Speaker. This role gave him the power to award or block the committee appointments of fellow assemblymen, a tactic he used to maintain a loyal following. [15] And as chairman of the Rules Committee, Sweet could decide which bills would be released for a vote on the assembly floor, and which would languish in committee. Only a majority vote by the assembly could overrule Sweet. [16] Sweet's continuing hold on power rested on the structure of the New

York State government, a structure that gave disproportionate representation to his supporters. New York State's apportionment system had been changed in 1894 to guarantee a large number of assembly seats to upstate districts. This system in turn had been created by conservative politicians trying to reduce the influence of New York City, with its large numbers of immigrant voters, in the legislature—a clear example of the ideological origins of state structure.[17] The dominance of representatives from upstate manufacturing and agricultural regions gave the assembly its solid Republican majority and Sweet his solid base of support.

It was Sweet's vow to kill the health insurance and other welfare bills that led the Women's Joint Legislative Conference to organize their April 3 mass meeting in Cooper Union and to concentrate their lobbying efforts on the Speaker. Following the rally, Mary Dreier of the WJLC led a delegation of women to meet with Speaker Sweet and two other Republican leaders. To the women's consternation, they found that "Speaker Sweet in all his questions exhibited a concern for the manufacturers rather than for the women workers of the state."[18] Ignoring the public outcry, Sweet continued to sit on the women's welfare bills, including health insurance, in the Rules Committee. On April 17, Assemblyman Donohue, co-sponsor of the health insurance bill, moved to discharge Sweet's committee of the legislation. The motion lost, eighty-four to fifty-eight.[19] As described in Chapter 7, despite the senate's support for the welfare measures, the 1919 assembly battle over health insurance had ended in defeat for the reformers.

Sweet's sabotage of the reform bills sparked widespread anger throughout the state. The New York press, as the AALL put it, was "a Unit in Denouncing" Sweet's strong-arm tactics. The editorial pages of the New York *Evening World*, *American*, *Evening Journal*, *Evening Mail*, and *Globe*, as well as the Albany *Argus* and Rochester *Times-Union*, rang with condemnations of Sweet's dominance of the voting process and his heartless annihilation of social legislation. An editorial in the Democratic New York *World* warned that Sweet's intent was "not only to usurp the power of the people but to use it against the people. If Mr. Sweet can do that, he has practically abolished the assembly and established a dictatorship over the Legislature of New York." Other papers described Sweet as a "steam-roller," a "Bourbon," and a "modern Machiavelli" who slavishly served the interests of a "plutocracy."[20]

The reformers who had fought the battle for the welfare bills were outraged. A joint meeting of the New York State Federation of Labor and the Women's Legislative Conference condemned the destruction of their bills and resolved to "call upon the voters of this state to recognize this challenge of autocracy to principles of democracy for which we have fought." The NYSFL announced that its legislative program had been "ruthlessly slaughtered and . . . the majority members of the Assembly are wholly to blame for the destruction." [21] In a letter to its supporters, the AALL denounced Sweet's tight control of the legislative process: "Regardless of their attitude toward health insurance all fair minded citizens should resent a situation which gives *one man* by virtue of his position as Chairman of the Rules Committee *power to refuse to give this measure of far-reaching public interest* opportunity for discussion by the Assembly." [22] Even the gentlemanly Davenport had harsh words for the conspirators against health insurance, calling the business groups who had influenced Sweet "these smooth tools of privilege." [23]

The reformers' fury at their loss was not met with complacency on the part of their opponents. Mark Daly and his allies, in fact, realized that health insurance had been defeated only narrowly, so that the threat of passage loomed large in 1920 if a majority of assemblymen could be persuaded to overrule Sweet. Daly told members of his AMM that despite Sweet's blockage of the bill, health insurance still represented "a pressing menace." He warned that the reformers had managed to convert much of the public to the health insurance cause; their "skillful and persistent propaganda . . . has made a distinct impression on many people who have not given the subject careful thought." [24] P. T. Sherman stirred up a NCF meeting by declaring that "the campaign for health insurance in the state is built up upon a tissue of gross, deadly lies, lies, lies!" but he went on to suggest that public opinion had been swayed in favor of health insurance; the reformers "are trying to delude the people and . . . I am afraid now . . . they have deluded the people." [25]

Mark Daly did not sway from his determination to lead the opponents of health insurance to a final, decisive victory in 1920. In June of 1919 he called "a meeting of the forces opposed to compulsory health insurance" in his Manhattan hotel room to map out a strategy for the next legislative session. The group he gathered was a powerhouse of men representing employers, insurance companies, and the medical profession. Together in Daly's room were Magnus Alexander of the National Industrial Conference Board; Dr. G. B. Beach of the New York State Dental Society; William Gale Curtis of the Insurance Economics Society (founder of the New York League for Americanism); Lee Frankel of the Metropolitan Life Insurance Company and the NCF; Eugene Hardin of the United Commercial Travelers; John L. Train, "representing mutual compensation insurance organizations"; and Dr. Henry L. Winters of the Medical Society of the State of New York.[26] The public outcry against Sweet's obstruction of the welfare bills drove Daly and his colleagues to concentrate on capturing public opinion in their favor. If, as so many newspapers and reformers claimed, the citizenry would punish Sweet's Republicans by voting them out of office, opponents needed to convince New York voters that health insurance was not in their interests. To this end, the group decided to target the workforce of upstate factories. In the summer of 1919, Mark Daly asked members of the AMM "to send him the names and addresses of employees who are not trouble makers in order that he may place them on a mailing list to receive the real facts about health insurance."[27] According to the NYSFL, "[S]uddenly telegrams from our opponents went out all through the up-state country for the foremen to go in to the mills and get the workers, men and women, to sign . . . petitions against these human welfare measures." Factory owners responded to the telegrams by circulating anti–health insurance petitions among their employees. The results seemed overwhelmingly in Daly's favor; in one Utica factory, 12,875 out of 13,000 workers signed the petitions against health insurance.[28] Sweet and other Republican assemblymen used the petitions to argue that their upstate constituencies wanted them to vote against health insurance.

Even some historians have taken these petitions as a signal of strong feeling against health insurance among factory workers.[29] But evidence suggests that many signatures were coerced and thus represent pressure from employers rather than the sentiments of workers. Some upstate factory operatives testified that they had been pressured to sign the petitions. The editor of a Polish newspaper in Utica said he had heard that factory foremen were in charge of getting workers to sign and achieved the desired result by "telling the people that everybody would have to pay for himself 50 cents a week from his pocket, to be insured and to receive the sick benefit." The result, the editor told Frederick Davenport, was "to produce false statements of the working people against your Bill in Albany."[30] An employee at a knitting mill reported, "I felt that it was unfair for all the workers to sign these petitions, when . . . the workers almost as a whole didn't understand this [health insurance] bill." Foremen had told the millworkers that money would be taken from their paychecks to pay for medical care, but they "mentioned no other benefits of the proposed health insurance bill," including sick pay. The worker complained that "these petitions came from the office," making him fear that if he made "a protest to the workers against signing the petition . . . it might cost me my job."[31] Similarly, a report on the petition campaign by the League of Women Voters charged that workers had been given false or partial information about the health insurance bill. The information distributed to workers not only failed to mention coverage for lost time during sickness but also kept silent about the health insurance bill's benefits for dependent wives and children. Petition organizers told employees that the government would force them to hire certain doctors, and "elaborated on the expense."[32]

While condemning Daly's petition drive among wage earners as coercive, reformers nevertheless were forced to ask why they had never attempted similar tactics themselves. Noting that the AALL had achieved a high level of public and press support in the New York metropolitan area, John B. Andrews conceded that "[o]ur fundamental weakness . . . lay in the lack of education upstate." [33] And the AALL had neglected not only upstate workers but workers in general. The AALL's association with the labor movement had been limited to correspondence and meetings with union officials and virtually no contact with the rank and file. In 1919 Frederick Davenport hoped that "when the fight opens again at Albany, there should be a bona fide petition from wage earners themselves a mile long, backing the men who are the proponents of these measures." [34] Repeating an often-heard criticism of the AALL, Davenport said that many members of the assembly "wouldn't have opposed [health insurance] if they could only have heard from the workers themselves . . . [but] they didn't hear from anybody except those blooming reformers." But it was not until June of 1919 that James Lynch began working on materials to distribute to upstate workers explaining the health insurance proposal — very late in the game for supporters to begin rallying ordinary workers to their cause.[35] The AALL's lack of a strategy to amass support among the potential beneficiaries of health insurance carried a high political cost.

The political strategy of the AALL's opponents, meanwhile, was rapidly taking on a new, even more effective form. In 1920 the NYLA, headed by Carleton D. Babcock of the Insurance Economics Society, became the instrument for an unprecedented alliance of physicians, employers, and insurance companies opposed to the health insurance bill. The league's letterhead claimed that its purpose was to "promote the spirit of true Americanism among all the people of the State of New York; to uphold and defend the constitution and laws of the United States and of the State of New York; to oppose radical and impractical doctrines and laws and racial customs which are fundamentally anti-American and not in harmony with our high ideals and free institutions; to initiate, conduct and aid educational campaigns in support of the foregoing objects." [36] While the league's public pronouncements called for "a million volunteers to fight un-Americanism wherever it appears," Babcock had no doubts about which manifestation of un-Americanism the league would target; he vowed "to kill Health Insurance definitely and finally." [37]

Reformers who had greeted the sudden appearance of the NYLA with disdain became increasingly alarmed as the most powerful enemies of health insurance — insurers, employers, physicians, and some members of the American Federation of Labor — threw their support behind Babcock. The Insurance

Economics Society provided the league with start-up funds, and Mark Daly's
AMM intensified its association with the NYLA as part its 1920 strategy to defeat
health insurance. Reformers claimed that the AMM "had raised a fund of between $100,000 and $200,000 for propaganda purposes . . . this fund has been
used for the support of the so-called New York League for Americanism." [38]
Babcock struck up a regular correspondence with Gertrude Easley to keep the
NCF informed of the league's activities.

Conservative physicians, too, found themselves welcomed under the umbrella of the NYLA. In response to the passage of the bill in the senate, upstate
doctors began organizing "guilds" or "protective leagues" to fight health insurance. At a meeting of Erie County physicians shortly after the bill's passage,
450 of the 550 doctors present joined the new Physicians Protective Association
"as rapidly as men could sign their names," paying the princely sum of ten dollars each "for the purpose of fighting compulsory health insurance and killing
it." [39] In Rennselaer County, a "Physicians', Dentists', and Nurses' Protective
Society" was formed in April 1919 "for the purpose of combating Compulsory
Health Insurance, and other vicious legislation inimical to the interests of the
medical and allied professions and to the welfare of the people at large." [40] In
Brooklyn, lawyer-physician John J. A. O'Reilly headed the new Professional
Guild of Kings County. The guild, according to O'Reilly, had "a practical, scientific plan for welding the Doctors, Dentists and Pharmacists of the State of
New York into a compact, working unit" to oppose health insurance. Such
organization would make the guild "a FORCE which must be reckoned with by
those who Frame and those who Pass our Laws." O'Reilly asked upstate practitioners to "start the work in your own County" so that New York physicians
might be "ORGANIZED SIMULTANEOUSLY ON IDENTICAL LINES." [41]

The new physicians' guilds worked closely not only with each other but also
with the NYLA. John B. Andrews reported that doctors were embracing the
anti–health insurance arguments put forward by Babcock's league, which was
"distributing [its] literature at meetings of the doctors, while the leaflets of
the Kings County Professional Guild . . . may be obtained from the New York
League for Americanism." In Buffalo, the secretary of the Physician's Protective Association and the local branch of the NYLA shared the same address. [42]
With physician cooperation, the league could invoke the "expert" opinion of
the medical profession in its opposition to health insurance. The participation of doctors gave greater force to league arguments that otherwise would
be based only on the interests of manufacturers and insurers.

Although not officially associated with the NYLA, conservative members
of the AFL participated in its activities. Sara Conboy, for example, allowed
herself to be quoted extensively in league propaganda (see Chapter 6). The

NYLA pamphlet titled "Labor's Attitude towards Compulsory State Health Insurance" was a typical example of the organization's rhetorical strategy. Its cover displayed the alarming-looking German words for health insurance ("Reichskranken-Versicherung") and announced that "Socialistic leaders endorse this scheme" while a "Majority of Others Oppose" it, including the "foremost woman labor leader," Sara Conboy. The pamphlet accused health insurance supporters both of representing "the autocrats of Germany" and of acting "in the name of the Socialist party of America." A cartoon depicted workers handing over their pay to a greedy bureaucrat, and the NYLA's address was displayed under a statement advertising "Free Literature on Compulsory Health Insurance on Request."[43] Nothing in the pamphlet hinted that the league was an association of employers, physicians, and insurance companies.

Aware that the league was vulnerable to charges of being a front organization for private interests opposed to health insurance, in December of 1919 Babcock sent a physician member of the NYLA on a "patriotic lecture tour . . . to give the League standing as an organization with some purpose in life other than to oppose Compulsory Health Insurance."[44] Reformers were infuriated that the league rallied its supporters under the banner of patriotism. The League of Women Voters fumed that Babcock's organization, despite its name, "has, in fact, no patriotic nor constructive objects beyond the particular and selfish ends of its sponsors." The guise of patriotism camouflaged the NYLA's ultimate aim, which was "to obstruct as long as possible any progressive industrial legislation in this State." Frederick Davenport was offended by the NYLA's invocation of American values to condemn health insurance, declaring, "[T]he story of the gross and impudent and unscrupulous means by which this propagandism has been carried on by the so-called New York League for Americanism will some day be told to the disgust of all decent people." Reformer John A. Lapp was amused that "the Casualty Insurance companies" had become "the particular guarantors of Americanism."[45]

In addition to their contempt for Babcock's organization, reformers were dismayed by its effectiveness. The NYLA's greatest triumph was its success in uniting contentious groups of physicians, employers, and insurers in a single-minded cause. Its prolific output of propaganda ensured that the health insurance battle would continue to be fought over the ground of Americanism. Repeatedly accused of unpatriotic activity, reformers were forced to spend their time defending their loyalty to the nation rather than the benefits of their health insurance bill.

To make matters worse for the reformers, the Red Scare was reaching a fever pitch. Throughout 1919, press and government reports of a murderous "reign of terror" in Russia described "decrees abolishing private ownership, confis-

LABOR'S ATTITUDE
TOWARDS
COMPULSORY
STATE HEALTH
INSURANCE

(Known in Germany as Reichskranken-Versicherung)

Socialistic leaders endorse this scheme
Majority of others Oppose

MRS. SARA A. CONBOY,
conceded to be the foremost woman labor leader,

is opposed to Compulsory Health Insurance

Bulletin No. 8
of the

NEW YORK LEAGUE *for* AMERICANISM

General Offices: 471 South Salina Street, Syracuse, N. Y.

Buffalo Office: 153 Delaware Avenue

The cover of a New York League for Americanism anti–health insurance pamphlet (Kheel Center for Labor-Management Documentation and Archives, Cornell School of Industrial and Labor Relations).

cating land, nationalizing industry, and establishing 'free love' bureaus." A general strike in Seattle, nationwide May Day rioting, and the discovery of an apparent bomb plot inflamed fears of a Bolshevik-inspired conspiracy of immigrants and radicals to overthrow the U.S. government. In the words of historian Robert Murray, "[W]hat was a mere theoretical possibility of radical revolution gradually became in the minds of many a horrible reality." In March 1919 the New York State legislature created a committee to investigate "seditious activities." Headed by Senator Clayton R. Lusk, the Lusk Committee, as it became known, targeted New York's left-wing organizations as centers of the Bolshevik conspiracy in America. The Lusk Committee raids resulted in hundreds of arrests, the seizure of vast amounts of printed material, and the deportation of aliens accused of being Red supporters.[46]

Supporters of health insurance also came under the Lusk Committee's fire. James Holland, president of the NYSFL, was hauled in front of the committee in 1919. Its members questioned him closely about the federation's association with the Women's Trade Union League, a major target of the committee's investigations. To reformers' dismay, Holland agreed with Lusk investigators that the WTUL did indeed exhibit Bolshevik sympathies. Elsewhere, he referred to WTUL leader Rose Schneiderman as "Red Rose." As a result, Schneiderman and the WTUL held a prominent place in the Lusk Committee's published report on sedition in New York State.[47]

At the following NYSFL convention, angry delegates accused Holland of betraying labor through his cooperation with the committee. Schneiderman herself rose to attack the New York Assembly's Red Scare tactics, and specifically linked the activities of the Lusk Committee to the efforts of the assembly to quash Progressive labor legislation: "[S]ome of us feel that this [Lusk] committee . . . were going out and yelling 'Bolshevism' so that . . . we would forget that Speaker Sweet smothered and killed legislation which would bring relief to hundreds of thousands of women in this state." Holland defended himself by reminding the convention that he had only testified before the Lusk Committee because he "was placed under arrest and subpoenaed and brought there." He went on to complain that other labor leaders, particularly Hugh Frayne of the AFL, had made far more damning accusations about Bolshevism in the labor movement, and that he felt unfairly attacked for his testimony in the New York socialist press.[48] At the same time that the defense of "Americanism" had unified the anti–health insurance forces in the form of the New York League for Americanism, the Red Scare bitterly divided health insurance advocates and weakened their ability to speak with a unified voice.

The antiradicalism of 1919 was also wielded in support of Speaker Sweet's campaign for reelection against Marion Dickerman (described in Chapter 7).

In addition to Sweet's attacks on the supposed Bolshevism of Dickerman and her supporters, Senator Lusk himself traveled to Fulton, Dickerman's hometown in Oswego County, just before the election to make a campaign speech for Sweet on behalf of the Committee to Investigate Seditious Activities. The New York Senate's preeminent foe of socialism reminded his audience of Sweet's singular ability to control the legislative process. "If Tad Sweet is beaten," Lusk told the crowd, "you'll lose your powerful officer. My God! What a calamity if he were beaten!"[49] The reelection of Speaker Sweet would guarantee protection from the twin calamities of socialism and Progressive labor legislation.

Indeed, shortly after he regained his assembly seat, Speaker Sweet oversaw one of the most notorious episodes of the Red Scare: the January 7, 1920, expulsion of five Socialist members of the New York legislature. The Socialist platform, Sweet declared, was "absolutely inimical to the best interests of the State of New York and of the United States," and hence he refused to seat the elected members. His autocratic action caused a nationwide sensation.[50] Even the fiercely antisocialist Ralph Easley of the NCF was "disgusted" that "Speaker Sweet should have gone at this matter in such a brutal fashion," since the expulsions had aroused sympathy for the Socialists. However, Easley told Samuel Gompers, it was still their duty to stand behind Sweet, because "every enemy of the American Federation of Labor or the National Civic Federation and the things for which either institution stands is out against Sweet."[51] In the eyes of the opponents of health insurance, Sweet's violation of civil liberties was a small price to pay for the defeat of reform legislation.

After the rout of the welfare bills in 1919, women's groups and the AALL had identified Speaker Sweet as the culprit, and they ran Marion Dickerman as candidate in his district in hopes of unseating him. After their efforts failed, reformers found a new target. This time it was Mark Daly, who was labeled "the most malign influence in the state,"[52] and his unsavory alliance with the New York League for Americanism. The great threat to Progressive legislation lay not simply within the government, as it had with Speaker Sweet, but with sinister outside influences and powerful camouflaged interests.

The NYSFL was indignant at the cabal of private interests that had shaped the outcome of the health insurance battle: "[W]e all know . . . that the public mind has been deliberately poisoned against this great social measure by the propaganda brought about by the influence of the Medical Fraternity and the Manufacturers' Association. This has been carried on in a great measure through the so-called Americanization League."[53] Nothing aroused more outrage in reformers than the NYLA's manipulation of patriotic sentiment. Supporters of health insurance tried to reclaim the term "Americanism" for their side, with the League of Women Voters charging, "We know of no organization that uses more un-American methods than this Daly-Babcock 'League,' and we regard it as one of the chief obstacles in this State to any genuine Americanism." [54] An editorial condemning Babcock's organization in the New York *World* brandished the headline "Un-American 'Americanism'" and insisted that compulsory health insurance was "a measure praised by many Americans of the purest type, which can in no sense be called subversive or dangerous." [55]

Once again, it was not the AALL but a women's organization that took the lead in publicly denouncing reform's enemies. In the spring of 1920, the New York State League of Women Voters, which was a major force in the WJLC, released and widely circulated a pamphlet that attacked Daly's and the NYLA's efforts to block the welfare bills. Its elaborate title displayed reformers' outrage at the purported business conspiracy: "Report and Protest to the Governor, the Legislature and the People of the State of New York—Danger Confronting Popular Government—The Daly Lobby and Propaganda and the So-Called New York League for Americanism—A Powerful and Perilous Influence Backed by the Upstate Associated Manufacturers and Merchants.... This Combination Is a Menace to Progress through Orderly and Intelligent Legislative Methods." Mark Daly not only had concealed his business interests behind the facade of the NYLA, the pamphlet charged, but also had exercised direct control of the political process. Daly enjoyed casual and comradely relations with some elected representatives and apparently had shared an apartment at an Albany hotel with one of Sweet's "loyal assemblymen." "'Playfellows,'" the pamphlet noted indignantly, "is the term employed by Daly to describe certain members of the Legislature." Daly would also meet with Sweet on the train journey between Albany and New York City. [56]

As if this weren't evidence enough of Daly's influence over politicians, Thaddeus Sweet actually allowed Daly to use part of his office in the capitol as the Albany headquarters of the AMM. On reporting this arrangement, an Albany political journal charged that, instead of a government "of the people, for the people and by the people," New York's "government is 'Associated Industries of New York State, Inc.'... and Lobbyist Mark A. Daly is the Governor." [57] To supporters of Progressive legislation, Daly's close proximity and literal physical connection to Sweet's milieu were proof of the inseparability of private economic interest and political power.

Despite the fiery tone of their attacks on the Daly-Babcock alliance, the reformers' 1920 campaign for health insurance was lackluster. Davenport reintroduced the health insurance bill in March, but it garnered little attention and once again met death in the Rules Committee.[58] Davenport and his supporters were deeply disheartened by Sweet's continuing hold on the assembly and by the relentless assaults from the NYLA. It was the effectiveness of the league's propaganda that led Davenport to relinquish hopes for passage of health insurance in 1920; instead, he "announced that the advocates of the bill would content themselves with a campaign of education this year."[59] Later, Davenport criticized his opponents' "war psychology" that had led to the intolerant atmosphere of the Red Scare. Turning the opposing side's anti-German rhetoric against them, Davenport argued that the obsession with anti-Bolshevism was leading to an era in which "we shall have developed in our American life here the sort of organized repression that is Prussian and warlike in its quality."[60]

John B. Andrews, too, attributed the AALL's surrender to being worn down by attacks on the "un-American" character of compulsory insurance. "We are in the most serious situation," Andrews said in 1920, "when thinking men and women do not propose reforms without having their patriotism attacked."[61] Even the tireless League of Women Voters was demoralized by the intransigence of its foes. The women's attempt to expose Daly and the NYLA apparently succeeded in driving Carleton Babcock from New York State, but not in dislodging the powerful cabal of manufacturers and legislators he had masterminded. The League of Women Voters' annual report for 1921 gloomily reported, "We endorsed our usual bills, the minimum wage and eight hour day for women in industry, without much hope that any progress would be made toward making them law."[62]

One thing was clear: the AALL had underestimated its opposition. Reformers had not predicted their enemies' ability to form a broad and unified coalition in the NYLA. Physicians, employers, insurance companies, and conservative labor disregarded their differences in 1919 to create a single-minded resistance to compulsory health insurance. And the AALL not only underestimated this opposition but also was unprepared and unwilling to fight it. John B. Andrews had little interest in developing a strategy for all-out rebuttal of his opponents. One upstate reformer wrote to Andrews in 1920 asking why he refused to respond to a local attack on health insurance. He was angered by the AALL's seeming passivity and criticized Andrews's "inability to see that it was a big man's job to turn a hostile attitude into at least a neutral one."[63] Andrews replied, in a characteristically mild-mannered fashion, that he was uncertain of the "wisdom of putting the health insurance movement upon the defensive and devoting our energies to reply to the opposition rather than to devote them [to] conquering fresh territory."[64]

After five years of pushing the health insurance bill, Andrews was ready to give up the fight. The methods of rational argument and statistical persuasion that the AALL preferred were impotent against the rhetorical frenzy of the Red Scare. "[I]t seems to me," wrote Andrews in 1920, "that we are in a period of such reaction that [the AALL's opponents] cannot be brought around to seeing the justice of health insurance by any process of reasoning. The emotional effects of the reactionary period make this impossible." [65] Unable to meet his opponents on emotional grounds, Andrews preferred not to meet them at all. By 1921, he was informing the AALL membership that the organization had "decided to await a more favorable time before again devoting so important a part of its modest resources to [the health insurance] campaign." [66]

The glowing promise of compulsory health insurance, Andrews told AALL members, had been "swept away by a tide of reaction." [67] The turn against reform demoralized and saddened the AALL leader; Dr. Alexander Lambert wrote to Andrews at the end of 1920, "I felt sorry to see you so blue about things." [68] But Andrews insisted that his gloom was temporary and that he was not a "prophet of despair;" within two or three years, he predicted, the tide would turn back in favor of labor legislation once again. "[A]nd when that time comes," Andrews said, "I want to have a definite program and a few thousand rather unusually alert and well-informed people ready." [69] Even in the face of defeat, Andrews still clung to his faith in the leadership of experts.

But in reality, health insurance vanished entirely from the AALL's agenda. The organization ceased all efforts on behalf of insuring workers' illness in 1921, turning instead to strengthening workmen's compensation laws (mostly successfully) and introducing legislation for unemployment insurance (which failed repeatedly). The topic of health insurance was barely mentioned in the AALL's journal throughout the 1920s. [70] The other organizations that had sponsored health insurance were no more eager than the AALL to continue the fight. The WJLC had showed its mettle with its highly public attacks on Mark Daly and Thaddeus Sweet, but the women's skillful exercise of propaganda would no longer be used in the cause of health insurance. By March of 1920, compulsory health insurance was removed from the WJLC's program. Women's groups had not initiated that legislation, and in the face of the AALL's retreat the WJLC turned its full attention back to protective legislation. The NYSFL also retreated from its support for health insurance. Health insurance remained an official part of the federation's agenda, but in the absence of the AALL's prodding the labor group made no effort to reintroduce the legislation on its own. [71]

Even if women, labor, and the AALL had not given up the struggle for health insurance, they would have faced formidable obstacles. In the pursuit of defeating health insurance, the opponents of reform had devised a uniquely powerful merger of private economic interest, patriotic bombast, and political control.

Although critics claimed that opponents' patriotic rhetoric was a smokescreen for their self-interest, the Americanism invoked by physicians, manufacturers, insurers, and labor leaders was in fact inseparable from their defense of their material interests. The opponents of health insurance championed a definition of Americanism that embodied hostility to government interference in economic affairs. True Americanism would protect business and professional autonomy and profits (and organizational autonomy, in the case of the AFL) and at the same time put the brakes on the development of a welfare state.

This union of Americanism and material interests was not just a rhetorical victory but had immediate and practical consequences when coupled with political power. The economic interests represented by the NYLA had direct influence on powerful legislators like Sweet who were intent on building their anti-Bolshevik credentials. Sweet dedicated himself to demonstrating his "true Americanism" as a leader of the Red Scare by blocking labor legislation and protecting business. Reformers were aware of this symbiotic relationship between patriotic propaganda and business influence on politicians. When manipulated by private economic interests, what had simply been rhetoric became an instrument of political power. As the League of Women Voters astutely expressed it, "The propagandism as created and financed by certain powerful, vested interests is assuming a highly potent, though unregulated, political and governmental function."[72]

This formulation of propaganda exercising a government function points to a useful description of the American state. Throughout the health insurance campaign, the state was not autonomous or independent of outside pressures.[73] State politicians were influenced both by interest groups and by the powerful language of Americanism. Employers, insurers, and physicians wielded patriotic, anti-German, and Red Scare rhetoric to persuade politicians to defend them from the threat of health insurance. In turn, Speaker Sweet used the power of Americanism and antiradicalism to defend his political position against reformist (and socialist) challenges from both within and outside of his party.

Americanist language and antiradical ideology combined with powerful economic interests to influence state action. Politician Sweet's decisions were shaped both by his own background as a manufacturer—an example of the highly permeable boundaries between business and government—and by his close relationships with the interest groups he found ideologically and personally congenial. This convergence of interest and ideology gave the opponents of health insurance direct—and unequal—access to the state.

Health insurance supporters, especially those from the women's and labor movements, effectively demonstrated their fury at the decisive influence of the

Red Scare and of private economic interests on the legislative process. But their vigorous attack on the Sweet-Daly-NYLA alliance failed to sway anti–health insurance legislators or to bring about reforms in a political system unduly responsive to the demands of certain interest groups. Instead, their dismay at the exposure of the complicated and seemingly intractable web of influences that had destroyed their bills left reformers so discouraged that they abandoned the campaign for health insurance.

EPILOGUE

On April 27, 1920, the American Medical Association passed a definitive resolution against compulsory medical insurance at its annual meeting. Supported by "ninety per cent of the delegates," the nation's preeminent physicians' organization declared its opposition to "any plan embodying the system of compulsory contributory insurance against illness."[1] Along with the American Association for Labor Legislation's surrender, the AMA resolution marked the end of the Progressive Era campaign for health insurance. Outside of New York, commissions in Connecticut, Illinois, and Wisconsin reported against compulsory health insurance, while favorable commission reports in other states, including Ohio and New Jersey, failed to generate political movements for the measure. For the next decade, health insurance was a dead issue.

By the time reformers began to speak again of compulsory health insurance, American medicine had changed dramatically. At the end of the 1920s the cost of medical care had risen so much that reformers "regarded medical costs as a more serious problem than the wage loss of sickness."[2] As a result, universal health insurance became a means to control health care expenditures as well as to protect workers. But reformers were no more successful in bringing such proposals to fruition than they had been during the Progressive Era. All the major attempts to pass universal health legislation at the national level—during the administrations of Franklin Roosevelt, Truman, Kennedy, Nixon, and finally Clinton—met with defeat.

The configuration of interests shaping the fate of these reform proposals was similar, but not identical, to that of the Progressive Era battle. Missing from the anti–health insurance coalition after 1920 was organized labor, which became one of the most avid backers of a national health plan. In contrast to his predecessor Samuel Gompers, American Federation of Labor president William Green worked with liberals in the Truman administration to press for health insurance legislation.[3] The AFL-CIO has kept health care reform on its agenda, and at the century's end service industry and public sector unions were among the most important advocates of universal health coverage.

But the major opponents of universal health insurance remained the same.

During the Great Depression, and again in the 1940s, schemes for national health coverage were vigorously attacked by the medical profession, employers, and insurance companies. Medical insurance and sick pay, the two pillars of Progressive Era proposals, were left out of the Social Security Act because New Dealers feared attacks from the medical profession and insurance companies would derail the legislation. In the 1940s, physicians amassed a multimillion dollar war chest to defeat Harry Truman's health insurance plan. American employers and insurance companies were the most significant opponents of the Clinton health care reform in the 1990s.[4]

Its refusal to adopt universal health insurance has left the United States with a fragmented health care system and a stunted welfare state. "[P]eculiar, constantly evolving, even Byzantine" is how health policy historian Rosemary Stevens describes American health care financing.[5] The 1920s saw the disappearance of traditional methods of providing medical care to the working class: the fraternal society, the dispensary, and the free hospital. At the same time, employer coverage of sickness and medical care expanded, spurring the proliferation of private health insurance plans and the growth of the commercial insurance industry. After World War II, a majority of American workers received private health insurance through their employers, but a significant and growing number have remained without coverage of any kind.[6] The American health care system is still a patchwork that leaves many out in the cold.

The AFL-CIO's efforts on behalf of universal health care were mitigated by the massive growth of employer-sponsored medical benefits after World War II and the inclusion of health care in collective bargaining agreements. With most of their members covered by private insurance plans, unions between the 1940s and the 1970s came to have less of a stake in advocating national health insurance.[7] As health care costs continued to rise, however, medical benefits were often the first to go in concessions demanded by employers. Well into her old age, labor leader Pauline Newman warned, "True, the employer can give you all these benefits as a condition of employment—*but he can also take them away from you whenever he chooses to do so.*"[8] After the deindustrialization and corporate restructuring of the 1980s and 1990s, fewer employers offered health benefits and employees paid more of the total cost.[9] And the employment-based system of health insurance means that employees lose benefits when they lose or change jobs. As the AFL long ago feared, health benefits do indeed tie workers to their jobs.[10]

Mandatory sick pay, the cash benefit of Progressive Era proposals, has also been left out of the American welfare state. Five states established temporary disability insurance programs during the 1940s, but no others have followed suit, and there is no federal requirement for paid sick leave.[11] As with health insurance, the primary providers of sickness benefits are employers. These benefits have taken the form of either disability leave or paid sick days. But such programs are far less common than health coverage. In 1992–93, 52 percent of small firms and 65 percent of large ones provided paid sick leave; long-term disability was offered by only 23 percent of small and 41 percent of large businesses.[12] Long-term disability benefits were added to the Social Security Act in 1956, but these are restricted to the severely disabled who are unlikely to reenter the workforce.[13]

Provision for maternity leave in the United States has been even more inadequate. The defeat of compulsory health insurance silenced further cries for maternity coverage until the upsurge of women's labor force participation during and after World War II. But feminist and labor demands for maternity pay went unheeded. By the 1990s, only 2 to 3 percent of private businesses offered paid leave for childbirth, making the United States by far the least generous industrialized nation in the protection of mothers' incomes. Leave without pay has been more common, meaning that only more affluent women can afford to take the time off. The most significant federal legislation to date on this issue, the Family and Medical Leave Act of 1993, mandates only *unpaid* parental leave for employees (and only those of large firms.)[14] Federal policy thus continues to separate the protection of childbearing from the protection of women's wages.

American resistance to universal insurance coverage has not meant a lack of government involvement in health care—quite the contrary. The federal Hospital Survey and Construction Act of 1946 (known as Hill-Burton) channeled billions of government dollars into building the modern hospital system, and the establishment of the Centers for Disease Control and National Institutes of Health have made the federal government the nation's primary provider of funds for medical research. And, of course, in the 1960s the United States did establish a kind of national health insurance—Medicare and Medicaid, which cover the elderly and the very poor.[15]

This patchwork system of private and government provision has served to maintain the interests of the very groups that have opposed state guarantees of universal insurance coverage. The political and cultural power of physicians, employers, and insurance companies, consolidated in part in the crucible of the early health insurance debate, helped these groups turn medical and social policy to their advantage, and enabled them to preserve their autonomy even in the face of increased governmental funding of medical care. When the rising cost of medical care and the threat of compulsory insurance finally led the AMA to endorse voluntary health insurance in the 1940s,[16] it paved the way for a profitable accommodation between doctors, employers, and insurance companies. The growth of private health insurance allowed employers to increasingly provide group insurance on a voluntary basis, without the threat of government mandates. Employer control of health coverage after World War II has massively enriched the commercial insurance companies that offer group health plans; as Paul Starr notes, the "campaign that they had waged thirty years earlier against a government program was finally paying off."[17] Perhaps the greatest beneficiaries of the private insurance system were physicians, whose incomes rose dramatically as third-party insurers paid for escalating medical costs while preserving physician autonomy and fee-for-service payment until the 1980s.[18]

When the federal government became involved in providing health insurance during the War on Poverty, the structure of the programs it created continued to protect the interests and autonomy of private groups. Medicare and Medicaid cover the aged and the indigent, who would otherwise be unable to afford private health plans, so the programs minimized government infringement on the private insurance market and on employer control of health care coverage. Although the AMA originally opposed Medicare, it supported Medicaid because it was restricted to the poor, "who would otherwise be unable to pay the doctor."[19] Both Medicaid and Medicare benefited the medical profession financially; the greatest rise in physician income in history came after 1965, when the two programs began channeling federal funds into paying doctors.[20] Until the 1980s, government subsidy of medical care also met physicians' demands for continuing autonomy. Hospitals and physicians retained significant independence even as federal funding poured in; Hill-Burton allowed hospitals to maintain local rather than federal control, and physicians under Medicare charged the government whatever fees they saw fit.[21]

But, after decades of seeing their incomes rise and their autonomy preserved, physicians are losing their long professional struggle. The inefficiencies of America's public-private system led to unacceptably high medical costs by the 1980s, and to new government restrictions on payments to doctors and hospitals under Medicare and Medicaid. The private system, too, is no longer willing to tolerate physician autonomy. In the 1990s, employers and insurance companies allied against the medical profession. Employers demanded lower medical costs to reduce the expense of employee health benefits; the insurance industry insisted on cost accounting from doctors, more and more of whom were becoming servants of that very industry. With the growth of managed care, the *New York Times* reported in 1996, physicians are "losing control over working conditions, treatments and incomes . . . so stripped of their independence that they have become de facto employees of the . . . [insurance] companies." As a result, the American Medical Association announced that between 1993 and 1994 doctors' incomes had begun to fall for the first time in the century.[22] Physicians' resistance to outsider threats to their autonomy throughout the century had finally failed.

Despite a consensus for reform, attempts in the 1990s to address the deficiencies in the American health care system fared little better than in the Progressive Era. The fate of the 1993–94 Clinton health plan was shaped by the profound reconfiguration of American politics, the economy, and the health care system since the New Deal, but in many ways it also bore striking similarities to the AALL's failed attempt during the 1910s. The greatest difference, of course, was that the proposal was initiated at the highest levels of federal government. Also, the Clinton administration's plan would have been universal, covering all Americans instead of just industrial workers. Rejecting calls for a Canadian-style single-payer system, policy makers devised a complex plan with both public and private elements. Employers would be required to provide health coverage through local "health alliances" that retained most features of the private insurance system, with government picking up the tab for the elderly and unemployed.[23]

The makeup of reform supporters had changed by the 1990s. The greatest contrast with the 1910s was the steadfast support of organized labor for universal health insurance. A constituency unheard from during the Progressive Era were senior citizens, who have formed a huge and influential interest group since the creation of Social Security. Health insurance supporters had also in preceding decades managed to gain increased leverage over government through lobbying organizations. Labor, senior citizens, and the pro-reform nursing profession in 1993 had their own nationwide organizations and a major lobbying presence in Washington. However, these groups found it difficult, if not impossible, to mobilize their constituencies around a reform plan whose provisions seemed overly complex and bewildering to most Americans.

Clinton's chosen method for formulating the legislation would have seemed familiar to the AALL. Rather than approaching the various interest groups first, the administration created a "Task Force on Health Care Reform," chaired by Hillary Rodham Clinton and made up of "disinterested" policy experts.[24] The secrecy of the task force's deliberations contributed to the spread of fears and rumors about what Clinton had in store for the nation, and when the plan was finally released, the task force's policy experts, like the AALL before them, were dismayed at the fury of interest groups' opposition.

With the exception of labor, the forces arrayed against health care reform were the same as before: physicians, insurance companies, and employers. Despite its attempt to preserve private involvement, the Clinton plan still threatened the interests of each of these groups. Large and small businesses would be subject to "employer mandates," the commercial insurance industry stood to lose control over the health care market, and physicians again faced a reduction in their autonomy and incomes.

But once again, opponents could not nakedly defend their private interests before a public decidedly eager for reform. Like their Progressive Era counterparts, interest groups used rhetoric and ideology to attack the Clinton plan. Opponents had throughout the century equated "socialized medicine" with Bolshevism and Communism. With the end of the Cold War, the Soviet menace was replaced by the welfare state and "big government" as the greatest threats to the nation. As journalists Haynes Johnson and David S. Broder write of the Clinton reform's failure, "Interest groups opposed to change were spectacularly successful in making government appear to be the enemy."[25] Opponents still emphasized the foreignness of universal health care, but this time it was not the United States's enemies but its allies whose health insurance systems were condemned. Tales abounded of British or Canadian citizens forced to wait endlessly for surgery or other life-saving measures under their nations' rigid health care bureaucracies.[26]

The "propagandism" cited as a major factor in the defeat of the 1919 health insurance proposal took a new form with a barrage of television advertisements against health care reform. A well-orchestrated advertising campaign featured "Harry and Louise," middle-class Americans who feared that "government health insurance" would take away their excellent health benefits and their freedom to choose their own doctor. These spots were financed by the Health Insurance Association of America, a "front group" of the commercial insurance industry, illustrating the continuing potency of cultural images that mask private interest with appeals to the public interest.[27]

Finally, and familiarly, the combination of private and political interest led health care reform to defeat. Opponents collaborated with politicians who shared their ideological opposition to liberal activist government. In turn, conservative Republicans rightly saw in their effort to kill the Clinton plan an opportunity for their own resurgence. In 1994, the coalition of insurance companies, employers, organized physicians, and conservative politicians not only defeated the proposal and ended hopes for universal health insurance but also sparked a "Republican Revolution" in Congress.

Battles over health care reform, in the Progressive Era and today, have displayed the ability of private interest groups to shape the actions of the American state. But alliances and interests shift. With labor now on the side of reform and physician autonomy threatened more by private insurance than by government interference, the coalition against universal coverage weakens.

Opponents fought the Clinton plan successfully, but they had to fight harder—spending an unprecedented four million dollars a month on advertising and lobbying [28]—because of the growing public demands for a restructuring of the health care system. "Reactionary legislators, selfish interests, paid lackeys and their like may succeed, for a while, to stem the tide for a comprehensive health insurance system," wrote Pauline Newman in 1954. "However, I am satisfied that the demand for [health insurance] on the part of those most concerned will finally override the ignorance and the willful misrepresentation of such a system by the opposition." [29] As their numbers continue to rise beyond the current forty-three million, the uninsured may someday find the power to shape politics in their own interests.

NOTES

ABBREVIATIONS

AALLP American Association for Labor Legislation Papers (Microfilm Edition, Glen Rock, N.J., 1974)

ALLR *American Labor Legislation Review*

CSSP Community Service Society Papers, Rare Book Room, Columbia University, New York, N.Y.

FDP Frederick Davenport Papers, Syracuse University Archives

FLHP Frederick Ludwig Hoffman Papers, Rare Book Room, Columbia University, New York, N.Y.

JAMA *Journal of the American Medical Association*

KC Kheel Center for Labor-Management Documentation and Archives, School of Industrial and Labor Relations, Cornell University, Ithaca, N.Y.

MBS Mutual Benefit Societies Constitutions and Bylaws, New York Public Library, New York, N.Y.

MDP Marion Dickerman Papers, Franklin D. Roosevelt Library, Hyde Park, N.Y.

NCFP National Civic Federation Papers, Rare Book Room, New York Public Library, New York, N.Y.

NICBP National Industrial Conference Board Papers, Hagley Museum and Library, Wilmington, Del.

NYAM New York Academy of Medicine, New York, N.Y.

NYPL New York Public Library, New York, N.Y.

NYSJM *New York State Journal of Medicine*

PNYWTUL Papers of the New York Women's Trade Union League, Women's Trade Union League and Its Principal Leaders (Microfilm Edition, Woodbridge, Conn., 1981)

RAC Rockefeller Archive Center, Tarrytown, N.Y.

RAWILAS Records of the American West Indian Ladies' Aid Society, Schomburg Center, New York, N.Y.

RG Record Group

YWCAP   Young Women's Christian Association Papers, Sophia Smith Archive,
          Northampton, Mass.

INTRODUCTION

1. According to a 1999 survey by the Discovery Channel and *Newsweek* magazine, 61 percent of Americans were "frustrated and angry" with the health care system (*Newsweek*, November 8, 1999: 60). In 1999, the number of uninsured in the United States was forty-three million (*Wall Street Journal*, May 17, 1999, A5).

2. Hirshfield, *Lost Reform*. Here I also respectfully disagree with health policy historian Daniel Fox, who argues that to study this failed attempt is to "focus on what did not happen . . . rather than on what did occur" ("History and Health Policy," 350).

3. Surgeon General Rupert Blue, quoted in Numbers, *Almost Persuaded*, 1.

4. New York did not face the same constitutional constraints as California, since it already had a constitutional amendment allowing the adoption of social insurance measures. The amendment, adopted in 1913, stated: "Nothing contained in this constitution shall be construed to limit the power of the Legislature to enact laws for the protection of the lives, health or safety of employees" (Article 1, Section 19, *New York State Constitution Annotated*, 12–13).

5. The most complete account of physicians' responses to health insurance in the Progressive Era is Numbers, *Almost Persuaded*. See also Stevens, *American Medicine and the Public Interest*, 136–39, and Starr, *Social Transformation of American Medicine*, 243–57. While Numbers focuses on physicians, he acknowledges that other interest groups had important roles to play in the debate (see *Almost Persuaded*, xi).

6. Scholars have been divided over the question of whether unity or differences among women were more important in the creation of the U.S. welfare state. Works that emphasize the unity of Progressive Era women reformers and their successes in advocating social legislation include Muncy, *Creating a Female Dominion*; Sklar, "Two Political Cultures"; and Skocpol, *Protecting Soldiers and Mothers*. Scholars who analyze divisions among women in the formation of the welfare state include Linda Gordon, *Pitied but Not Entitled*; Goodwin, *Gender and the Politics of Welfare Reform*; and Mink, *Wages of Motherhood*.

7. On gender inequality in welfare provision, see Mink, *Wages of Motherhood*; Goodwin, *Gender and the Politics of Welfare Reform*; Linda Gordon, *Pitied but Not Entitled*; Barbara Nelson, "The Origins of the Two-Channel Welfare State," in Linda Gordon, ed., *Women, the State, and Welfare*. In Europe, most pre–World War I health insurance systems included maternity insurance (see Chapter 7), and today European welfare states offer generous paid maternity leave to women workers, ranging from twelve to twenty-eight weeks (and up to one year at less than full pay in Scandinavian countries). See "U.N. Surveys Paid Leave for Mothers," *New York Times*, February 16, 1998.

8. Some influential recent writings have argued, from a perspective known as state-

centered or historical-institutionalist, that the state is an autonomous actor and that existing policies and state capacities and structures determine the outcomes of policy battles, more than social, economic, or ideological forces. Theda Skocpol, *Protecting Soldiers and Mothers*, has been the most prominent advocate of this approach. See also Orloff, "Gender in Early U.S. Social Policy" (she writes that the "existing capacities of the American state . . . precluded the establishment of contributory social insurance programs for any group" in the Progressive Era [261]) and *Politics of Pensions*; Robertson, "Bias of American Federalism"; and Skowronek, *Building a New American State*.

CHAPTER ONE

1. Russell Sage Foundation, "Committee on Women's Work for Six Months Ending March 31, 1915," Box 100, Van Kleeck Papers, Sophia Smith Archive.

2. "Wage Earner's Illness" (ca. 1917), 3, Box 99, Van Kleeck Papers, Sophia Smith Archive. This unpublished study contains a wealth of information on health and economic conditions for workers in New York City. Russell Sage Foundation researchers surveyed two groups of wage earners: 690 applicants to the Charity Organization Society and the United Hebrew Charities, and 539 seekers of medical care at the Cornell Out-Patient Department (dispensary) ("Wage Earner's Illness," 2).

3. John Kingsbury to Carol Aronovici, June 10, 1918, Box 25, CSSP. Kingsbury earlier reported that sickness accounted for the poverty of 43 percent of the applicants to the AICP (Kingsbury to Simon Lipschitz, September 27, 1911, Box 25, CSSP).

4. B. S. Warren and Edgar Sydenstricker, *Health Insurance: Its Relation to Public Health*, Public Health Bulletin No. 76 (Washington, 1916), 6; quoted in Numbers, *Almost Persuaded*, 2.

5. "Facts about Health Insurance: A Text-book for Speakers, Writers, and Workers," Box 3, Folder 13, AALL Pamphlet Collection, KC.

6. Coverage under workmen's compensation varied widely, and in some states participation in the system was optional (Skocpol, *Protecting Soldiers and Mothers*, 293–97). The majority of states excluded agricultural and domestic laborers from compensation plans (Moss, *Socializing Security*, 199 n. 63).

7. Rosner, ed., *Hives of Sickness*, 13–14; *Report of the Health Insurance Commission of Pennsylvania*, 120. Also see Rosner and Markowitz, eds., *Deadly Dust*, and Derickson, "Federal Intervention in the Joplin Silicosis Epidemic."

8. "Report of Elizabeth L. Meigs," February 1916, 3, Box 100, Van Kleeck Papers, Sophia Smith Archive.

9. Anna Mann Richardson, M.D., "Opportunities for Preventive Medical Work in the Dispensary Clinic," August 1, 1916, Box 99, Van Kleeck Papers, Sophia Smith Archive.

10. Bailey Burritt to Franklin B. Kirkbride, February 5, 1918, Box 36, CSSP.

11. Among African Americans in New York City, "[a]s a rule the unmarried mother is a wage earner and must remain one until her last months of pregnancy. . . . The mother as a wage earner exists also to a great extent among our married mothers, as a large percentage work to supplement the men's wages." In one New York City district in 1917, the infant mortality rate was 35 per 1,000 for whites, but 105 per 1,000 for "colored" (Report of Columbus Hill Health Center, March 1921, Box 36, and Bailey Burritt to Franklin B. Kirkbride, March 30, 1917, Box 36, CSSP). For further discussion of maternal and infant mortality, see Chapter 7.

12. Beito, "Mutual Aid," 420–21. Beito's book, *From Mutual Aid to the Welfare State* (Chapel Hill, N.C., 2000), was not in print at the time of this writing.

13. Beito makes the 30 percent calculation (ibid., 431 n. 5). Estimates for the industrial states are from Lubove, *Struggle for Social Security*, 75. In the Sage report, 16 to 19 percent of the New York City families surveyed belonged to benefit societies ("Wage Earner's Illness," 100).

14. Carnes, *Secret Ritual and Manhood in Victorian America*; Clawson, *Constructing Brotherhood*.

15. Beito, "Mutual Aid," 421. On African American mutual aid and insurance, see also Stuart, *Economic Detour*.

16. "Wage Earner's Illness," 100.

17. Ibid., 108.

18. Minutes, February 3, 1916, Box 1, Progress Mutual Aid Society Records, Landsmanshaftn Archive, YIVO Institute. The Landsmanshaftn were Jewish fraternal societies whose members were immigrants from the same Eastern European village. The societies were instrumental in maintaining ethnic traditions in the New World; see Weisser, *Brotherhood of Memory*.

19. Beito, " 'Program That Looks to . . .,' " 3–4. Leaders of the Woman's Benefit Association would fiercely oppose compulsory health insurance.

20. On black women's fraternal societies, see Linda Gordon, *Pitied but Not Entitled*, 115–16. Black societies that admitted women on equal terms with men included the United Order of True Reformers, the International Order of Twelve Knights and Daughters of Tabor, and the Independent Order of St. Luke (Beito, "Mutual Aid," 425, 433 n. 19).

21. Anna Kalet, "Voluntary Health Insurance in New York City," *ALLR* 6 (June 1916): 144; "Wage Earner's Illness," 107.

22. An AALL study found that twelve out of fourteen fraternal societies required a medical examination of applicants; for each of these, "those ill at the time of application (whether chronic or acute) are not admitted" (Kalet, "Voluntary Health Insurance," 143).

23. "Wage Earner's Illness," 123. Annual median income in 1918 was $1,140 (around $22 a week) (Howell and McLaughlin, "Race, Income, and the Purchase of Medical Care," 452).

24. "Wage Earner's Illness," 101; Minutes, April 17, 1914, Sojourna Household of Ruth, Box 10, Knights of Pythias Records, Schomburg Center.

25. "Wage Earner's Illness," 102.

26. Ibid., 107, 110; Minutes, June 21, 1918, and November 15, 1918, Sojourna Household of Ruth, Box 10, Knights of Pythias Records, Schomburg Center.

27. *Constitution of the Workmen's Sick and Death Benefit Fund.*

28. Minutes, January 9, 1913, Box 1, Progress Mutual Aid Society Records, Landsmanshaftn Archive, YIVO Institute.

29. Minutes of the Salamanca Rebekah Lodge, December 15, 1911, Salamanca Public Library.

30. Beito, "Mutual Aid," 424–26.

31. *Monthly Bulletin*, 1915–17, Box 5, Ceres Union Records, Landsmanshaftn Archive, YIVO Institute.

32. Beito, "Mutual Aid," 430.

33. Minutes, November 16, 1917, Sojourna Household of Ruth, Box 10, Knights of Pythias Records, Schomburg Center.

34. Kalet, "Voluntary Health Insurance," 148.

35. Victoria Elliot and Joseph Forbes to the Society, October 5, 1933, and Beatrice B. Matthews to the President, Officers and Members, February 28, 1928, Box 1, RAWILAS.

36. Minutes, April 16, 1917, Sojourna Household of Ruth, Box 10, Knights of Pythias Records, Schomburg Center.

37. "Wage Earner's Illness," 111.

38. Minutes of the Salamanca Rebekah Lodge, January 21, 1910, Salamanca Public Library.

39. Minutes, May 21, 1915, Sojourna Household of Ruth, Box 10, Knights of Pythias Records, Schomburg Center.

40. *Monthly Bulletin*, 1915–17, Ceres Union Records, Landsmanshaftn Archive, YIVO Institute.

41. Beito, "Mutual Aid," 423.

42. Minutes, April 20, 1908, and June 5, 1913, Box 1, Progress Mutual Aid Society Records, Landsmanshaftn Archive, YIVO Institute.

43. Starr, *Social Transformation of American Medicine*, 207.

44. "Wage Earner's Illness," 121.

45. Minutes, December 11, 1919, Box 1, Progress Mutual Aid Society Records, Landsmanshaftn Archive, YIVO Institute; Starr, *Social Transformation of American Medicine*, 206.

46. Minutes, November 20, 1913, Box 1, Progress Mutual Aid Society Records, Landsmanshaftn Archive, YIVO Institute.

47. Kalet, "Voluntary Health Insurance," 149.

48. Galloway, "Speech to National Fraternal Congress of America," 7–8.

49. Russell Sage Foundation, "Committee on Women's Work Report," 16.

50. State of New York Insurance Department, "Report on Examination of Supreme Council of the Catholic Mutual Benefit Association," 1919, Miscellaneous Pamphlets — Mutual Aid, NYPL. The Illinois Health Insurance Commission found that the influenza epidemic ruined many small mutual aid societies in that state (Cohen, *Making a New Deal*, 67).

51. Minutes, October 12, 1920, Ceres Union Records, Landsmanshaftn Archive, YIVO Institute.

52. Irene Sylvester to Mr. Mortimer, March 9, 1917, reel 17, AALLP. In 1910, 5.5 percent of U.S. industrial workers were unionized (Yellowitz, *Labor and the Progressive Movement*, 19).

53. Kalet, "Voluntary Health Insurance," 148.

54. Derickson, *Workers' Health, Workers' Democracy*; Derickson, "From Company Doctors to Union Hospitals"; interview with Pauline Newman, January 26, 1965, International Ladies' Garment Workers' Union Papers, KC. For further discussion of union health benefits, see Chapter 6.

55. A fine recent study of employer motivations in creating welfare programs (and workers' responses to the programs) is Andrea Tone, *Business of Benevolence*. Tone's study says little, however, about sick pay or medical care. Also see Brandes, *American Welfare Capitalism*, 92–97.

56. "Wage Earner's Illness," 103.

57. Kalet, "Voluntary Health Insurance," 149; New York Factory Investigating Committee, "Cost of Living Report, Draft, and Background Notes," 85, reel A3016-1, New York State Factory Investigating Commission Records, New York State Archives; RB&CCES Benefit Association, Rome, N.Y., "Constitution and By-laws"; The American Food Co., Newark N.J., "Constitution and By-laws" (n.d.), Mutual Benefit Societies Constitutions and Bylaws, NYPL.

58. Helping Hand Benefit Association of Standard Sanitary Manufacturing Co., Louisville, Ky., "Constitution and By-laws," 1914; "Regulations of the Hospital Department," Southern Pacific Company, 1915, Mutual Benefit Societies Constitutions and Bylaws, NYPL.

59. Tone, *Business of Benevolence*, 94.

60. "Lidgerwood Aid Society," Brooklyn, N.Y., 1908, Miscellaneous Pamphlets — Mutual Aid, NYPL.

61. Minutes of the meeting of the Social Insurance Dept., January 22, 1917, Box 70, NCFP.

62. "Constitution and By-Laws," Dain Manufacturing Company, Ottumwa, Iowa (n.d.), Mutual Benefit Societies Constitutions and Bylaws, NYPL.

63. "Constitution and By-Laws," Westinghouse Air Brake Company Relief Department, 1916, Mutual Benefit Societies Constitutions and Bylaws, NYPL.

64. National Industrial Conference Board, *Experience with Mutual Benefit Associations*.

65. "Regulations of the Hospital Department"; Derickson, *Workers' Health, Workers' Democracy*; Korneski, "Louisiana Lumber Workers and Patent Medicines."

66. Starr, *Social Transformation of American Medicine*, 200, 203; Nugent, "Fit for Work."

67. "Memorandum of Dr. Rector" to M. W. Alexander, June 28 and 19, 1920, Box 8, NICBP. In 1926, the Bureau of Labor Statistics reported that more than 400 large companies provided medical care for employees (Brandes, *American Welfare Capitalism*, 99). I was unable to determine the percentage of firms that provided medical services before 1920, which was undoubtedly much smaller than the 1926 figure. A majority of the "largest" firms in the country engaged in some sort of "welfare work" by 1920 (Tone, *Business of Benevolence*, 33–34), but this included nonmedical programs. On the growth of welfare capitalism in the 1920s, see Cohen, *Making a New Deal*, and Brandes, *American Welfare Capitalism*.

68. "Memorandum[s] from Dr. Rector" to M. W. Alexander, June 29, July 19, July 20, July 23, and July 30, 1920, Box 8, NICBP.

69. "Memorandum from Dr. Rector" to M. W. Alexander, July 20, 1920, Box 8, NICBP; Zahavi, *Workers, Managers, and Welfare Capitalism*, 47–49.

70. Starr, *Social Transformation of American Medicine*, 202–3; Derickson, *Workers' Health, Workers' Democracy*, 206–8.

71. Korneski, "Louisiana Lumber Workers and Patent Medicines."

72. Arthur E. Childs, *Address to 9th Annual Convention of the International Association of Casualty and Surety Underwriters*, 1919, Insurance — Uncatalogued Pamphlets, NYPL.

73. Harbaugh, *Industrial Claim Adjustor*.

74. *Joint Stock Company Health Insurance* (n.a., n.p., ca. 1910), Insurance — Uncatalogued Pamphlets, NYPL.

75. The Russell Sage study found that "[o]nly one person among the entire number included carried sickness insurance in a commercial company" ("Wage Earner's Illness," 101).

76. On the history of industrial insurance, see Dublin, *Family of 30 Million*, and Carr, *"From Three Cents a Week."*

77. More, *Wage-Earners Budgets*, 44; "Wage Earner's Illness," 48.

78. Frankel and Dublin, "Community Sickness Survey," 634. Quoted in Numbers, *Almost Persuaded*, 2.

79. Rosenberg, "Social Class and Medical Care."

80. Ernst C. Meyer, "Relative Value of Hospitals and Dispensaries as Public Health Agencies and as Fields of Activity for the Rockefeller Foundation," 1919, RG 1.1, Series 200, Box 23, Rockefeller Foundation Archives, RAC.

81. E. Lewinski-Corwin speech in *Proceedings of the Twentieth New York State Conference of Charities and Corrections*.

82. "Report from the Dispensary Committee of Gouverneur Hospital, 1914," Pub-

lic Health Committee of the New York Academy of Medicine Papers, NYAM; "New York Academy of Medicine Dispensary Study, 1918–1919," RG 1.1, Series 200, Box 102, Rockefeller Foundation Archives, RAC; Alexander Candlish to W. H. Matthews, September 9, 1915, Box 22, CSSP.

83. Meyer, "Relative Value of Hospitals and Dispensaries"; "New York Academy of Medicine Dispensary Study," 1918–19, RG 1.1, Series 200, Box 102, Rockefeller Foundation Archives, RAC. Their suggestions were never implemented; the dispensary system went into decline shortly afterward (see Rosner, *Once Charitable Enterprise*).

84. Chapin, *Standard of Living*.

85. On dispensary abuse, see Rosner, *Once Charitable Enterprise*, ch. 6; Rosenberg, "Social Class and Medical Care"; and Brieger, "Use and Abuse of Medical Charities," 264–67.

86. J. Whitridge Williams, "Dispensary Abuse and Certain Problems of Medical Practice," *JAMA* 66 (June 17, 1916): 1903.

87. "New York Academy of Medicine Dispensary Study."

88. "Bellevue Departmental Estimate for 1915," Box 25, CSSP; "Report from the Dispensary Committee of Gouverneur Hospital."

89. "New York Academy of Medicine Dispensary Study."

90. Alexander Candlish to W. H. Matthews, September 11, 1915, Box 22, CSSP.

91. Form letter from Charity Organization Society director to New York hospitals, May 20, 1913, Box 133, CSSP.

92. Walsh, "Physicians' Fees Down the Ages"; Williams, "Dispensary Abuse," 1903; Rosner, *Once Charitable Enterprise*.

93. "Wage Earner's Illness," 37a.

94. Buhler-Wilkerson, *False Dawn*, 68–69.

95. Dye, "Modern Obstetrics and Working-Class Women"; Korneski, "Louisiana Lumber Workers"; Howell and McLaughlin, "Race, Income, and the Purchase of Medical Care," 456.

96. Starr, *Social Transformation of American Medicine*, 185.

97. On racial differences in health care access, see Beardsley, *History of Neglect*; Love, *One Blood*; and Smith, *Sick and Tired*.

98. Starr, *Social Transformation of American Medicine*, 185. Three excellent books on New York City's public health system are Duffy, *History of Public Health in New York City*; Rosner, ed., *Hives of Sickness*; and Opdycke, *No One Was Turned Away*.

99. On quarantine and confinement of tuberculars, see Rothman, *Living in the Shadow of Death*, 186–93.

100. In 1911 the State Hospital for Incipient Tuberculosis in Buffalo, New York, had a waiting list of 200 ("Memorandum regarding the B— family . . . ," May 5, 1911, Box 19, CSSP). On sanatorium care for the poor, see Rothman, *Living in the Shadow of Death*, 201–10.

101. Lillian L. Foster to Cornelius Bliss, April 17, 1916, Box 25, CSSP. There is no record of Bliss's response to Foster.

102. Anna M. Richardson, M.D., "Cornell Clinic Work," ca. 1916, 8, Box 99, Van Kleeck Papers, Sophia Smith Archive.

103. "Wage Earner's Illness," 131.

104. On fraternals' opposition to compulsory health insurance, see Beito, "It Substitutes Paternalism for Fraternalism." Fraternal societies were not, however, significant political players in the New York health insurance battle, and did not play a central role in the legislation's defeat.

105. Both the ILGWU and the United Mine Workers, which had the most extensive worker health programs in the nation, supported compulsory health insurance. On the United Mine Workers, see Derickson, "Health Security for All?" This was also the position of the Typographical Union, which had its own benefits. See James Lynch, "Trade Union Sickness Insurance," *ALLR* 4 (March 1917): 91-95. See Chapter 6 for further discussion of these unions.

CHAPTER TWO

1. Moss, *Socializing Security*, 19-20; Kathryn Kish Sklar, "The Historical Foundations of Women's Power in the Creation of the American Welfare State, 1830-1930," in Koven and Michel, eds., *Mothers of a New World*, 58-59. Moss's book is the most comprehensive history of the AALL. Frederick Hoffman is not related to the author.

2. Moss, *Socializing Security*, 4.

3. Andrews probably made around $5,000 a year in 1914 as AALL secretary; see Frederick Hoffman to Henry R. Seager, January 13, 1914, Hoffman Correspondence, Hagley Museum and Library. The other AALL staff members likely made significantly less since they were female, but I have found no records detailing their compensation.

Critics of the AALL have accused the organization of being in the thrall of John D. Rockefeller and other major capitalists because they made occasional contributions to the AALL's coffers. Their views, however, never shaped the AALL agenda, any more than did the views of the labor leaders associated with the AALL. Rockefeller certainly had no hand in the health insurance campaign. Skocpol, *Protecting Soldiers and Mothers*, 183-87, and Moss, *Socializing Security*, 190 n. 11, decisively dismiss interpretations of the AALL as a tool of capitalist interests.

4. Sklar, "Two Political Cultures," 42.

5. Hofstadter, *Age of Reform*, sets forth the "status-anxiety thesis." David Moss (*Socializing Security*, 25) argues that status anxiety was one of the "primary motivations" of AALL leaders, although "not wholly applicable."

6. John E. Ransom, "Memorandum to the Rockefeller Foundation Concerning the

Improvement of Dispensaries in New York City," February 7, 1920, RG 1.1, Series 200, Box 23, Rockefeller Foundation Archives, RAC.

7. On the AALL's campaign against phosphorus, see Sellers, *Hazards of the Job*, 62–66, and Moss, *Socializing Security*, ch. 5. On workmen's compensation, see Skocpol, *Protecting Soldiers and Mothers*, 293–302, and Lubove, *Struggle for Social Security*, ch. 3.

8. Lambert, "Health Insurance," *Proceedings of the International Conference of Women Physicians*, 1919, Box 30A, Young Women's Christian Association Papers, Sophia Smith Archive; Dr. Percy Stickney Grant to Assemblymen, March 27, 1919, reel 19, AALLP.

9. Dr. John A. Lapp, "Health Insurance," *Proceedings of the Twentieth New York State Conference of Charities and Corrections*.

10. Moss, *Socializing Security*, 10–11.

11. This obstacle did not prevent Socialist congressman Meyer London from (unsuccessfully) introducing health insurance legislation in the U.S. House of Representatives in 1916. London's legislation would have created a "federal commission to investigate the need for health insurance." The Committee on Labor held two days of hearings on his proposal in April of 1916, but the bill "fell 29 votes short of passage in the House." See Numbers, *Almost Persuaded*, 60.

12. The original members were Edward Devine, Henry Seager, Miles Dawson, Dr. I. M. Rubinow, Dr. S. S. Goldwater, Charles R. Henderson, Henry J. Harris, Frederick Hoffman, and John Koren. Olga Halsey attended some of their meetings but did not appear to be a voting member; see minutes of the Social Insurance Committee meeting, January 3, 1916, reel 61, AALLP.

13. "Health Insurance — Tentative Draft of an Act," *ALLR* 6 (June 1916): 239–68. Besides Wald, the other new members were Carroll W. Doten and Dr. Alexander Lambert.

14. "Health Insurance — Tentative Draft."

15. Olga Halsey, "Health Insurance: A Positive Statement in Answer to Opponents," *ALLR* 7 (December 1917): 652.

16. Massachusetts, Connecticut, New Jersey, Pennsylvania, Ohio, Illinois, Wisconsin, and California all established commissions between 1915 and 1919 to investigate the need for compulsory health insurance. Of these, California, New Jersey, and Ohio produced favorable reports; Connecticut, Illinois, and Wisconsin produced negative reports; and the reports of Massachusetts and Pennsylvania were divided on the question. Only in New York and California did the AALL's bill go further in the political process than the commission stage. On health insurance in Illinois, see Bennett, "Movement for Compulsory Health Insurance in Illinois"; on California, see Viseltear, "Compulsory Health Insurance in California."

17. C. D. Stuart to John B. Andrews, November 10, 1918, reel 18, AALLP.

18. Margaret Hobbs to Elizabeth McShane, November 18, 1919, reel 20, AALLP.

19. Despite its exclusions, the AALL's bill could still have been a model for universal health insurance in the United States. European plans originally applied to industrial

workers only, but after World War II they evolved into full-fledged national insurance systems covering all citizens.

20. "Facts about Health Insurance: A Text-book for Speakers, Writers, and Workers," Box 3, Folder 13, AALL Pamphlet Collection, KC.

21. Moss, *Socializing Security*, 8.

22. John A. Lapp, "Health Insurance and the Hospitals," address before the American Hospital Association, September 27, 1918, Box 3, Folder 12, AALL Pamphlet Collection, KC.

23. Irene Andrews to Armand Wylie, July 29, 1919, reel 20, AALLP.

24. On the exclusion of African Americans from social provision, see, for example, Goodwin, *Gender and the Politics of Welfare Reform*; Alice Kessler-Harris, "Designing Women and Old Fools," in Kerber et al., *U.S. History as Women's History*, 87–106; Quadagno, *Color of Welfare*, 4, 10, 21, 157, 160–62; and Poole, "Securing Race and Ensuring Dependence."

25. Social Insurance Committee member Dr. S. S. Goldwater later argued for the inclusion of "servants" in the bill, but the AALL never took up his suggestion. See "Minority Report to the House of Delegates," *NYSJM* 19 (1919): 403.

26. Rubinow, *Social Insurance*, 256.

27. As David Moss notes in his study of the AALL, "references to race are rare in the AALL papers, and references to blacks in particular are virtually nonexistent" (*Socializing Security*, 195 n. 19).

28. John R. Commons published *Races and Immigrants in America*, a tract with scientific racist leanings, in 1907. I am grateful to Mary Poole for calling my attention to this reference. See Chapter 3 for a discussion of Hoffman's racial ideology.

29. On the entry of blacks into industrial labor in New York, see Oshofsky, *Harlem*, 137.

30. *ALLR* 2 (June 1912), facing 284.

31. On black Progressivism in New York, see Oshofsky, *Harlem*, 55–67; Linda Gordon, *Pitied but Not Entitled*, ch. 5; and Cash, "Radicals or Realists."

32. John B. Andrews to Margarite L. Smith, March 22, 1920, reel 21, AALLP.

33. Numbers, *Almost Persuaded*, 40, 37–38. The New Jersey and Massachusetts bills made little progress; see ibid., 44–46, 70–71, 99–100.

34. Ibid., 41.

35. On the California health insurance campaign, see Moss, *Socializing Security*, 148–51; Lubove, *Struggle for Social Security*, 83; and especially Viseltear, "Compulsory Health Insurance in California."

36. Ansley K. Salz to John B. Andrews, n.d. [ca. October 1918], reel 18, AALLP.

37. Christian Scientists played little part in the New York debate. They were far more numerous and organized in California.

38. The most detailed account of the AMA's switch on health insurance is Numbers, *Almost Persuaded*, which also includes a careful discussion of Lambert's role.

39. Dr. Eden Delphey, quoted in *Monitor* 3 (March 1917): 24.

40. *Monitor* 2 (November 1915): 3.

41. John B. Andrews to Dr. W. A. Evans, July 17, 1919, reel 20, AALLP.

42. Minutes of the meeting of the Social Insurance Dept., December 6, 1915, Box 70, NCFP. Gompers was also angered at the AALL's support of the 1915 New York Industrial Commission bill that would have reduced labor's influence on the commission; see Moss, *Socializing Security*, 32.

43. Moss, *Socializing Security*, 32; Samuel Gompers, "Labor vs. Its Barnacles," *American Federationist* 13 (April 1916): 268, 272.

44. Sklar, "Two Political Cultures," 57.

45. See Chapter 6.

46. Weinstein, *Corporate Ideal in the Liberal State*, discusses the Civic Federation's role in the workmen's compensation movement. On commercial insurance companies and workmen's compensation, see Lubove, *Struggle for Social Security*, 61-64.

47. AALL circular letter to "Dear Friend," December 29, 1916, reel 17, AALLP.

48. Moss, *Socializing Security*, 141.

49. *Monitor* 2 (November 1915): 25; John B. Andrews to Mrs. Raymond Robins, April?, 1919, reel 19, AALLP; illegible author, Dock and Mill Lumber Company to John B. Andrews, April 27, 1920, reel 22, AALLP.

50. See Chapter 5.

51. Numbers, *Almost Persuaded*, 21-22.

52. Leff, "Consensus for Reform," 403-4.

53. AICP form letter, March 6, 1919, reel 19, AALLP.

54. John Kingsbury to Carol Aronovici, June 10, 1918, Box 25, CSSP.

55. Mary M. Sturges, "Report on a Study of 64 Cases of Dependency for the NY AICP," 1916, Box 19, CSSP.

56. *Monitor* 3 (March 1917): 45.

57. See n. 11, above.

58. "Interview with Miss Pauline Newman," June 15, 1965, Oral History Collection, 10, 12-13, Columbia University. On Newman's life, see Orleck, *Common Sense and a Little Fire*, and Chapters 6 and 7 of this book.

59. Quoted in Numbers, *Almost Persuaded*, 95. On the assembly expulsions, see Chapter 8.

60. On the "American Plan" or "American System," see Lubove, *Struggle for Social Security*, 172, and Linda Gordon, *Pitied but Not Entitled*, 155.

61. Sklar, in "Two Political Cultures," 62, uses the phrase "male expertise and power" to describe the AALL's reform strategy. Theda Skocpol (*Protecting Soldiers and Mothers*, 176-204, 354) argues that the AALL represented the "paternalist" strand of the Progressive movement (organizations run by men and advocating legislation to protect male workers).

62. John B. Andrews to Belle Moskowitz, July 20, 1919, reel 20, AALLP.

63. Somehow her position as a woman in the AALL has made Olga Halsey invisible to both traditional and feminist historians. Studies of the AALL omit her achievements, and Halsey does not even merit a listing in the index of the most recent history of the organization. See Moss, *Socializing Security*. Ronald Numbers's *Almost Persuaded*, 22, includes an index entry for Halsey and mentions her role as special investigator for the AALL. Historians of women reformers, too, have ignored Halsey. Her career clearly upsets the distinction between men's social insurance advocacy and women's welfare activism.

64. Mary Beard to John B. Andrews, July 15, 1918, reel 18, AALLP.

Halsey joined the New Deal administration in the 1930s, receiving a post in the newly created Bureau of Employment Security. Halsey's commitment to social insurance was lifelong. In a tribute to Halsey upon her retirement from the bureau in 1959, Wisconsin economist Edwin Witte wrote, "Miss Halsey was a devoted and staunch believer in social security. . . . Employment security I know is in [her] veins." See Scrapbook, Halsey Family Papers, Manuscripts and Archives, Cornell University; Mrs. F. A. Halsey to Senators, March 16, 1919, reel 19, AALLP; Halsey to E. Lewinski-Corwin, April 4, 1916, reel 16, AALLP; and Edwin E. Witte to R. G. Wagenet, July 31, 1959, Halsey Family Papers, Manuscripts and Archives, Cornell University. Like many Progressive and New Deal women, Halsey never married.

65. Rodgers, *Atlantic Crossings*, is a thorough analysis of transatlantic Progressivism.

66. "Medical Benefit . . ." and "Sickness in Twelve Industries . . . ," 1916; and "Childbirth Protection," 1917, reel 62, AALLP. AALL records from 1915 to 1918 contain numerous other examples of Halsey's research.

67. For example, Halsey to James Holland, March 21, 1916, reel 16; Halsey, "Arguments of Those Opposed to Health Insurance to Which a Reply Should Be Made," reel 62; Halsey, "Objections of Mr. Gompers to the Mills Health Insurance Bill Answered," reel 63; Halsey, "Advantages of Health Insurance to Employers," reel 63; and correspondence between Halsey and Ralph Easley, reel 16, AALLP.

68. Linda Gordon, *Pitied but Not Entitled*, 167–68.

69. Irene Sylvester to John B. Andrews, March 12, 1919, reel 19, AALLP.

70. On this legislation, also known as Kern-McGillicudy, see Moss, *Socializing Security*, 223 n. 47.

After moving to St. Louis in 1923 Sylvester became active in the League of Women Voters and continued to agitate for social insurance legislation (Alumnae Trustee Candidate Blank, 1938; "Club Women Urged by Mrs. Chubb to Support Unemployment Insurance," *St. Louis Star Times* [undated clipping], Irene Sylvester Papers, Mount Holyoke College Archives and Special Collections).

71. Sellers, *Hazards of the Job*, 66–67.

72. Irene Andrews to [?] Thomas, July 29, 1919, reel 20, AALLP.

73. Minutes of the meeting of the Social Insurance Dept., December 20, 1916, Box 70, NCFP.

74. See Chapter 7 for Olga Halsey's advocacy of maternity insurance. Irene Andrews began investigating maternity insurance as early as 1913, and she became a major backer of the federal Sheppard-Towner Maternity and Infancy Protection Act in the 1920s.

75. Sklar, "Two Political Cultures," 54.

76. Dr. Eden Delphey, transcript of the hearing on Mills Health Insurance Bill, *Monitor* 3 (March 1917): 22.

77. Mark Daly to Gertrude Beeks, March 9, 1917, Box 69, NCFP.

78. Sklar, "Two Political Cultures," 54.

79. Rubinow, *Quest for Security*, 210; Moss, *Socializing Security*, 143.

CHAPTER THREE

1. "The Need for Health Insurance in America," 1916, reel 70, AALLP.

2. For a thoughtful discussion of the language of Americanism, see Gerstle, *Working-Class Americanism*, 5–13.

3. The nations, and the dates they established health insurance, were Germany (1883), Austria (1888), Hungary (1891), Luxembourg (1901), Norway (1909), Serbia (1910), Great Britain (1911), Russia (1912), Romania (1912), and the Netherlands (1913). *Report of the Health Insurance Commission of Pennsylvania*; Rubinow, *Social Insurance*, ch. 2.

4. Rimlinger, *Welfare Policy and Industrialization*, 122–30; Dawson, *Bismarck and State Socialism*, 114.

5. In 1883 the income ceiling was 2,000 marks ($476). Employers contributed one-third, and employees two-thirds of the insurance funds (Willoughby, *Workingmen's Insurance*, 36–59).

6. For an interesting exception to this general rule in Germany, see Quataert, "Social Insurance and the Family Work of Oberlausitz Home Weavers," which describes some German craft workers' discontent with the legislation.

7. Quoted in Dawson, *Social Insurance in Germany*, 239; for additional favorable testimony of German employers on health insurance, see 239–44; on fraudulent claims, see 248–52.

8. Dawson, *Social Insurance in Germany*, 258–65; Rodgers, *Atlantic Crossings*, 225; Detlev Zoellner, "Germany," in Köhler and Zacher, eds., *Evolution of Social Insurance*, 35.

9. Zoellner, "Germany," 37.

10. Fraser, *Evolution of the British Welfare State*, 144–46, 150, 153–54. For an analysis of the relationship of British imperialism to the rise of the welfare state, see Davin, "Imperialism and Motherhood."

11. Fraser, *Evolution of the British Welfare State*, 155; De Schweinitz, *England's Road to Social Security*, 207. Friendly societies were temporarily preserved in Germany but

were not a major part of the system (Willoughby, *Workingmen's Insurance*, 39–40). For the AALL's exclusion of commercial insurers, see Chapter 5.

12. British Ministry of Health, statement, August 12, 1919, reel 20, AALLP. Thane, in "Working Class and State 'Welfare,'" 895, notes that British labor tended to support new social insurance policies, but "only *after* they were implemented."

13. Gilbert, *Evolution of National Insurance*, 400–416.

14. Alfred Cox, "Seven Years of National Health Insurance in England: A Retrospect," *JAMA* 76 (1921): 1313–14.

15. On American Progressives' contact with Europeans, see Rodgers, *Atlantic Crossings*; on additional American reports of European social insurance, see ibid., 241–45.

16. I. M. Rubinow, "Sickness Insurance," *ALLR* 3 (1913): 163; "Health Insurance: Standards and Tentative Draft of an Act," 1915, reel 62, AALLP.

17. Clarence Poe, "Lloyd George's England," *World's Work* 25 (November 1912): 101–11.

18. "Britain's Medical-Insurance Law," *Literary Digest* (February 8, 1913): 271; "England's National Insurance," *Literary Digest* (August 3, 1912): 182.

19. Gary Land, "American Images of British Compulsory Health Insurance," in Numbers, ed., *Compulsory Health Insurance*.

20. For a discussion of federalism and social insurance, see Robertson, "Bias of American Federalism," and Moss, *Socializing Security*, ch. 8.

21. Because of pressure from the industry, British National Insurance allowed commercial companies to participate in the system. Commercial insurance opposition to the German system was nonexistent because "the German commercial insurance industry was in its infancy in the 1880s"; see Rodgers, *Atlantic Crossings*, 233–34.

22. National Civic Federation, *Report of the Committee*.

23. Land, "American Images," 59; J. McCrea to Foster Kennedy, February 5, 1920, Public Health Committee of the New York Academy of Medicine Papers, NYAM; Minutes of the meeting of the Social Insurance Dept., January 9, 1920, Box 70, NCFP. Numbers, *Almost Persuaded*, does an excellent job of tracing changes in *JAMA*'s coverage of British developments.

24. James W. Gerard, quoted in "Labor's Attitude towards Compulsory State Health Insurance," Bulletin No. 8 of New York League for Americanism (n.d.), Rare Pamphlet Collection, KC.

25. Bulletin No. 1-b, "To All Members," from Mark A. Daly, February 23, 1918, reel 18, AALLP.

26. For example, see Irene Sylvester to Mr. Mortimer, March 9, 1917, reel 17, AALLP, and Irving Fisher, "General Discussion," *ALLR* 7 (March 1917): 128.

27. British Manufacturers Association to John B. Andrews, August 19, 1919, reel 20, AALLP; *New York Herald*, February 9, 1916.

28. See Chapter 6 for a more detailed discussion of the NCF.

29. National Civic Federation, *Report of the Committee*, 34–35.

30. Ibid., 55–56; Olga Halsey, "Compulsory Health Insurance in Great Britain," *ALLR* 6 (June 1916): 128, 136.

31. Halsey, "Compulsory Health Insurance," 135–36; National Civic Federation, *Report of the Committee*, 55.

32. National Civic Federation, *Report of the Committee*, 64, 52; Halsey, "Compulsory Health Insurance," 127.

33. Halsey, "Compulsory Health Insurance," 137.

34. National Civic Federation, *Report of the Committee*, 89, 92, 96.

35. Olga Halsey to Floyd S. Leach, March 17, 1916, reel 16, AALLP.

36. Minutes of the meeting of the Social Insurance Dept., December 20, 1916, Box 70, NCFP.

37. Halsey, "Compulsory Health Insurance," 130–34.

38. "Sickness Insurance," 1914, reel 62, AALLP; *New York Times*, March 8, 1917.

39. *New York Times*, May 28, 1917; Higham, *Strangers in the Land*, 197–208.

40. *New York Times*, February 10, 1916, March 15, 1919; "Compulsory Welfare Insurance Condemned," *The Insurance Press*, August 29, 1917; Viseltear, "Compulsory Health Insurance in California," 177–78.

41. Irving Fisher, "The Need for Health Insurance," *ALLR* 7 (March 1917): 10.

42. *ALLR* 8 (December 1918): 320.

43. Quoted in *ALLR* 7 (June 1919): 255.

44. Frederick M. Davenport, "Address before United Meeting of Women's Conference of the State of New York and the State Federation of Labor," Syracuse, August 27, 1919, reel 63, AALLP; Davenport speech, *Proceedings of the New York State Federation of Labor*, 1919, 181.

45. Harry B. Mason, "What Compulsory Health Insurance Would Mean to the Druggist," *Detroit Bulletin of Pharmacy*, January 1916, reel 62, AALLP.

46. Dr. John A. Lapp, "Health Insurance," *Proceedings of the Twentieth New York State Conference of Charities and Corrections*, 191.

47. Testimony at New York Senate Judiciary Hearing, March 26, 1918, *Monitor* 4 (April 1918): 23.

48. Frederick Davenport to W. B. Romer, M.D., March 6, 1919, Box 2, FDP.

49. Boorstin, *America and the Image of Europe*, 22.

50. New York Board of Trade, "Shall Health Insurance Be Made Compulsory by Law?" 1916, reel 62, AALLP.

51. "Resolution Adopted by the National Civic Federation," January 1917, Box 70, NCFP.

52. Ralph Easley to Olga Halsey, April 25, 1916; Statement of Olga S. Halsey, 1916, reel 62, AALLP.

53. Minutes of the Social Insurance Dept. meeting, December 6, 1915, Box 70, NCFP.

54. Ibid., May 19, 1919.

55. "Statement Made by Mrs. Alice B. Locke, in Behalf of the Woman's Benefit Association of the Maccabees," April 1920, Box 69, NCFP.

56. "Report of the Committee on Social Insurance. Presented to the National Fraternal Congress of America," August 25, 1920, Box 69, NCFP.

57. "Germany: A Model or a Warning?" *World's Work* 26 (July 1913): 315–21; Testimony of Dr. John J. Hurley, "Hearing before the Special Commission on Social Insurance," reel 62, AALLP; Samuel Gompers, "Labor vs. Its Barnacles," *American Federationist* 13 (April 1916): 269.

58. Statement of New York League for Americanism, January 5, 1920, reel 21, AALLP (my emphasis).

59. Mink, *Old Labor and New Immigrants*, 125–26; Higham, *Strangers in the Land*, 197–208.

60. On Hoffman's career, see Cassedy, "Frederick Ludwig Hoffman"; Knopf, *History of the National Tuberculosis Association*, 453; Ella Hoffman Rigney, "Frederick L. Hoffman," 199, Box 31, FLHP; and Derickson, *Black Lung*, 62–69.

61. Hoffman, *Race Traits and Tendencies of the American Negro*, 328, 326.

62. Frederick Hoffman to Forrest F. Dryden, November 21, 1918, Box 6, FLHP; Minutes of the meeting of the Social Insurance Dept., May 19, 1919, Box 70, NCFP.

63. For Du Bois's response to Hoffman, see Aptheker, ed., *Book Reviews by W. E. B. Du Bois*, 117, and Miller, *Review of Hoffman's Race Traits and Tendencies*, 6.

64. Hoffman, *History of the Prudential*, 139, 208–11.

65. Ibid., 153. In 1915, following an investigation in Hawaii, Hoffman advised Prudential: "[F]ull-blooded Hawaiians—not generally eligible for insurance . . . Koreans, Filipinos, Porto [*sic*] Ricans, and other Polynesians—*not insurable* . . . American and other white applicants of pure stock—Eligible for insurance on *any plan*" (Hoffman to John K. Gore, June 3, 1915, Box 5, FLHP). On race discrimination in the insurance industry, including Hoffman's role, see Haller, "Race, Mortality, and Life Insurance."

66. Frederick Hoffman to Forrest F. Dryden, December 16, 1918, Box 6, FLHP.

67. "The Life Story of a Statistician, 1865–1884" (typescript, ca. 1919), Box 9, FLHP.

68. "New Verses of a Wanderer," 1923, Box 13, FLHP.

69. Hoffman, "On the Duty of Americans of German Birth," *Economic World*, April 7, 1917.

70. Frederick Hoffman to Forrest F. Dryden, May 8, 1919, Box 6, FLHP.

71. Frederick Hoffman to Forrest F. Dryden, February 13, 1918, Box 6, FLHP. Hoffman did not accept Creel's invitation for unknown reasons.

72. See Chapter 5 for Hoffman's defense of the insurance industry's economic interests.

73. Hoffman, *Facts and Fallacies of Compulsory Health Insurance*, 23; *Failure of German Compulsory Health Insurance*, 6.

74. Hoffman to Irving Fisher, February 5, 1917, reel 17, AALLP.

75. Hoffman, *Race Traits and Tendencies*, 324, 328.

76. *ALLR* 7 (March 1917): 10.

77. "Labor Laws in Wartime," 1917, reel 70, AALLP.

78. Mink, *Wages of Motherhood*, 15.

79. Sen. William E. Borah to John B. Andrews, January 22, 1917, reel 17, AALLP.

80. *Proceedings of the New York State Federation of Labor*, 1918, 132.

81. "Health Insurance. Report of Standing Committee Adopted by the Conference of State and Territorial Health Officers with the US Public Health Service, May 13, 1916," reel 62, AALLP.

82. *Proceedings of the New York State Federation of Labor*, 1918, 133.

83. Mrs. Lee S. Bernheim to Sen. C. W. Walton, March 24, 1919, reel 19, AALLP.

84. W. D. Alsener to Olga Halsey, November 11, 1919, reel 20, AALLP; Walter Winn to Frederick Davenport, March 15, 1919, Box 2, FDP.

85. *Proceedings of the New York State Federation of Labor*, 1918, 132.

86. Quoted in Lubove, *Struggle for Social Security*, 89; Numbers, *Almost Persuaded*, 87.

87. "Statement Made by Mrs. Alice B. Locke."

88. "Facts about Health Insurance: A Text-book for Speakers, Writers, and Workers," Box 3, Folder 13, AALL Pamphlet Collection, KC.

89. Testimony, March 26, 1918, *Monitor* 4 (April 1918): 23.

CHAPTER FOUR

1. Ronald Numbers, "The Specter of Socialized Medicine: American Physicians and Compulsory Health Insurance," in Numbers, ed., *Compulsory Health Insurance*, 5.

2. Numbers's *Almost Persuaded* is the classic account of the organized medical profession's response to compulsory health insurance. Despite its brief length, this book's narrative is so comprehensive and astute that I have not attempted to supplant it. Instead, I build on Numbers's work by exploring areas that were less central to his analysis, such as the role of nurses, the relationship between income and autonomy, and physicians' Americanist strategies (including their participation in the New York League for Americanism, described in Chapter 8).

3. "Health Insurance: Standards and Tentative Draft of an Act," *ALLR* 6 (June 1916): 239–45.

4. Burrow, *Organized Medicine in the Progressive Era*, 131–38.

5. Numbers, *Almost Persuaded*, 29–31; Gary Land, "American Images of British Compulsory Health Insurance," in Numbers, ed., *Compulsory Health Insurance*, 55–58.

6. Frederick R. Green, "A Model Bill for Health Insurance," *JAMA* 65 (1915): 824.

7. On the decreasing number of physicians, see Rosen, *Structure of American Medical Practice*, 64–65, and Starr, *Social Transformation of American Medicine*, 118–21, 126–27.

8. Stevens, *American Medicine and the Public Interest*, pt. 2; Rosen, *Structure of American Medical Practice*, 51.

9. Numbers, *Almost Persuaded*, 33–36.

10. Ibid., 22–24.

11. Ibid., 57.

12. S. S. Goldwater to John B. Andrews, February 25, 1919, reel 20, AALLP; B. S. Warren, quoted in "Recent American Opinion on Health Insurance," *ALLR* 6 (1916): 352.

13. Samuel Kopetzky, "Reply to Curtis," *NYSJM* 17 (February 1917): 80. On compulsory health measures in New York City, see Duffy, *History of Public Health in New York City*, and Rosner, ed., *Hives of Sickness*.

14. B. S. Warren, quoted in "Recent American Opinion on Health Insurance," 352; Lewinski-Corwin to Olga Halsey, January 28, 1916, reel 16, AALLP; Numbers, *Almost Persuaded*, 57.

15. John F. Anderson (former president, American Public Health Association), quoted in "Recent American Opinion on Health Insurance," 351.

16. John A. Lapp, "Health Insurance and the Hospitals," address before the American Hospital Association, September 27, 1918, Box 3, Folder 12, AALL Pamphlet Collection, KC; *ALLR* 8 (December 1918): 326. On the hospital's charity function and its decline, see Rosner, *Once Charitable Enterprise*.

17. Statement of Dr. William T. Bishop, in "Ninth Conference of Industrial Physicians and Surgeons," *Pennsylvania Medical Journal* 23 (January 1920): 207.

18. C. E. McDermid, M.D., to John B. Andrews, February 27, 1917, reel 17, AALLP.

19. "Second National Conference of Health Insurance Commissioners," *ALLR* 8 (1918): 189; "Facts about Health Insurance: A Text-book for Speakers, Writers, and Workers," Box 3, Folder 13, AALL Pamphlet Collection, KC.

20. Bishop statement, "Ninth Conference," 207.

21. The study was conducted for the National Industrial Conference Board in 1920 by a Dr. Rector. His reports are in a folder titled "Hygiene, Industrial," Box 8, NICBP.

22. Bishop statement, "Ninth Conference," 205–8; Sellers, *Hazards of the Job*, 33–34. (In another example of physician loyalty to the employer rather than to the worker, Alan Derickson describes a Western mining physician who "personally identified numerous union activists for arrest" in the 1890s [*Workers' Health, Workers' Democracy*, 89].) "Report of the Committee on Health Insurance of the American Association of Industrial Physicians and Surgeons," June 1917, Box 3, Folder 11, AALL Pamphlet Collection, KC.

23. Morantz-Sanchez, *Sympathy and Science*, ch. 10.

24. "Report of the Legislative Committee of the Woman's Medical Society of the State of New York," *Woman's Medical Journal* 19 (August 1919): 174.

25. "General Discussion," *ALLR* 7 (March 1917): 57. On the quota system and other types of discrimination against female practitioners, see Morantz-Sanchez, *Sympathy and Science*.

26. Linda Gordon has persuasively made this point about black women reformers; see *Pitied but Not Entitled*, ch. 5.

27. Numbers, "Specter of Socialized Medicine," 13. On African American physicians see Beardsley, *History of Neglect*, and Reitzes, *Negroes in Medicine*. On the National Medical Association, see Gamble, *Making a Place for Ourselves*, ch. 2.

28. *Fourteenth Annual Meeting*, 1915, 111, New York State Nurses' Association Historical Collection. On Metropolitan Life's visiting nurse service, see Buhler-Wilkerson, *False Dawn*, 68–69.

29. Pauline Newman, "What Will Health Insurance Mean to the Insured?" *American Journal of Nursing* 17 (1917): 944.

30. Minutes of the Massachusetts Social Insurance Commission meeting, October 3, 1916, reel 62, AALLP.

31. Edna Foley to John B. Andrews, September 25, 1916, reel 17, AALLP.

32. *Eighteenth Annual Meeting*, 1919, 138, New York State Nurses' Association Historical Collection.

33. Rosen, *Structure of American Medical Practice*, 57–59; Starr, *Social Transformation of American Medicine*, 125–26; Buhler-Wilkerson, *False Dawn*, ch. 4.

34. "Health Insurance," *American Journal of Nursing* 17 (1916): 188.

35. Martha M. Russell, R.N., "What Social Insurance Will Mean to Nurses," *American Journal of Nursing* 17 (1917): 390–91.

36. *Eighteenth Annual Meeting*, 1919, 77, New York State Nurses' Association Historical Collection.

37. Russell, "What Social Insurance Will Mean," 385. Susan Reverby (*Ordered to Care*, 98) estimates that private-duty nurses in the early twentieth century earned an average of $950 a year.

38. "Discussion," *Fifteenth Annual Meeting*, 1916, 188, 155, New York State Nurses' Association Historical Collection.

39. On professionalization, see Hine, *Black Women in White*, ch. 5, and Reverby, *Ordered to Care*, ch. 7.

40. The Nurse Practice Act was introduced repeatedly in the New York Assembly between 1916 and 1919, finally achieving passage in 1920 (*Nineteenth Annual Meeting*, 1920, New York State Nurses' Association Historical Collection). In 1916, the act was killed by the Speaker of the Assembly—one Thaddeus Sweet.

41. Minutes of the Social Insurance Committee meeting, November 2, 1916, reel 61, AALLP. Apparently Lillian Wald did not attend this meeting.

42. Anne Hansen to John B. Andrews, November 18, 1919, reel 20, AALLP.

43. Minutes of the Social Insurance Committee meeting, November 2, 1916, reel 61, AALLP.

44. Ella Phillips Crandall to John B. Andrews, March 29, 1916, reel 16, AALLP; "Evening Session," *Sixteenth and Seventeenth Annual Meetings*, 1917–18, 99–100, New York State Nurses' Association Historical Collection.

45. When Wald turned down Andrews's request to testify on behalf of health insurance at the 1920 hearing in Albany, she had her secretary write to Andrews: "Every minute of [Miss Wald's] time and all of her thought are absorbed in the publicity campaign to raise a million dollars for the Visiting Nursing Service administered by the Henry Street Settlement" (E. B. Sayre to John B. Andrews, March 17, 1920, reel 21, AALLP). Another reason for Wald's withdrawal from the AALL may have been her close friendship with Florence Kelley, who disliked the organization for reasons discussed in Chapter 7.

46. Alexander Lambert, "Medical Organization under Health Insurance," *ALLR* 7 (March 1917): 38–47.

47. Eden V. Delphey to AALL, January 16, 1916, reel 16, AALLP; Numbers, *Almost Persuaded*, 42–44.

48. *NYSJM* 17 (February 1917): 102–3; *NYSJM* 17 (March 1917): 154–56. The opposition of additional county societies is discussed in Numbers, *Almost Persuaded*, 67.

49. F. W. James, M.D., to Frederick Davenport, March 10, 1919, Box 2, FDP; Francis D. Tyson, "General Discussion" [Tenth Annual Meeting of the AALL], *ALLR* 7 (March 1917): 60.

50. Starr, *Social Transformation of American Medicine*, 122. See also Rosen, *Structure of American Medical Practice*, 117.

51. Numbers, *Almost Persuaded*, 38, 40.

52. William P. Cunningham, M.D., "A Bolshevik Bolus," pt. 1, *New York Medical Journal* 108 (December 21, 1918): 1062. On New York practitioners' resentment of public health activities, see Duffy, *History of Public Health in New York City*, 241–42, and Elizabeth Fee and Evelyn M. Hammonds, "Science, Politics, and the Art of Persuasion: Promoting the New Scientific Medicine in New York City," in Rosner, ed., *Hives of Sickness*, 175–78.

53. "Report of the Committee on Legislation," *NYSJM* 17 (April 1917): 237, 234.

54. "Medical Society of the County of Albany, Special Meeting," and "Medical Society of the County of Washington, Special Meeting, January 4, 1917," *NYSJM* 17 (March 1917): 155.

55. "Report of the Committee on Legislation," *NYSJM* 17 (June 1919): 227.

56. "Medical Society of the County of Monroe, Special Meeting, Rochester, January 23, 1917," and "Medical Society of the County of Erie, Regular Meeting, April 16, 1917," *NYSJM* 17 (April 1917): 103, 258.

57. Numbers, *Almost Persuaded*, 27–28.

58. Ibid., 69–70.

59. The AMA estimated that only 10 percent of American physicians were "comfortable"; figures for Wisconsin in 1914 showed the average annual income of physicians who earned enough to pay taxes to be $1,488 (Numbers, *Almost Persuaded*, 9).

60. Kopetzky quoted in Numbers, *Almost Persuaded*, 64; Frederick Davenport to Charles Miller, March 8, 1919, Box 2, FDP. In five British towns studied, "it is estimated

that the act has brought an average annual addition of $750 to $1,000" ("Health Insurance: A Positive Statement in Answer to Opponents," *ALLR* 7 [December 1917]: 671). See also Gilbert, *Evolution of National Insurance*, 400–416.

61. Numbers, *Almost Persuaded*, 113; Robertson, "Bias of American Federalism," 284.

62. Stevens, *American Medicine and the Public Interest*, 139; Michael M. Davis, "Organization of Medical Service," *ALLR* 6 (1916): 16–18; Rosen, *Structure of American Medical Practice*, 32.

63. Josephine Shatz to John B. Andrews, November 6, 1919, reel 20, AALLP.

64. Statement of Dr. David C. English, in "Ninth Conference of Industrial Physicians and Surgeons," *Pennsylvania Medical Journal* 23 (January 1920): 206–7.

65. Numbers, *Almost Persuaded*, 68.

66. M. R. Silvernail to Frederick Davenport, August 28, 1919, Box 2, FDP.

67. John A. Lapp, "Health Insurance," *Proceedings of the Twentieth New York State Conference of Charities and Corrections*, 191.

68. Numbers, *Almost Persuaded*, 91.

69. Transcript of Senate Judiciary Committee Hearing on Mills Bill, *Monitor* 3 (March 1917): 20.

70. "Special Meeting of the House of Delegates," *NYSJM* 19 (1919): 402.

71. Starr, *Social Transformation of American Medicine*, 26.

72. "Medical Society of the County of Schenectady, January 16, 1917," *NYSJM* 17 (March 1917): 155.

73. Luther Emerick, M.D., "The Honor of the Profession," *NYSJM* 17 (March 1917): 145.

74. Lapp, "Health Insurance" (discussion), 202.

75. Eden V. Delphey to AALL, January 16, 1916, reel 16, AALLP.

76. Cunningham, "Bolshevik Bolus," 1063.

77. Statement of Dr. G. Franklin Bell, in "Ninth Conference of Industrial Physicians and Surgeons," *Pennsylvania Medical Journal* 23 (January 1920): 208.

78. Kopetzky, "Reply to Curtis," 80.

79. Transcript of Senate Judiciary Committee Hearing on Mills Bill, 20.

80. Ibid., 32.

81. Cunningham, "Bolshevik Bolus," 1063.

82. Transcript of Senate Judiciary Committee Hearing on Mills Bill, 20; Lapp, "Health Insurance" (discussion), 202.

83. Transcript of Senate Judiciary Committee Hearing on Mills Bill, 32.

84. "Medical Society of the County of Schenectady," 155.

85. Dr. John J. A. O'Reilly, "To the Medical, Dental, and Pharmaceutical Societies of the State of New York," 1919, Folder 10, MDP.

86. Circular letter to Legislature, Committee on Legislation of the New York Physicians' Association, October 27, 1919, Folder 3, MDP.

87. "Notes on the Hearing of the Davenport Health Insurance Bill, April 7, 1920," Box 3, AALL Pamphlet Collection, KC.

88. Transcript of Senate Judiciary Committee Hearing on Mills Bill, 25, 23; Cunningham, "Bolshevik Bolus," 1063.

89. Physicians' linkage of autonomy and Americanism was alive and well in 1999. In a letter to the *New York Times* on medical unionization, a Florida doctor wrote, "[T]he private, autonomous physician was and will be a bargain for free Americans" (Pepi Granat, M.D., to the editor, *New York Times*, June 29, 1999, A22).

90. See Chapter 1 for a discussion of dispensary care.

91. Transcript of the hearing on Mills Health Insurance Bill, *Monitor* 2 (March 1916): 21; O'Reilly, "To the Medical . . . Societies"; Numbers, *Almost Persuaded*, 84.

92. Transcript of Senate Judiciary Committee Hearing on Mills Bill, 21.

93. "Utica Doctor Writes Vigorous Letter to Sen. Davenport on Health Bill," *Monitor* 6 (April 1919): 29.

94. J. Charles, M.D., to E. Lewinski-Corwin, November 28, 1919, "Legislation" Folder, Public Health Committee of the New York Academy of Medicine Papers, NYAM.

95. [Name illegible] to "Gentlemen," January 19, 1920, ibid.

96. C. E. McDermid, M.D., to John B. Andrews, February 27, 1917, reel 17, AALLP; Guy L. Howe, M.D., "Industrial versus Private Medical Practice," *NYSJM* 17 (February 1917): 88. On the prevalence of prepaid medical care plans in Western mining areas, see Derickson, *Workers' Health, Workers' Democracy*.

A correlation between cost and quality is also refuted by statistics indicating that the United States, with the highest health care expenditures of all industrial nations, ranks inferior to many European countries and Japan in national health status indicators, including life expectancy and infant mortality (Wilsford, *Doctors and the State*, 21).

97. Numbers, *Almost Persuaded*, 56.

98. Ibid., 89, 91; "Health Insurance Bill as Developed from 'Tentative Drafts,'" *ALLR* 19 (1919): 232–38.

99. Numbers, *Almost Persuaded*, 97.

100. O'Reilly, "To the Medical, Dental, and Pharmaceutical Societies."

101. "Report of the Committee on Medical Economics," and "Minutes of the House of Delegates," *NYSJM* 17 (1917): 237–38, 256.

102. Frederick R. Green, letter to editor, *Illinois Medical Journal* 32 (1917): 32, quoted in Numbers, *Almost Persuaded*, 84.

103. John J. O'Reilly, letter to editor, *Long Island Medical Journal* 13 (1919): 193.

104. William P. Cunningham, M.D., "Bolshevik Bolus," pt. 2, *New York Medical Journal* 108 (December 28, 1918): 1114.

CHAPTER FIVE

1. *Monitor* 2 (November 1915): 1–2.

2. *Monitor* 4 (July 1918): 25. I found little evidence of retail or other nonmanufacturing employers' response to health insurance. Although these sectors were represented in the business organizations opposed to health insurance, the vast majority of public pronouncements on the issue came from industrial employers. So, in this chapter "employers" refers to both large and small employers of industrial labor unless otherwise specified.

3. S. P. Bush, "General Discussion," Tenth Annual Meeting of the AALL, *ALLR* 7 (March 1917): 61. On business participation in the workmen's compensation movement, see Lubove, *Struggle for Social Security*, and Weinstein, *Corporate Ideal in the Liberal State*.

4. The most thorough discussions of the insurance industry in Progressive America are Grant, *Insurance Reform*, and Keller, *Life Insurance Enterprise*.

5. In contrast, much of the historiography of the Progressive Era has emphasized business *support* for Progressive legislation; see for example, Sklar, *Corporate Reconstruction of American Capitalism*; Weinstein, *Corporate Ideal in the Liberal State*; Kolko, *Triumph of Conservatism*; and Wiebe, *Businessmen and Reform*.

6. C. Cheney, NICB finance committee to John D. Rockefeller Jr., February 22, 1917, RG II2F, Box 13, Rockefeller Foundation Archives, RAC.

7. Gitelman, "Management's Crisis of Confidence."

8. "Second Annual Meeting of Associated Manufacturers and Merchants of New York State," December 10, 1915, Box 1, Associated Industries Papers, SUNY-Albany Special Collections; *Monitor* 2 (July 1915).

9. "Second Annual Meeting."

10. I was unable to find biographical material on Daly, so it is unclear whether he had been an employer himself before going to work for the AMM.

11. Twenty-Sixth Meeting of the Executive Committee, Thursday, August 14, 1919, and Sixteenth Meeting of the Executive Committee, Friday, October 25, 1918, Series 2, NICBP.

12. Twenty-Fourth Meeting of the Executive Committee, Wednesday, May 21, 1919, Series 2, and Meeting of National Industrial Conference Board, February 19, 1920, Series 3, NICBP.

13. Gertrude Beeks Easley to Lee Frankel, January 26, 1920, Box 69, NCFP.

14. Annual Meeting, January 29, 1920, Box 136, NCFP.

15. Irene Sylvester Chubb to I. M. Rubinow, July 26, 1919, reel 20, AALLP.

16. *Monitor* 2 (November 1915): 3.

17. *Monitor* 3 (March 1917): 18.

18. Frederick Hoffman to John R. Dryden, January 14, 1918, Box 6, FLHP.

19. Irving Fisher, "General Discussion," *ALLR* 7 (March 1917): 98. This amount was

an estimate; what compulsory health insurance would actually cost employers was unclear. The bill that finally passed in the New York Senate did not specify an exact percentage of payroll; instead, employer contributions would be based on the needs of the insurance funds and on the rate of sickness in each industry. In its model bill, the AALL estimated that "the premium for a person earning $50 a month would be about $2," of which the employer would pay 40 percent ("Health Insurance Bill as Developed from 'Tentative Drafts,'" 217; Numbers, *Almost Persuaded*, 26).

20. E. M. Roberts to Frederick Davenport, March 15, 1920, Box 2, FDP.

21. John L. Whiting to John B. Andrews, December 12, 1916, reel 17, AALLP.

22. Haley Fiske, "The Future of Industrial Life Insurance," 1911, Haley Fiske Speeches Vertical File, Metropolitan Life Insurance Company Archives.

23. Annual Meeting, January 29, 1920, Box 136, NCFP.

24. John L. Whiting to John B. Andrews, December 12, 1916, reel 17, AALLP.

25. *Monitor* 2 (March 1916): 24.

26. On *Muller v. Oregon*, see Kessler-Harris, *Out to Work*, 186–90, and Woloch, *Muller v. Oregon*.

27. "Facts about Health Insurance: A Text-book for Speakers, Writers, and Workers," Box 3, Folder 13, AALL Pamphlet Collection, KC. See Chapter 1 for further discussion of work-related illness.

28. Circular letter to "Dear Friend," December 29, 1916, reel 17, AALLP.

29. Frederick M. Davenport, "Address before United Meeting of Women's Conference of the State of New York and State Federation of Labor," Syracuse, August 27, 1919, reel 63, AALLP.

30. L. C. Hammond to "Assemblymen," March 27, 1919, reel 19, AALLP.

31. F. A. Reinhard to "Senators," March 18, 1919, reel 19, AALLP.

32. John B. Andrews to Mrs. Charles E. Stevenson, March 27, 1919, reel 19, AALLP.

33. Meeting transcript, March 31, 1919, Box 9, NICBP.

34. M. W. Alexander to Ogden Mills, April 9, 1920, Series 3, NICBP.

35. Meeting transcript, March 31, 1919, Box 9, NICBP.

36. Quoted in Gertrude Beeks Easley to Lee Frankel, January 26, 1920, Box 69, NCFP.

37. E. M. Roberts to Frederick Davenport, March 15, 1920, Box 2, FDP.

38. John L. Whiting to John B. Andrews, December 12, 1916, reel 16, AALLP.

39. "Compulsory Health Insurance: Statement Issued by Social Insurance Department, National Civic Federation," n.d., Box 70, NCFP.

40. Roy D. Barber to Frederick Davenport, March 18, 1919, Box 2, FDP.

41. Meeting transcript, March 31, 1919, Box 9, and Meeting, December 21, 1916, Series 3, NICBP.

42. Frederick Davenport to Frank Munsey, January 30, 1919, Box 2, FDP.

43. Dr. Joseph Catton, "Malingering," *Military Surgeon* 45 (December 1919): 706.

44. Ibid., 709.

45. Judson C. Fisher, M.D., "Malingering—Involving the Problem of Getting the

Sick or Injured Employee Back to Work," *Journal of Industrial Hygiene* 1 (December 1919): 409.

46. *Practitioner* 99 (July 1917): 90.

47. E. M. Roberts to Frederick Davenport, March 15, 1920, Box 2, FDP.

48. H. S. Powell to Frederick Davenport, March 25, 1919, Box 2, FDP.

49. "Wage Earner's Illness" (ca. 1917), 120–21, Box 99, Van Kleeck Papers, Sophia Smith Archive; Frederick L. Hoffman, article reprint (from unidentified periodical), Rare Pamphlet Collection, KC. See also Dawson, *Social Insurance in Germany*, 248–49.

50. Fisher, "Malingering," 410. Using sick benefits as unemployment or retirement insurance would not have been possible under the AALL's scheme, since coverage was tied to employment.

51. Fisher, "Malingering," 409.

52. Thornton R. Richardson, "Group Health Insurance for Employees of the Metropolitan Life Insurance Company," 1917, Group Insurance Vertical File, Metropolitan Life Insurance Company Archives.

53. Warren Stone, minutes of the meeting of the Social Insurance Dept., May 19, 1919, Box 70, NCFP. Interestingly, Stone was an opponent of compulsory health insurance.

54. Irene Sylvester to Mr. Mortimer, March 9, 1917, reel 17, AALLP.

55. Quoted in James Lynch to editor, *Evening Sun*, April 2, 1919, reel 19, AALLP.

56. "Facts about Health Insurance."

57. See Chapter 1.

58. John A. Lapp, "Health Insurance and the Hospitals," address before the American Hospital Association, September 27, 1918, Box 3, Folder 12, AALL Pamphlet Collection, KC.

59. Charles G. DuBois, "Sickness Insurance in the Bell Telephone System," January 22, 1917, Box 70, NCFP.

60. "Meeting of the National Industrial Conference Board," May 19, 1921, Series 3, NICBP.

61. Eugenius H. Outerbridge, "Group Insurance as an Influence in Promoting Stability in Labor Groups," address delivered at the 12th Annual Meeting of the Association of Life Insurance Presidents, 1918, Insurance—Uncatalogued Pamphlets, NYPL; Edward J. Barcalo to John B. Andrews, June 2, 1920, reel 22, AALLP; Executive Committee Meeting, December 4, 1919, NICBP; Minutes of the meeting of the Social Insurance Dept., January 22, 1917, Box 70, NCFP. On the NCF's welfare work, see Tone, *Business of Benevolence*, 45–48. For more on employer-sponsored health care, see Chapter 1.

62. Tone, *Business of Benevolence*, 7.

63. Brandes, *American Welfare Capitalism*, 97, 99. On the explosive growth of welfare capitalism in the 1920s, see Brandes, *American Welfare Capitalism*; Zahavi, *Workers, Managers, and Welfare Capitalism*, chs. 2–4; and Cohen, *Making a New Deal*.

64. Hiram J. Messenger, "The Rate of Sickness," 1917, Insurance—Uncatalogued Pamphlets, NYPL.

65. "Report of the Committee on Social Insurance. Presented to the National Fraternal Congress of America, Chicago, Aug. 31, 1921," Box 69, NCFP.

66. Insurance Federation of New York, "To our New York Agents," January 27, 1916, reel 16, AALLP. Also quoted in Lubove, *Struggle for Social Security*, 86, and Moss, *Socializing Security*, 146.

67. Policies provided by the Metropolitan, however, included the services of visiting nurses. See Chapter 4, note 28.

68. "Health Insurance: Tentative Draft of an Act," *ALLR* 6 (June 1916): 245.

69. R. P. Shorts to John B. Andrews, January 27, 1916, reel 16, AALLP.

70. Frederick Hoffman to Forrest F. Dryden, January 5, 1917, Box 5, FLHP.

71. R. P. Shorts to John B. Andrews, January 27, 1916, reel 16, AALLP.

72. Grant, *Insurance Reform*, 23, 41–42.

73. James Holland, "Annual Report of President Holland of Federation," August 23, 1916, *Monitor* 3 (October 1916): 9.

74. John B. Andrews to Mary M. Lilly, March 27, 1919, reel 19, AALLP; press release, League of Women Voters, April 5, 1920, reel 22, AALLP.

75. Haley Fiske, "Insurance" (address to National Civic Federation), 1908, Haley Fiske Speeches Vertical File, Metropolitan Life Insurance Company Archives.

76. Lee Frankel, "The Sickness Problem—Is Social Insurance the Remedy?" n.d., Box 70, NCFP.

77. Sidney Webb to Olga S. Halsey, August 26, 1916, reel 17, AALLP.

78. "Health Insurance for Workers," resolution of the International Fur Workers' Union (AFL), July 18, 1918, reel 18, AALLP.

79. J. Chamberlain to unidentified recipient, February 18, 1916, reel 16, AALLP.

80. Olga S. Halsey to William Lander, May 18, 1916, reel 17, AALLP.

81. Potts, *Addresses and Papers on Insurance*, 95.

82. Meeting, December 21, 1916, Series 3, NICBP.

83. Frederick Hoffman to Forrest F. Dryden, October 20, 1920, Box 8, and December 12, 1916, Box 5, FLHP.

84. "Report on European trip by Gertrude Beeks Easley," June 30, 1919, Box 70, NCFP.

85. Frederick Hoffman to Forrest F. Dryden, September 22, 1916, and December 13, 1916, Box 5, FLHP.

86. Insurance Federation of New York, "To our New York Agents."

87. Frederick Hoffman to Forrest F. Dryden, March 27, 1918, and December 2, 1918, Box 6, FLHP.

88. Frederick Hoffman to Irving Fisher, February 5, 1917, reel 17, AALLP.

89. Frederick Hoffman to Forrest F. Dryden, May 20, 1919, Box 6, and December 7, 1920, Box 8, FLHP.

90. Frederick Hoffman to Forrest F. Dryden, May 21, 1918, Box 6, FLHP. For a summary of the state commission reports, see Numbers, *Almost Persuaded*, 99.

91. Frederick Hoffman to Forrest F. Dryden, October 20, 1920, Box 8, FLHP.

92. Ibid., January 20, 1919.

93. On Babcock and the Insurance Economics Society, see Numbers, *Almost Persuaded*, 61, 81. Senator Davenport alleged that the league was backed with $100,000 from the insurance industry, and Babcock's own propaganda stated that he charged no membership dues because "[t]he League is amply supported by patriotic men" (Frederick Davenport to John B. Andrews, September 27, 1919, reel 10, AALLP; "New York League for Americanism Wants Million Members," *Monitor* 6 [January 1920]: 13).

94. Richardson, "Group Health Insurance for Employees."

95. Faulkner, *Accident-and-Health Insurance*, 15–18.

96. AALL (unknown author) to "Dear Friend," December 29, 1916, reel 17, AALLP.

97. Frederick Hoffman to Forrest F. Dryden, December 4, 1916, Box 5, FLHP.

98. Augustus H. Knoll, "Notice to Physicians," February 28, 1920, reel 21, AALLP.

99. Messenger, "Rate of Sickness."

100. May, *Prudential*, 175; Klein, "Managing Security," 51; Carr, *"From Three Cents a Week,"* 193. Prudential did not sell individual health plans between 1877 and 1951. Dublin, *Family of 30 Million*; Starr, *Social Transformation of American Medicine*, 294.

101. *Proceedings of the New York State Federation of Labor*, 1918, 185.

102. Gertrude Beeks Easley to Warren Stone, July 8, 1919, Box 69, NCFP.

103. Frederick Hoffman to Forrest F. Dryden, March 8, 1917, Box 6, FLHP.

104. Mark Daly to Ralph Easley, August 13, 1919, Box 69, NCFP; press release, League of Women Voters, April 5, 1920, reel 22, AALLP.

CHAPTER SIX

1. On labor support for health insurance after 1930, see Derickson, "Health Security for All?" and Munts, *Bargaining for Health*.

2. Samuel Gompers, "Labor vs. Its Barnacles," *American Federationist* 13 (April 1916): 270. Scholars, too, have erroneously taken the AFL opposition to stand for the entire labor movement; historian Daniel Levine, for example, concludes from the AFL's stance that "in the United States, organized labor before the Great Depression opposed social insurance" (*Poverty and Society*, 168, 174–75, 278).

3. James W. Lynch, "To the Editor," March 15, 1919, reel 19, AALLP.

4. Moss, *Socializing Security*, 32. The bill would have merged New York's Labor Department into a new industrial commission. Organized labor feared it would lose representation on the new commission.

5. Gompers, "Labor vs. Its Barnacles," 270–71.

6. J. G. Skemp to John B. Andrews, April 13, 1916, reel 16, AALLP.

7. Meaning the adult, white, male worker. Gompers and the AFL supported state regulation of only women, children, and immigrant workers. As this chapter argues,

Gompers did not include women, children, and nonwhites in his definition of the true American worker.

8. Gompers, "Labor vs. Its Barnacles," 271, 273.

9. "Objections of President Holland of the New York State Federation of Labor to the Mills Health Insurance Bill," n.d., reel 16, AALLP.

10. Minutes of the meeting of the Social Insurance Dept., December 20, 1916, Box 70, NCFP; transcript of the hearing on Mills Health Insurance Bill, *Monitor* 2 (March 1916).

11. Olga Halsey to James Holland, March 21, 1916, reel 16, AALLP.

12. Mary Van Kleeck to John B. Andrews, March 28, 1916, reel 16, AALLP.

13. Olga Halsey to James Holland, March 21, 1916, reel 16, AALLP.

14. John B. Andrews to J. G. Skemp, April 17, 1916, reel 16, AALLP.

15. James Duncan to John B. Andrews, February 21, 1916, reel 16, AALLP.

16. William Green, "Trade Union Sick Funds and Compulsory Health Insurance," *ALLR* 7 (March 1917): 93–95.

17. On Green's work for health insurance during his AFL presidency, see Derickson, "Health Security for All?"

18. John P. Coryell to Sen. J. Henry Walters, February 26, 1916, reel 16, AALLP.

19. Chas. Bradley to John B. Andrews, February 12, 1919, reel 19, AALLP.

20. *Proceedings of the New York State Federation of Labor*, 1917, 67.

21. Ibid., 1918, 185.

22. James Lynch, "Health and Humor," *Typographical Journal* 53 (November 1918): 442.

23. *Proceedings of the New York State Federation of Labor*, 1918, 132.

24. "Health Insurance Discussion, Executive Council Meeting, New York State Federation of Labor, January 8, 1918," Box 3, Folder 12, AALL Pamphlet Collection, KC.

25. *Proceedings of the New York State Federation of Labor*, 1918, 186, 187, 184.

26. "Facts about Health Insurance: A Text-book for Speakers, Writers, and Workers," Box 3, Folder 13, AALL Pamphlet Collection, KC.

27. In a discussion at the NYSFL convention, Lynch mentioned that he and another union member "fought together for Ireland" (*Proceedings of the New York State Federation of Labor*, 1918, 184). On Lynch and Gompers in the printers' strike, see Greene, *Pure and Simple Politics*, 103.

28. Lynch, "Health and Humor"; "Health Insurance for Workers," *Typographical Journal* 50 (April 1917): 304.

29. "Health Insurance for Workers"; John Mitchell to the editor, *Evening Post*, n.d., reel 63, AALLP.

30. Fink, *Labor's Search for Political Order*, 168–73; Skocpol, *Protecting Soldiers and Mothers*, 233–45; Greene, *Pure and Simple Politics*, 193–96.

31. Skocpol, *Protecting Soldiers and Mothers*, 240.

32. See Chapter 7.

33. Orleck, *Common Sense and a Little Fire*, 45.

34. For an illuminating biography of Newman, see ibid.

35. *Monitor* 2 (March 1916): 34.

36. John B. Andrews to John R. Commons, March 16, 1916, reel 16, AALLP.

37. Mary Laird to unknown recipient, April 27, 1917, Box 6, Pauline Newman Papers, Schlesinger Library.

38. Transcript of Health Insurance Hearing, March 7, 1917, *Monitor* 3 (March 1917): 41.

39. This phrase is Orleck's (*Common Sense and a Little Fire*, 65).

40. Political scientist Gwendolyn Mink has pointed out that American gender ideology, based on republican notions, decreed that "men's dependency was the sign of men's inadequacy" but "woman's dependency was the mainspring of woman's virtue" ("The Lady and the Tramp: Gender, Race, and the Origins of the American Welfare State," in Linda Gordon, ed., *Women, the State, and Welfare*, 96).

41. *American Journal of Nursing* 17 (1917): 943.

42. See, for example, Hattam, *Labor Visions and State Power*, and Forbath, *Law and the Shaping of the American Labor Movement*.

43. Pauline Newman, "What Will Health Insurance Mean to the Insured?" *American Journal of Nursing* 17 (1917): 942; "New York Senate Judiciary hearing, March 7, 1917," reel 62, AALLP.

44. *Report of the Proceedings of the American Federation of Labor*, 1918, 282; "Report of the Social Insurance Committee, American Federation of Labor," n.d., Folder 19, Box 3, AALL Pamphlet Collection, KC.

45. New York State Federation of Labor, "Health Insurance Discussion, Executive Council Meeting," January 8, 1918, Folder 12, Box 3, AALL Pamphlet Collection, KC; Meeting of the National Industrial Conference Board, December 21, 1916, Series 3, NICBP.

46. Frederick Hoffman to Forrest F. Dryden, November 4, 1920, Box 8, and October 9, 1919, Box 7, FLHP; Bulletin No. 1-b, "To All Members" from Mark A. Daly, February 23, 1918, reel 18, AALLP.

47. Delegate Rander (unidentified affiliation), "Health Insurance Discussion," 125. In 1910, 5.5 percent of U.S. industrial workers were unionized (Yellowitz, *Labor and the Progressive Movement*, 19).

48. Delegate Gernon (unidentified affiliation), "Health Insurance Discussion," 131.

49. J. G. Skemp to John B. Andrews, April 13, 1916, reel 16, AALLP.

50. Thomas J. Curtis at meeting of the Social Insurance Dept., January 22, 1917, Box 70, NCFP.

51. "Health Insurance and Trade Unionism," typescript, n.p., AALL Pamphlet Collection, KC; "Health Insurance Discussion." For a more detailed discussion of voluntary insurance coverage, see Chapter 1.

52. Green, "Trade Union Sickness Funds," 91–92.

53. *Typographical Journal* 51 (September 1917): 218. This statement referred to a resolution approving old-age pensions.

54. On union benefits in the mining industry, see Derickson, *Workers' Health, Workers' Democracy*, ch. 3.

55. "Address Delivered before the Conference on Social Insurance," December 7, 1916, Washington, D.C., Box 70, NCFP.

56. John R. Commons, "Group Insurance and Universal Insurance," May 27, 1918, reel 18, and WTUL, "Resolution," n.d., reel 20, AALLP.

57. Frank A. Byrne, Pipe Caulkers and Tappers Union (AFL), "Why Workers Need Health Insurance Laws," n.d., Folder 13, Box 3, AALL Pamphlet Collection, KC.

58. "Health Insurance Discussion."

59. Editorial, *Union Labor Bulletin*, quoted in *ALLR* 9 (June 1919): 283.

60. James Maurer to John B. Andrews, February 21, 1916, reel 16, AALLP.

61. "Health Insurance for Workers," resolution of the International Fur Workers' Union (AFL), July 18, 1918, reel 18, AALLP.

62. "Health Insurance Discussion," 103.

63. Lubove, *Struggle for Social Security*, 86.

64. Alfred Lussier Jr., "Health Insurance," *Typographical Journal* 53 (November 1918): 442.

65. *Proceedings of the New York State Federation of Labor*, 1918, 183–84.

66. Quoted in Rosner and Markowitz, eds., *Dying for Work*, xiii; "Address Delivered before the Conference on Social Insurance."

67. "Report of the Social Insurance Committee."

68. "Address Delivered before the Conference on Social Insurance."

69. Minutes of the Social Insurance Dept. meeting, May 19, 1919, and January 22, 1917, Box 70, NCFP.

70. Historians, too, have disagreed on the nature of the state's relationship to the American labor movement. Forbath, *Law and the Shaping of the American Labor Movement*, Hattam, *Labor Visions and State Power*, and Tomlins, *State and the Unions*, argue that the state has primarily been a repressive force; Dubofsky, *State and Labor in Modern America*, contends that state intervention has at times strengthened American labor.

71. James Lynch, "Trade Union Sickness Insurance," *ALLR* 4 (March 1917): 91–95.

72. *Proceedings of the New York State Federation of Labor*, 1918, 184.

73. Resolution No. 135, introduced by Benjamin Schlesinger, J. Heller, I. Feinberg, Max Gorenstein, Mollie Friedman, and Alfred Laporta, Delegates of the International Ladies' Garment Workers' Union, in "Report of the Social Insurance Committee"; *Report of the Proceedings of the American Federation of Labor*, 1918, 282.

74. Green, *National Civic Federation*, 6, 14. The NCF's New York offices were in the Metropolitan Life Building, which also housed the AALL. The most detailed discussion

of the NCF and workmen's compensation is Weinstein, *Corporate Ideal in the Liberal State*, chs. 1–3. David Moss, however, argues that Weinstein exaggerates business's role in shaping the legislation; see *Socializing Security*, 130–31, 224 n. 54.

75. Green, *National Civic Federation*, 143–44.

76. Samuel Gompers to Ralph Easley, July 21, 1920, and R. Lee Guard to Ralph Easley, July 7, 1920, 3, Box 4, NCFP.

77. Ralph Easley to Olga Halsey, April 25, 1916, reel 17, AALLP.

78. Green, *National Civic Federation*.

79. Frederick L. Hoffman to Forrest F. Dryden, March 11, 1918, Box 6, FLHP.

80. Gertrude Beeks Easley to Louis A. Coolidge, February 22, 1917, Box 69, NCFP.

81. Gertrude Beeks Easley to Samuel Gompers, March 7, 1918, Box 43, NCFP.

82. Gertrude Beeks Easley to Samuel Gompers, September 24, 1919, Box 69, NCFP.

83. Gertrude Beeks Easley, notes on conversation with Lee Frankel, December 7, 1918, Box 69, NCFP.

84. P. Tecumseh Sherman to Gertrude Beeks Easley, August 30, 1919, Box 69, NCFP.

85. Gertrude Beeks Easley to W. S. Stone, February 12, 1919, Box 69, NCFP.

86. *Report of the Proceedings of the American Federation of Labor*, 1919, 144–45.

87. National Civic Federation, *Report of the Committee on Preliminary Foreign Inquiry*; Green, *National Civic Federation*, 306–11.

88. Gompers's racial views are analyzed in Mink, "Lady and the Tramp."

89. Minutes of the meeting of the Social Insurance Dept., September 19, 1919, Box 70, NCFP.

90. "Labor's Attitude towards Compulsory State Health Insurance," Bulletin No. 8 of the New York League for Americanism (n.d.), Rare Pamphlet Collection, KC.

91. "Labor's Attitude towards Compulsory State Health Insurance"; "Memorandum of Suggestions for Answer(s) by Mrs. Conboy," n.d., Box 70; Gertrude Beeks Easley to Mark Daly, November 1, 1919, Box 69; press release, n.d., Box 70, all in NCFP. I have been unable to locate biographical material on the intriguing Conboy.

92. Gertrude Easley to Matthew Woll, May 5, 1920, Box 70, NCFP.

93. Report of the *Proceedings of the American Federation of Labor*, 1920, 176, 387; "Minutes of Meetings," February 25, 1920, American Federation of Labor Executive Council Minutes, Meany Archive Center. The resolution read in part, "[W]e recommend to the convention that the entire subject-matter be referred to a committee to be selected by the EC."

94. Report of the *Proceedings of the American Federation of Labor*, 1920, 176; "Minutes of Meetings," May 17, 1920, American Federation of Labor Executive Council Minutes, Meany Archive Center.

95. Frederick Hoffman to Forrest F. Dryden, November 4, 1920, Box 8, FLHP (emphasis added).

96. Ibid.

97. Gompers's work with the NCF fits Julie Greene's argument that the AFL was

antistatist but not antipolitics (*Pure and Simple Politics*, 3 n. 3). In the case of health insurance, Gompers took political action to work for an antistatist end.

98. Quoted in Green, *National Civic Federation*, 166.

99. William Green to James Duncan, July 24, 1919, William Green Papers (RG 1-019), Box 1, Folder 7, American Federation of Labor, Office of the President, Meany Archive Center.

100. Samuel Z. Batten to Samuel Gompers, February 19, 1921, Box 43, NCFP.

101. On socialist opposition to Gompers's participation in the NCF, see Green, *National Civic Federation*, ch. 4.

102. Fink, *Labor's Search for Political Order*; Skocpol, *Protecting Soldiers and Mothers*, 233–45.

CHAPTER SEVEN

1. Olga Halsey, "Maternity Insurance," November 10, 1915, reel 62, AALLP.

2. "Necessary Standards of Sickness Insurance," 1914, reel 62, AALLP.

3. Ladd-Taylor, *Raising a Baby the Government Way*, 14.

4. Mrs. John S. Rogers to John B. Andrews, February 10, 1919, reel 62, AALLP.

5. *Proceedings of the New York State Federation of Labor*, 1918, 186.

6. Halsey, "Maternity Insurance."

7. The Progressives' equation of midwifery with high mortality rates was incorrect. Researchers have determined that between 1890 and 1935 "the infant and maternal mortality rates of the midwife were equal to or even lower than that of the average general practitioner" (Judy Barrett Litoff, "Midwives and History," in Apple, ed., *Women, Health, and Medicine in America*, 439, 440 n. 9). On the persistence of midwifery alongside the medicalization of childbirth in New York, see Dye, "Modern Obstetrics and Working-Class Women."

8. "A Maternity Center," press release, January 24, 1918, reel 18, AALLP; Ladd-Taylor, *Raising a Baby the Government Way*, 6.

9. John B. Andrews to Frances Perkins, February 15, 1916, reel 16, AALLP.

10. Olga Halsey, "Objections to Maternity Benefits Answered," reel 62, AALLP.

11. Ladd-Taylor, *Raising a Baby the Government Way*, 135.

12. Halsey, "Maternity Insurance."

13. See Kessler-Harris, *Woman's Wage*, 6–32.

14. Moss, *Socializing Security*, 109–10.

15. The definitive biography of Kelley's early life is Sklar, *Florence Kelley and the Nation's Work*. On the minimum-wage campaign, see Sklar, "Two Political Cultures."

16. Florence Kelley, "Memorandum on the Maternity Features of the Proposed Health Insurance Act," 1915, reel 62, AALLP.

17. Kessler-Harris, *Woman's Wage*, 29–20.

18. Kelley, "Memorandum on the Maternity Features."

19. On the AALL's opposition to the Consumers' League wage campaign, see Sklar, "Two Political Cultures," 60–61.

20. Florence Kelley, "Maternity Benefits," December 1916, reel 62, AALLP.

21. The term "maternalism" used here refers to a particular strain of political thought and a strategy by which women invoked the primary importance of motherhood in order both to champion women's growing activity in the public sphere and to demand welfare programs to protect mothers and children. My approach emphasizes maternalism as an ideology and strategy that could coexist with other types of political thinking (as in the case of the AALL and Florence Kelley) rather than as a cohesive movement. Works that analyze maternalism as the motivating force behind many early welfare-state proposals include Skocpol, *Protecting Soldiers and Mothers*, pt. 3, and Koven and Michel, eds., *Mothers of a New World*. Other scholars, including Linda Gordon, in "Putting Children First: Women, Maternalism, and Welfare in the Early Twentieth Century," in Kerber et al., *U.S. History as Women's History*, 63–86, and Mink, in *Wages of Motherhood*, have critiqued the maternalist paradigm, arguing that maternalism worked against the creation of an equitable welfare state.

22. Kelley, "Maternity Benefits."

23. Kelley, "Memorandum on the Maternity Features," 2. Kelley seemed unaware that health insurance would exclude most African Americans.

24. Halsey, "Objections to Maternity Benefits Answered."

25. Minutes of the Social Insurance Committee meeting, January 3, 1916, reel 61, AALLP.

26. John B. Andrews to Alice Henry, February 23, 1916, reel 16, AALLP.

27. Pauline Newman to Rose Schneiderman, June 19, 1912, File 18-A, Rose Schneiderman Papers, Wagner Labor Archives.

28. Orleck, *Common Sense and a Little Fire*, 64, 67–68.

29. Pauline Newman, "Woman and Her Interests" (interview in *The American Hebrew*), September 15, 1916, Box 10, Pauline Newman Papers, Schlesinger Library; Pauline Newman, "What Will Health Insurance Mean to the Insured?" *American Journal of Nursing* 17 (1917): 942–45.

30. Newman, "Woman and Her Interests," and "What Will Health Insurance Mean?"

31. Newman, "What Will Health Insurance Mean?"

32. By 1920, 23 percent of American working women were married, and 9 percent of all married women worked (Moss, *Socializing Security*, 218 n. 75).

33. Transcript of Health Insurance Hearing, *Monitor* 2 (March 1916): 34.

34. Kathryn Kish Sklar, "The Historical Foundations of Women's Power in the Creation of the American Welfare State, 1830–1930," in Koven and Michel, eds., *Mothers of a New World*, 45.

35. Orleck, *Common Sense and a Little Fire*, 125.

36. Pauline Newman, "Part of an Address Delivered before the Canadian Trades and Labor Congress," September 1919, Box 4, Pauline Newman Papers, Schlesinger Library.

37. Newman, "Woman and Her Interests."

38. Olga S. Halsey to Julia Lathrop, February 3, 1916, reel 16, AALLP.

39. Mary Macarthur to Olga Halsey, December 1916; Sophy Sanger to John B. Andrews, February 28, 1916, and n.d.; and M. Smith to John B. Andrews, December 11, 1916, all on reel 16, AALLP. For a discussion of the milieu in which these women operated, see Pat Thane, "Women in the British Labour Party and the Construction of State Welfare, 1906–1939," in Koven and Michel, eds., *Mothers of a New World*, 343–77, and Pedersen, "Gender, Welfare, and Citizenship."

40. Mrs. M. R. Smith to John B. Andrews, December 11, 1916, reel 16, AALLP.

41. Mary Conyngton to John B. Andrews, December 11, 1916, reel 16, AALLP.

42. Mary Van Kleeck to John B. Andrews, February 17, 1916; Alice Henry to Andrews, February 15, 1916; and AALL (unknown writer) to Frances Perkins, February 15, 1916, all on reel 16, AALLP.

43. Ella Phillips Crandall to John B. Andrews, March 29, 1916, reel 16, AALLP.

44. John B. Andrews to John R. Commons, March 16, 1916, reel 16, AALLP. As they assessed the support for maternity benefits, AALL correspondence took on a gleefully triumphant tone, which is further evidence of the acrimony between the organization and Kelley. "Since Mrs. Kelley is prominent both as a socialist and a suffragist," Andrews wrote to Commons, "she will probably be kept busy explaining to her own groups." AALL board member Henry Seager agreed that Kelley would now be forced "to defend her position even in her own special spheres of influence." Irene Osgood Andrews wrote to her husband, "I am glad you put it over Miss Kelley and particularly glad you did it 'so politely.' Its [*sic*] amazing how long she will hold out on a proposition, isn't it, with everybody else against her?" AALL secretary Andrews, later admitting that deleting the benefit had been a mistake, couldn't resist another stab at Kelley: "The bills were criticized more for that one omission than for any other single thing. The criticisms came, as far as I know, never from 'avaricious husbands' who would force their wives into the factories that they might profit, but almost without exception from women, and from unmarried women, some of them very prominent suffragists, some of them very prominent socialists" (Henry Seager to Andrews, February 27, 1916; Irene Osgood Andrews to Andrews, June 12, 1916; and Andrews to Commons, March 16, 1916, all on reel 16, AALLP).

45. Press release, 1917, reel 62, AALLP.

46. *New York Times*, March 4, 1917; "Facts about Health Insurance," Folder 13, Box 3, AALL Pamphlet Collection, KC. I have been unable to determine exactly why or how Kelley gave in on the matter; apparently she withdrew from the debate and chose not to intervene when the league endorsed the measure.

47. "Wage Earner's Illness" (ca. 1917), 34–35, Box 99, Van Kleeck Papers, Sophia Smith Archive.

48. Press release, 1917, reel 62, AALLP.

49. *Report of the Health Insurance Commission of Pennsylvania*, 51.

50. "Wage Earner's Illness," 16–17.

51. Mrs. F. A. Halsey to Senators, March 16, 1919, reel 19, AALLP.

52. John B. Andrews to Alice Henry, February 23, 1916, reel 16, AALLP; Irene Osgood Andrews, "A Tentative Outline for Maternity Protection Legislation," *ALLR* 10 (December 1920): 251.

53. Excerpt of *Report of the California Health Insurance Commission*, AALLP; Irene Sylvester Chubb to James Lowell Putnam, February 3, 1920, reel 21, AALLP.

54. Lillian Wald to Jane Addams, November 13, 1917, reel 1, Lillian Wald Papers, NYPL. On Wald's crucial role in the success of the 1917 suffrage vote, see Daniels, "Building a Winning Coalition."

55. "Meeting of the Women's Joint Legislative Conference," July 7, 1919, AALL Pamphlet Collection, KC.

56. "Report of the Secretary for 1918–1919," reel 2, PNYWTUL.

57. For a history of the WTUL, see Nancy Schrom Dye, *As Equals and as Sisters*.

58. "The Story of a Legislative Fight," reel 6, PNYWTUL.

59. "Legislative and Publicity Report from January Third to April Eighteenth," no author (likely Irene Sylvester Chubb), 1919, Folder 23, Box 5, AALL Pamphlet Collection, KC.

60. New York *Globe*, March 4, 1919.

61. *Monitor* 5 (March 1919): 1.

62. "Story of a Legislative Fight."

63. New York *World*, April 18, 1919.

64. Ibid., April 1, 1919, 28.

65. *New York Times*, April 2, 1919.

66. New York *World*, March 22, 1919, 11.

67. *Monitor* 5 (March 1919): 41.

68. New York State League of Women Voters, "Report and Protest to the Governor, the Legislature and the People of the State of New York," March 1920, Rare Pamphlet Collection, KC.

69. New York *World*, March 27, 1919, 15.

70. Report of the Secretary, April 1919, reel 2, PNYWTUL.

71. Harriet Laidlaw to Marion Dickerman, September 22, 1919, Folder 11, MDP; "Story of a Legislative Fight."

72. Although her harrowing experience in the Oswego campaign discouraged Dickerman from a political career, she later became part of Eleanor Roosevelt's inner circle. See Cooke, *Eleanor Roosevelt*, and Orleck, *Common Sense and a Little Fire*, 142–45.

73. Dye, *As Equals and as Sisters*, 155–56, and Lehrer, *Origins of Protective Labor Legislation*, 128–30, discuss the origins of the LEO.

74. Minutes of the Executive Board Meeting, October 20, 1919, reel 2, PNYWTUL; Lemons, *Woman Citizen*, 24.

75. Lemons, *Woman Citizen*, 24; Lehrer, *Origins of Protective Labor Legislation*, 162.

76. *Monitor* 5 (March 1919): 9, 13.

77. "Women in Politics" scrapbook, MDP.

78. Suffragist Harriet Stanton Blatch, for example, distanced herself from the LEO leadership's extreme conservatism, but she still supported Sweet against Dickerman because of his opposition to protective legislation (DuBois, *Harriet Stanton Blatch*, 220–21).

There was a bizarre contradiction in the LEO's work for Sweet: he was credited with killing the eight-hour and minimum-wage bills, but no LEO member blamed him for passage of the elevator and transportation bills. There are several possible explanations for why Sweet allowed the elevator and transportation bills out of his committee in April of 1919. He may have distinguished between legislation that would cost employers money and nonredistributive measures like a ban on night work. Restrictions on women in the "new" elevator and transportation industries, which women had only recently entered, may have accorded more with Sweet's view of gender propriety. But for Rose Schneiderman, the passage of the two bills reflected even more sinister motives on the part of Sweet and his colleagues. "The same Republican Assemblymen and the same leader Mr. Sweet, who refused to permit the other bills to come up for a vote, on the floor of the Assembly," Schneiderman wrote to Marion Dickerman's campaign manager, "rushed the Transportation bill through the last night of the session in the last Legislature. None of us ever dreamed that it would go through. *It was a trick by which to get these women opposed to all our legislative work*" (Rose Schneiderman to Bertha Funk, October 20, 1919, reel 6, PNYWTUL [emphasis added]). I have not been able to find further evidence to support Schneiderman's theory.

79. "Women in Politics" scrapbook, MDP.

80. "Rousing Sweet Rally Last Night at Sullivan's Hall," *The Fulton Patriot*, October 29, 1919.

81. "Women in Politics" scrapbook, MDP. See Chapter 8 for further discussion of the opposition's petitioning methods.

82. New York State League of Women Voters, "Report and Protest to the Governor."

83. "Women in Politics" scrapbook, MDP.

84. "Equal Opportunity for Women Wage Earners: Fact vs. Fiction," Box 49, New York Consumers' League Papers, KC.

85. "Some Questions Answered," typescript, n.d., Box 6, Pauline Newman Papers, Schlesinger Library. LEO members were renegades within their union; the Typographical Union "did not support them" and championed protective legislation and health insurance, as discussed in Chapter 6 (Lehrer, *Origins of Protective Labor Legislation*, 168).

86. *Monitor* 5 (March 1919): 9.

87. Dickerman told her supporters, "I would undertake the campaign, but could not accept the plank on compulsory health insurance for I felt totally unprepared to meet this issue" ("Mary Elizabeth Dreier" typescript, MDP).

88. Report of the Secretary, November 1919, reel 2, PNYWTUL.

89. John B. Andrews to Frederick Davenport, May 27, 1919, reel 20, AALLP; "Legislative and Publicity Report."

90. Vira Whitehouse to John B. Andrews, May 15, 1919, reel 20, AALLP.

91. John B. Andrews to Frederick Davenport, May 27, 1919, reel 20, AALLP. Andrews continued, "This resulted in some merriment and I think not a little embarrassment on the part of some of the local Consumers' League members."

92. Sweet commented of Dickerman, "The 'Health Insurance Bill' which was most urgently demanded last winter, and early in the present campaign advocated by my opponent, is now by her repudiated" (Thaddeus C. Sweet to "Fellow Electors," October 28, 1919, MDP).

93. Minutes of the Regular Meeting of the Women's Trade Union League, November 10, 1919, reel 2, PNYWTUL.

94. The 1918 campaigns were run by Rose Schneiderman of the WTUL and the WJLC (Orleck, *Common Sense and a Little Fire*, 110).

95. On female voter disunity on the national level after passage of the Nineteenth Amendment, see Muncy, *Creating a Female Dominion*, 126–28, and Cott, *Grounding of Modern Feminism*.

96. Alice Kessler-Harris, "The Paradox of Motherhood: Night Work Restrictions in the United States," in Wikander et al., *Protecting Women*, 341.

97. Sheppard-Towner also did little to reorganize the American health care system. Because of opposition from the medical profession, the act did not provide mothers with physician or hospital services. For more detailed histories of Sheppard-Towner, see Ladd-Taylor, *Mother-Work*, ch. 6, and Muncy, *Creating a Female Dominion*, ch. 4. Despite its moderation, Sheppard-Towner still represented enough government involvement in health care to earn the enmity of physicians and conservatives, and it was finally eliminated by Congress in 1929. The rhetoric of protection for mothers and babies was unable to shield this successful women's program from the political opponents of the welfare state.

98. Irene Osgood Andrews, "A Tentative Outline for Maternity Protection Legislation," *ALLR* 10 (December 1920): 250–51; Irene Sylvester Chubb to Arthur Suffern, June 9, 1920, reel 22, AALLP.

99. Ladd-Taylor, *Mother-Work*, 174–75. For an excellent analysis of the struggle over the "endowment of motherhood" in Britain, see Pedersen, "Failure of Feminism."

CHAPTER EIGHT

1. The split among New York's Republicans dated to 1912, when the New York Progressive Party was created (Yellowitz, *Labor and the Progressive Movement*, 229–30; Perry, *Belle Moskowitz*, 76–77). Republican control of the New York legislature had been entrenched since 1894; see Moscow, *Politics in the Empire State*, 166–67.

2. AMM Circular letter, January 20, 1920, reel 21, AALLP; *New York State Assembly Journal* 1 (1919): 191; *ALLR* 9 (March 1919): 239; Hon. Eberly Hutchinson to Sam S. Lewisohn, March 14, 1919, reel 19, AALLP.

3. Frederick Hoffman to Forrest F. Dryden, January 20, 1919, Box 6, FLHP.

4. Perry, *Belle Moskowitz*, 120–21.

5. John Robert Greene, "Frederick Morgan Davenport: Portrait of a Progressive," *Theodore Roosevelt Association Journal*, n.d., 12–13, Box 1, FDP; "Reminiscences of Frederick M. Davenport," 1952, 39–44, Oral History Collection, Columbia University.

6. Frederick Davenport, Campaign Letter, July 8, 1908, Box 34, FDP. On New York State politics, see McCormick, "Prelude to Progressivism" and *From Realignment to Reform.*

7. Frederick Davenport to Charles B. Rogers, December 19, 1919, and Davenport to James Lynch, June 30, 1919, Box 2, FDP.

8. *Proceedings of the New York State Federation of Labor*, 1919, 183.

9. F. W. James, M.D., to Frederick Davenport, March 10, 1919, Box 2, FDP.

10. Gertrude Beeks Easley to Samuel Gompers, September 24, 1919, Box 69, NCFP.

11. New York *World*, March 22, 1919, 11, April 3, 1919, 10.

12. "Health Insurance: Digest of the Speech of Honorable Frederick Davenport," *Seventh Report of the Committee on Health, New York State Federation of Labor*, 1919, 16, Box 34, FDP.

13. New York *World*, April 13, 1919, 20; "Legislative and Publicity Report from January Third to April Eighteenth," no author (likely Irene Sylvester Chubb), 1919, Folder 23, Box 5, AALL Pamphlet Collection, KC.

14. John B. Andrews to John R. Commons, April 29, 1919, reel 19, AALLP.

15. Sauers, "Thaddeus C. Sweet"; telephone interview with Kenneth Sweet (grandson of Thaddeus Sweet), Phoenix, New York, January 12, 1994 (unfortunately, Mr. Sweet informed me that Thaddeus Sweet's personal papers had been destroyed in a fire); New York State League of Women Voters, "Report and Protest to the Governor, the Legislature and the People of the State of New York," March 1920, Rare Pamphlet Collection, KC.

16. Irene Sylvester Chubb to Mrs. Frank J. Tone, May 5, 1920, reel 22, AALLP.

17. Moscow, *Politics in the Empire State*, 166–67. This type of apportionment was the norm for state governments until challenged in the 1960s; therefore, "rural interests [have] largely controlled the enactments of state legislation" in the United States (Buechner, *State Government in the Twentieth Century*, 92). See also Holcombe, *State Government in the United States*, 253–56.

18. "Legislative and Publicity Report."

19. Numbers, *Almost Persuaded*, 91.

20. *ALLR* 9 (June 1919): 265–74; New York *World*, April 15, 1919, 12.

21. *Proceedings of New York State Federation of Labor*, 1919, 193, 141.

22. AALL letter to membership, April 12, 1919, reel 19, AALLP.

23. Frederick Davenport to James Lynch, June 13, 1919, Box 2, FDP.

24. "Second Annual Meeting of Associated Manufacturers and Merchants of New York State," December 10, 1915, Buffalo, N.Y., Box 1, Associated Industries, Inc., Papers, SUNY-Albany Special Collections.

25. Minutes of the meeting of the Social Insurance Dept., May 19, 1919, Box 70, NCFP.

26. Mark Daly to Gertrude Beeks Easley, June 9, 1919, Box 69, NCFP. The United Commercial Travelers was an organization of traveling salesmen.

27. Irene Sylvester Chubb to Mrs. Frank J. Tone, July 28, 1919, reel 20, AALLP.

28. Proceedings of the New York State Federation of Labor, 1919, 181; Numbers, Almost Persuaded, 91.

29. David Beito cites the petitions as evidence of working-class antipathy to health insurance in " 'It Substitutes Paternalism for Fraternalism,' " 2. Ronald Numbers writes that the petitions were "an obvious embarrassment" to the AALL, "an association that claimed to represent the working class" (Almost Persuaded, 91).

30. Walter Kozlowski to Frederick Davenport, n.d., Box 2, FDP.

31. Proceedings of the New York State Federation of Labor, 1919, 181.

32. New York State League of Women Voters, "Report and Protest to the Governor."

33. John B. Andrews to Frederick Almy, April 23, 1919, reel 19, AALLP.

34. Proceedings of the New York State Federation of Labor, 1919, 183.

35. Frederick Davenport to James Lynch, June 13, 1919, Box 2, FDP.

36. New York League for Americanism, letterhead, January 5, 1920, reel 21, AALLP.

37. Consumers' League Bulletin 9 (December 1919); Carleton D. Babcock to Gertrude Beeks Easley, December 20, 1919, Box 69, NCFP.

38. New York State League of Women Voters, "Report and Protest to the Governor." Frederick Davenport reported that "[t]he League has funds of $100,000 for surveys and propaganda campaign against any form of social insurance" (Frederick Davenport to John B. Andrews, September 27, 1919, reel 19, AALLP).

39. "Ninth Conference of Industrial Physicians and Surgeons," Pennsylvania Medical Journal 23 (January 1920): 205.

40. "Medical Society of the County of Rennselaer, Special Meeting, April 29, 1919," NYSJM 19 (May 1919): 198.

41. Dr. John J. A. O'Reilly, "To the Medical, Dental, and Pharmaceutical Societies of the State of New York," 1919, Folder 10, MDP.

42. John B. Andrews to Josephine Shatz, November 8, 1919, reel 20, AALLP; Numbers, Almost Persuaded, 96. See also John B. Andrews to Dr. Herbert Schenck, April 16, 1920, reel 22, AALLP.

43. "Labor's Attitude towards Compulsory State Health Insurance," 1, 2, 16, Bulletin No. 8 of the New York League for Americanism (n.d.), Rare Pamphlet Collection, KC.

44. Carleton D. Babcock to Gertrude Beeks Easley, December 20, 1919, Box 69, NCFP.

45. New York State League of Women Voters, "Report and Protest to the Governor"; Frederick Davenport to Charles Russell, December 2, 1919, Box 2, FDP; John A. Lapp, "Health Insurance," *Proceedings of the Twentieth New York State Conference of Charities and Corrections*, 190.

46. Murray, *Red Scare*, 97, 83, 197.

47. Orleck, *Common Sense and a Little Fire*, 138.

48. *Proceedings of the New York State Federation of Labor*, 1919, 245.

49. New York State League of Women Voters, "Report and Protest to the Governor."

50. Murray, *Red Scare*, 236.

51. Ralph Easley to Samuel Gompers, January 14, 1920, and Easley to Gompers, January 16, 1920, Box 43, NCFP.

52. Report of Miss Olive Williams, March 11, 1925, Box 41, New York League of Women Voters Papers, Rare Book Room, Columbia University.

53. *Proceedings of the New York State Federation of Labor*, 1919, 12.

54. New York State League of Women Voters, "Report and Protest to the Governor."

55. New York *World*, November 30, 1919, quoted in *Consumers' League Bulletin* 9 (December 1919).

56. New York State League of Women Voters, "Report and Protest to the Governor"; Gertrude Easley to Sweet, March 20, 1920, Box 70, NCFP.

57. *The Constitution* (Albany, N.Y.), February 22, 1920, 2, February 28, 1920, 1. The Associated Industries was the new name of the Associated Manufacturers and Merchants of New York.

58. Mrs. Irving Lehman to John B. Andrews, April 3, 1920, reel 22, AALLP.

59. *Proceedings of the New York State Federation of Labor*, 1919, 12.

60. Annual Meeting of the National Civic Federation, January 29, 1920, Box 136, NCFP.

61. John B. Andrews to Fred Kenkel, January 3, 1920, reel 21, AALLP.

62. Annual Report, 1921, Box 71, New York League of Women Voters Papers, Rare Book Room, Columbia University. On the fate of protective legislation, see Wikander et al., *Protecting Women*, and Lehrer, *Origins of Protective Labor Legislation*.

63. Armand Wyle to John B. Andrews, March 3, 1920, reel 21, AALLP.

64. John B. Andrews to Armand Wyle, March 5, 1920, reel 21, AALLP.

65. Ibid.

66. "Report of Work," 1921, reel 61, AALLP. I was unable to find evidence of other AALL staff members' response to Andrews's decision.

67. John B. Andrews, "To our members and friends," November 23, 1920, reel 21, AALLP.

68. Alexander Lambert to John B. Andrews, December 1, 1920, reel 21, AALLP.

69. John B. Andrews to Alexander Lambert, November 20, 1920, reel 21, AALLP.

70. Moss, *Socializing Security*, 159–60.

71. A WJLC form letter (March 3, 1920, reel 21, AALLP) announcing its 1920 legisla-

tive program did not mention health insurance. Although the NYSFL's 1920 legislative program included "Universal Health Insurance," "[t]he Health Insurance bill [was] not introduced because of the illness of the chairman of our Health Committee [probably Thomas Fitzgerald]." See Bulletin No. 1, New York State Federation of Labor, February 27, 1920, reel 21, AALLP.

72. New York State League of Women Voters, "Report and Protest to the Governor."

73. On scholarly arguments for state autonomy, see Introduction, note 10.

EPILOGUE

1. "Minutes of the House of Delegates," *JAMA* 74 (1920): 1319.

2. Starr, *Social Transformation of American Medicine*, 258.

3. Poen, *Harry S. Truman versus the Medical Lobby*, 34; Derickson, "Health Security for All?"

4. Moss, *Socializing Security*, 171; Hirshfield, *Lost Reform*; Poen, *Harry S. Truman versus the Medical Lobby*; Ronald Numbers, "The Third Party: Health Insurance in America," in Leavitt and Numbers, eds., *Sickness and Health in America*, 269–83; Skocpol, *Boomerang*; Johnson and Broder, *System*.

5. Rosemary Stevens, foreword to Cunningham and Cunningham, *Blues*, vii.

6. On the decline of free hospitals and dispensaries, see Rosner, *Once Charitable Enterprise*; on the decline of fraternal medicine, see Beito, "The 'Lodge Practice Evil' Reconsidered." The number of uninsured Americans has increased from 37 million in 1993 to 43 million in 1999 (Skocpol, *Boomerang*, 4; *Wall Street Journal*, May 17, 1999, A5).

7. On collective bargaining and health insurance, see Munts, *Bargaining for Health*, and Rosner and Markowitz, eds., "Hospitals, Insurance, and the American Labor Movement."

8. Pauline Newman, "Concerning American Working Women," n.d. (ca. 1960), Box 6, Pauline Newman Papers, Schlesinger Library. In this piece, Newman notes that "the writer of these lines . . . began her battle with indifferent legislators way back in 1914!"

9. Tone, *Business of Benevolence*, 256.

10. The 1996 Kassebaum-Kennedy Act provides some insurance portability for job changers, but only for those who can afford to pay market rates for the insurance (Johnson and Broder, *System*, 650–52).

11. Berkowitz, *America's Welfare State*, 158–60. The states with temporary disability insurance are New York, New Jersey, California, Rhode Island, and Hawaii. The Family and Medical Leave Act of 1993 requires large employers to offer up to twelve weeks of *unpaid* medical leave.

12. In contrast, in 1992–93, 71 percent of small employers and 82 percent of large employers provided medical insurance (U.S. Bureau of Labor Statistics, *Employee Benefits in Small Private Establishments, 1992*, 5–6; *Employee Benefits in Medium and Large Private Establishments, 1993*, 8–10).

13. Berkowitz, *America's Welfare State*, 164–66.

14. Dorothy McBride Stetson, "The Political History of Parental Leave Policy," in Hyde and Essex, eds., *Parental Leave and Child Care*, 406–32. Western Europe and Canada average sixty-eight weeks of leave, thirty-three of which are paid ("U.N. Surveys Paid Leave for Mothers," *New York Times*, February 16, 1998; Scharlach and Grosswald, "Family and Medical Leave Act of 1993").

15. Stevens, *In Sickness and in Wealth*, 216–26; Starr, *Social Transformation of American Medicine*, 342–51.

16. Starr, *Social Transformation of American Medicine*, 313.

17. Tone, *Business of Benevolence*, epilogue; Starr, *Social Transformation of American Medicine*, 328.

18. Numbers, "Third Party," 274–77.

19. Berkowitz, *America's Welfare State*, 173.

20. Numbers, "Third Party," 278; Katz, *In the Shadow of the Poorhouse*, 264; Wilsford, *Doctors and the State*, 9. In the late 1990s cost pressures had begun to significantly reduce Medicare and Medicaid payments to doctors and hospitals.

21. Starr, *Social Transformation of American Medicine*, 349–51, 385.

22. "Feeling Devalued by Change, Doctors Seek Union Banner," *New York Times*, May 30, 1996, A1.

23. On the specifics of the Clinton plan, see Skocpol, *Boomerang*, and Johnson and Broder, *System*.

24. Reform opponents' "demonization" of the First Lady for her role in formulating the health care plan is described in Skocpol, *Boomerang*, 150–53.

25. Johnson and Broder, *System*, 207.

26. Skocpol, *Boomerang*, 149.

27. Johnson and Broder, *System*, 204, 205–13; Skocpol, *Boomerang*, 137–38. Just as the Progressives' campaign paved the way for growth of private health benefits, the failure of the Clinton reform accelerated mergers of big insurance companies and the massive growth of private managed care; by 1996 at least half of privately insured Americans were in managed-care health plans. Recently, government programs have begun to subsidize the private insurance industry as well as physicians, with some states and the federal government encouraging (and probably soon requiring) Medicare and Medicaid recipients to join for-profit Health Maintenance Organizations (HMOs) (Skocpol, *Boomerang*, 196–97; Russell Baker, "Harry! Louise! You Lied," *New York Times*, June 1, 1996; "U.S. Lets State Shift Poor into Managed Care Plan," *New York Times*, May 27, 1999, A27).

28. Johnson and Broder, *System*, 212–13.

29. Untitled typescript, June 7, 1954, Box 10, Pauline Newman Papers, Schlesinger Library.

BIBLIOGRAPHY

MANUSCRIPT AND ARCHIVAL COLLECTIONS

American Association for Labor Legislation Papers (Microfilm Edition, Glen Rock, N.J., 1974)

Columbia University, New York, N.Y.

  Oral History Collection

    "Interview with Miss Pauline Newman," June 15, 1965

    "Reminiscences of Frederick M. Davenport," 1952

  Rare Book Room

    Community Service Society Papers

    Frederick Ludwig Hoffman Papers

    Samuel McCune Lindsay Papers

    New York League of Women Voters Papers

Cornell University Library, Ithaca, N.Y.

  Division of Rare and Manuscript Collections

    Halsey Family Papers

Hagley Museum and Library, Wilmington, Del.

  Frederick Hoffman Correspondence with the American Association for Labor Legislation

  National Industrial Conference Board Papers

Kheel Center for Labor-Management Documentation and Archives, School of Industrial and Labor Relations, Cornell University, Ithaca, N.Y.

  American Association for Labor Legislation Pamphlet Collection

  International Ladies' Garment Workers' Union Papers

  New York Consumers' League Papers

  Rare Pamphlet Collection

Meany Archive Center, Silver Spring, Md.

  American Federation of Labor, Office of the President

    William Green Papers

  American Federation of Labor Executive Council Minutes

Metropolitan Life Insurance Company Archives, New York, N.Y.

Mount Holyoke College Archives and Special Collections, South Hadley, Mass.

Irene Sylvester Papers
New York Academy of Medicine, New York, N.Y.
   Public Health Committee of the New York Academy of Medicine Papers
New York Public Library, New York, N.Y.
   Insurance — Uncatalogued Pamphlets
   Miscellaneous Pamphlets — Mutual Aid
   Mutual Benefit Societies Constitutions and Bylaws
   Rare Book Room
      Nicholas Kelley Papers
      National Civic Federation Papers
      New York Typographical Union Papers
      William Rhinelander Stewart Papers
      Lillian Wald Papers
New York State Archives, Albany, N.Y.
   Department of Health Records
   New York State Factory Investigating Commission Records
   Office of Governor Records
New York State Nurses' Association Historical Collection, Guilderland, N.Y.
Nursing Archives, Boston University, Boston, Mass.
   American Nurses' Association Collection
Rockefeller Archive Center, Tarrytown, N.Y.
   Laura Spelman Rockefeller Memorial Archives
   Rockefeller Family Archives
   Rockefeller Foundation Archives
   Rockefeller University Archives
   Russell Sage Foundation Records
Franklin D. Roosevelt Library, Hyde Park, N.Y.
   Marion Dickerman Papers
Salamanca Public Library, Salamanca, N.Y.
   Minutes of the Salamanca Rebekah Lodge
Schlesinger Library, Cambridge, Mass.
   Alice Hamilton Papers
   Pauline Newman Papers
   Elizabeth Lowell Putnam Papers
Schomburg Center, New York, N.Y.
   Knights of Pythias Records
   Records of the American West Indian Ladies' Aid Society
Sophia Smith Archive, Northampton, Mass.
   Mary Van Kleeck Papers
   Young Women's Christian Association Papers
SUNY-Albany Special Collections, Albany, N.Y.

Associated Industries, Inc., Papers
Syracuse University Archives, Syracuse, N.Y.
Frederick Davenport Papers
Robert F. Wagner Labor Archives, New York University, New York, N.Y.
Rose Schneiderman Papers
Women's Trade Union and Its Principal Leaders Papers (Microfilm Edition,
Woodbridge, Conn., 1981)
Papers of the National Women's Trade Union League
Papers of the New York Women's Trade Union League
YIVO Institute for Jewish Research, New York, N.Y.
Landsmanshaftn Archive
Ceres Union Records
Progress Mutual Aid Society Records

PERIODICALS

American Federationist
American Journal of Nursing
American Labor Legislation Review
The Constitution (Albany, N.Y.)
Fulton Patriot
Journal of the American Medical Association
Journal of the National Medical Association
Literary Digest
Long Island Medical Journal
The Monitor: Official Publication of the Associated Manufacturers and Merchants of New
York State
New York *Globe*
New York Medical Journal
New York State Assembly Journal
New York State Journal of Medicine
New York Times
New York *World*
Pennsylvania Medical Journal
Typographical Journal
Woman's Medical Journal

BOOKS, ARTICLES, PROCEEDINGS, AND REPORTS

Aptheker, Herbert, ed. *Book Reviews by W. E. B. Du Bois.* Millwood, N.Y., 1977.
Armstrong, Barbara Nachtrieb. *Insuring the Essentials.* New York, 1932.

Baker, Elizabeth Faulkner. *Protective Labor Legislation, with Special Reference to Women in the State of New York*. New York, 1925.

Chapin, Robert Coit. *The Standard of Living Among Workingmen's Families in New York City*. New York, 1909.

Constitution of the Workmen's Sick and Death Benefit Fund. New York, 1901.

Dawson, William Harbutt. *Bismarck and State Socialism*. 1890. Reprint, New York, 1973.

——. *Social Insurance in Germany, 1883–1911*. 1912. Reprint, Westport, Conn., 1979.

Dublin, Louis I. *A Family of 30 Million: The Story of the Metropolitan Life Insurance Company*. New York, 1943.

Faulkner, Edwin J. *Accident-and-Health Insurance*. New York and London, 1940.

Fisher, Judson C., M.D., "Malingering—Involving the Problem of Getting the Sick or Injured Employee Back to Work." *Journal of Industrial Hygiene* 1 (December 1919): 408–14.

Frankel, Lee K., and Louis I. Dublin. "Community Sickness Survey: Rochester, N.Y., September, 1915." *U.S. Public Health Reports* 31 (1916).

Galloway, George S. "Speech to National Fraternal Congress of America." *Medical Insurance and Health Conservation* 26 (October 1916): 1–10.

Harbaugh, Charles Hamilton. *Adjuster's Manual for the Settlement of Accident and Health Claims*. Chicago and New York, 1915.

——. *The Industrial Claim Adjustor*. New York, 1917.

Hoffman, Frederick. *Facts and Fallacies of Compulsory Health Insurance*. Newark, N.J., 1917.

——. *Failure of German Compulsory Health Insurance—A War Revelation*. Newark, N.J., 1918.

——. *History of the Prudential Insurance Company of America*. Newark, N.J., 1900.

——. *Race Traits and Tendencies of the American Negro*. New York, 1896.

Holcombe, Arthur N. *State Government in the United States*. New York, 1926.

Knopf, S. Adolphus. *A History of the National Tuberculosis Association*. New York, 1922.

Miller, Kelly. *A Review of Hoffman's Race Traits and Tendencies of the American Negro*. Occasional Papers of the American Negro Academy, No. 1. Washington, D.C., 1897.

More, Louise B. *Wage-Earners Budgets: A Study of Standards and Cost of Living in New York City*. New York, 1907.

National Civic Federation. *Report of the Committee on Preliminary Foreign Inquiry*. New York, 1914.

National Industrial Conference Board. *Experience with Mutual Benefit Associations in the United States*. Boston, 1923.

New York State Constitution Annotated. New York, 1915.

Potts, Rufus M. *Addresses and Papers on Insurance*. Springfield, 1917.

Proceedings of the Twentieth New York State Conference of Charities and Corrections, 11–13 November 1919, Syracuse, N.Y.

Proceedings of the New York State Federation of Labor.

Reilly, Thomas P. *Building a Profitable Practice*. Philadelphia, 1912.

Report of the Health Insurance Commission of Illinois. Springfield, 1919.

Report of the Health Insurance Commission of Pennsylvania. Harrisburg, 1919.

Report of the Proceedings of the American Federation of Labor.

Report of the Social Insurance Commission of the State of California. Sacramento, 1917.

Rubinow, I. M. *The Quest for Security*. New York, 1934.

———. *Social Insurance: With Special Reference to American Conditions*. New York, 1913.

Sommer, Armand. *Manual of Accident and Health Insurance: A Valuable Sales Aid and Text Book Dealing with Every-Day Problems*. Chicago, 1928.

Walsh, James J. "Physicians' Fees Down the Ages." *International Clinics*. Vol. 4, Series 20, 1910.

White, Lewis P. *Physicians' Collection Guide: A Practical Guide for the Physician in Collecting His Accounts*. Los Angeles, 1913.

Willoughby, William Franklin. *Workingmen's Insurance*. New York, 1898.

AUTHOR INTERVIEW

Kenneth Sweet, Phoenix, New York, January 12, 1994.

SECONDARY SOURCES

Apple, Rima D., ed. *Women, Health and Medicine in America: A Historical Handbook*. New Brunswick, N.J., 1990.

Beardsley, Edward H. *A History of Neglect: Health Care for Blacks and Mill Workers in the Twentieth-Century South*. Knoxville, 1987.

Beito, David. " 'It Substitutes Paternalism for Fraternalism': Fraternal Societies and Compulsory Health Insurance, 1916–1920." Paper delivered at the conference of the Organization of American Historians, April 1998.

———. "The 'Lodge Practice Evil' Reconsidered: Medical Care through Fraternal Societies, 1900–1930." *Journal of Urban History* 23 (July 1997): 569–600.

———. "Mutual Aid, State Welfare, and Organized Charity: Fraternal Societies and the 'Deserving' and 'Undeserving' Poor, 1900–1930." *Journal of Policy History* 5 (1993): 419–34.

———. "A 'Program That Looks to . . . the Nationalization of Women': The Woman's Benefit Association of the Maccabees and Compulsory Health Insurance, 1917–1920." Paper presented at the conference "From Redemption to Reaganism: American Conservatism in Historical Perspective, 1865–1980," Princeton University, May 3–4, 1996.

Bennett, Michael T. "The Movement for Compulsory Health Insurance in Illinois, 1912–1920." *Illinois Historical Journal* 89 (Winter 1996): 233–46.

Berkowitz, Edward D. *America's Welfare State*. Baltimore, 1991.

Beyer, Clara M. *History of Labor Legislation for Women in Three States*. Washington, D.C., 1932.

Boorstin, Daniel. *America and the Image of Europe*. Cleveland, 1960.

Brandes, Stuart D. *American Welfare Capitalism, 1880–1940*. Chicago, 1970.

Brandt, Allan M. *No Magic Bullet: A Social History of Venereal Disease in the United States*. New York, 1985.

Brieger, Gert H. "The Use and Abuse of Medical Charities in Late-Nineteenth-Century America." *American Journal of Public Health* 67 (March 1977): 264–67.

Buechner, John C. *State Government in the Twentieth Century*. Boston, 1967.

Buhler-Wilkerson, Karen. *False Dawn: The Rise and Decline of Public Health Nursing, 1900–1930*. New York, 1989.

Burrow, James. *Organized Medicine in the Progressive Era: The Move toward Monopoly*. Baltimore, 1977.

Carnes, Mark. *Secret Ritual and Manhood in Victorian America*. New Haven, 1989.

Carr, William H. A. *"From Three Cents a Week...": The Story of the Prudential Insurance Company of America*. Englewood Cliffs, N.J., 1975.

Cash, Florence Barnett. "Radicals or Realists: African American Women and the Settlement House Spirit in New York City." *Afro-Americans in New York Life and History* 15 (January 1991): 7–17.

Cassedy, John. "Frederick Ludwig Hoffman." *Dictionary of American Biography*, Supplement 4. New York, 1974.

Clawson, Mary Ann. *Constructing Brotherhood: Class, Gender, and Fraternalism*. Princeton, N.J., 1989.

Clemens, Elisabeth S. *The People's Lobby: Organizational Innovation and the Rise of Interest Group Politics in the United States, 1890–1925*. Chicago, 1997.

Cohen, Lizabeth. *Making a New Deal: Industrial Workers in Chicago, 1919–1939*. Cambridge, 1990.

Cooke, Blanche Wiesen. *Eleanor Roosevelt*. New York, 1992.

Cott, Nancy. *The Grounding of Modern Feminism*. New Haven, 1987.

Cunningham, Robert, III, and Robert M. Cunningham Jr. *The Blues: A History of the Blue Cross and Blue Shield System*. DeKalb, Ill., 1997.

Daniels, Doris. "Building a Winning Coalition: The Suffrage Fight in New York State." *New York History* 60 (January 1979): 59–80.

Davin, Anna. "Imperialism and Motherhood." *History Workshop Journal* 5 (1978): 61–113.

Dawley, Alan. *Struggles for Justice: Social Responsibility and the Liberal State*. Cambridge, Mass., 1991.

Derickson, Alan. *Black Lung: Anatomy of a Public Health Disaster*. Ithaca, N.Y., 1998.

———. "Federal Intervention in the Joplin Silicosis Epidemic, 1911–1916." *Bulletin of the History of Medicine* 62 (Summer 1988): 236–51.

————. "From Company Doctors to Union Hospitals: The First Democratic Health Care Experiments of the UMWA." *Labor History* 33 (Summer 1992): 325–42.

————. "Health Security for All? Social Unionism and Universal Health Insurance, 1935–1958." *Journal of American History* 80 (March 1994): 1333–56.

————. *Workers' Health, Workers' Democracy: The Western Miners' Struggle, 1891–1925.* Ithaca, N.Y., 1988.

De Schweinitz, Karl. *England's Road to Social Security.* New York, 1943.

Dubofsky, Melvyn. *The State and Labor in Modern America.* Chapel Hill, N.C., 1994.

DuBois, Ellen Carol. *Harriet Stanton Blatch and the Winning of Woman Suffrage.* New Haven, 1997.

Duffy, John. *A History of Public Health in New York City.* New York, 1968.

Dye, Nancy Schrom. *As Equals and as Sisters: Feminism, the Labor Movement, and the Women's Trade Union League of New York.* Columbia, Mo., 1980.

————. "Modern Obstetrics and Working-Class Women: The New York Midwifery Dispensary, 1890–1920." *Journal of Social History* 20 (Spring 1987): 549–64.

Eldot, Paula. *Governor Alfred E. Smith: The Politician as Reformer.* New York and London, 1983.

Evans, Peter B., Dietrich Rueschmeyer, and Theda Skocpol, eds. *Bringing the State Back In.* New York, 1985.

Fink, Gary. *Labor's Search for Political Order: The Political Behavior of the Missouri Labor Movement, 1890–1940.* Columbia, Mo., 1974.

Forbath, William E. *Law and the Shaping of the American Labor Movement.* Cambridge, Mass., 1991.

Fox, Daniel M. *Health Policies, Health Politics: The British and American Experience, 1911–1965.* Princeton, N.J., 1986.

————. "History and Health Policy: An Autobiographical Note on the Decline of Historicism." *Journal of Social History* 18 (Spring 1985): 350–51.

Fraser, Derek. *The Evolution of the British Welfare State.* London, 1973.

Gamble, Vanessa. *Making a Place for Ourselves: The Black Hospital Movement, 1920–1945.* New York, 1995.

Gerstle, Gary. *Working-Class Americanism: The Politics of Labor in a Textile City, 1914–1960.* Cambridge, U.K., 1989.

Gilbert, Bentley B. *The Evolution of National Insurance in Great Britain: The Origins of the Welfare State.* London, 1966.

Gitelman, H. M. "Management's Crisis of Confidence and the Origin of the National Industrial Conference Board, 1914–1916." *Business History Review* 58 (Summer 1984): 153–77.

Goebel, Thomas. "American Medicine and the 'Organizational Synthesis': Chicago Physicians and the Business of Medicine, 1900–1920." *Bulletin of the History of Medicine* 68 (1994): 639–63.

Goodwin, Joanne. *Gender and the Politics of Welfare Reform.* Chicago, 1997.

Gordon, Colin. *New Deals: Business, Labor, and Politics in America, 1920–1935.* New York, 1994.

Gordon, Linda. "Gender, State and Society: A Debate with Theda Skocpol." *Contention* 2 (Spring 1993): 139–56.

———. *Pitied but Not Entitled: Single Mothers and the History of Welfare.* New York, 1994.

———. "Social Insurance and Public Assistance: The Influence of Gender in Welfare Thought in the United States, 1890–1935." *American Historical Review* 97 (February 1992): 19–54.

———. ed. *Women, the State, and Welfare.* Madison, Wisc., 1990.

Grant, H. Roger. *Insurance Reform: Consumer Action in the Progressive Era.* Ames, Iowa, 1979.

Green, Marguerite. *The National Civic Federation and the American Labor Movement, 1900–1925.* 1956. Reprint, Westport, Conn., 1973.

Greene, Julie. *Pure and Simple Politics: The American Federation of Labor and Political Activism, 1881–1917.* Cambridge, U.K., 1998.

Greenwald, Maurine. *Women, War and Work: The Impact of World War I on Women Workers in the United States.* Westport, Conn., 1980.

Haller, John S., Jr. "Race, Mortality, and Life Insurance: Negro Vital Statistics in the Late Nineteenth Century." *Journal of the History of Medicine and Allied Sciences* 25 (1970): 247–61.

Hattam, Victoria. *Labor Visions and State Power: The Origins of Business Unionism in the United States.* Princeton, N.J., 1993.

Hennock, E. P. *British Social Reform and German Precedents: The Case of Social Insurance, 1880–1914.* Oxford, 1987.

Higham, John. *Strangers in the Land: Patterns of American Nativism, 1860–1925.* 2nd ed. New Brunswick, N.J., 1988.

Hine, Darlene Clark. *Black Women in White: Racial Conflict and Cooperation in the Nursing Profession, 1890–1950.* Bloomington and Indianapolis, 1989.

Hirshfield, David S. *The Lost Reform: The Campaign for Compulsory Health Insurance in the United States from 1932 to 1943.* Cambridge, Mass., 1970.

Hofstadter, Richard. *The Age of Reform: From Bryan to F. D. R.* New York, 1955.

Howell, Joel D., and Catherine G. McLaughlin. "Race, Income, and the Purchase of Medical Care by Selected 1917 Working-Class Urban Families." *Journal of the History of Medicine and Allied Sciences* 47 (October 1992): 439–61.

Hyde, Janet Shibley, and Marilyn J. Essex, eds. *Parental Leave and Child Care: Setting a Research and Policy Agenda.* Philadelphia, 1991.

Jacobs, Lawrence. *The Health of Nations: Public Opinion and the Making of American and British Health Policy.* Ithaca, N.Y., 1993.

Jacoby, Sanford M., ed. *Masters to Managers: Historical and Comparative Perspectives on American Employers.* New York, 1991.

Johnson, Haynes, and David S. Broder. *The System: The American Way of Politics at the Breaking Point.* Boston, 1996.

Kaiser Commission on Medicaid and the Uninsured and KPMG Peat Marwick. "Changes in Employee Health Coverage by Small Businesses." Report no. 1463. Menlo Park, Calif., February 1, 1999.

Kamerman, Sheila B., Alfred J. Kahn, and Paul Kingston. *Maternity Policies and Working Women.* New York, 1983.

Katz, Michael B. *In the Shadow of the Poorhouse: A Social History of Welfare in America.* New York, 1986.

Keller, Morton. *The Life Insurance Enterprise.* Cambridge, Mass., 1963.

Kerber, Linda K., Alice Kessler-Harris, and Kathryn Kish Sklar, eds. *U.S. History as Women's History: New Feminist Essays.* Chapel Hill, N.C., 1995.

Kessler-Harris, Alice. *Out to Work: A History of Wage-Earning Women in America.* New York, 1983.

―――. *A Woman's Wage: Historical Meanings and Social Consequences.* Lexington, Ky., 1990.

Klaus, Alisa. *Every Child a Lion: Maternity and Infant Policy in the United States and France.* Ithaca, N.Y., 1993.

Klein, Jennifer. "Managing Security: The Business of American Social Policy, 1910s–1960." Ph.D. diss., University of Virginia, 1999.

Kloppenberg, James T. *Uncertain Victory: Social Democracy and Progressivism in European and American Thought, 1870–1920.* New York, 1986.

Köhler, Peter A., and Hans F. Zacher. *The Evolution of Social Insurance, 1881–1981.* London, 1982.

Kolko, Gabriel. *The Triumph of Conservatism: A Reinterpretation of American History, 1900–1916.* New York, 1963.

Korneski, Kurt. "Louisiana Lumber Workers and Patent Medicines, 1910–1915." Unpublished paper, Northern Illinois University, 1998.

Koven, Seth, and Sonya Michel, eds. *Mothers of a New World: Maternalist Politics and the Origins of Welfare States.* New Haven, 1993.

―――. "Womanly Duties: Maternalist Politics and the Origins of Welfare States in France, Germany, Great Britain and the United States, 1880–1920." *American Historical Review* 95 (October 1990): 1076–108.

Ladd-Taylor, Molly. *Mother-Work: Women, Child Welfare, and the State, 1890–1930.* Urbana, Ill., 1994.

―――. *Raising a Baby the Government Way: Mothers' Letters to the Children's Bureau, 1915–1932.* New Brunswick, N.J., 1986.

Leavitt, Judith, and Ronald Numbers, eds. *Sickness and Health in America: Readings in the History of Medicine and Public Health.* Madison, Wisc., 1997.

Leff, Mark. "Consensus for Reform: The Mothers'-Pension Movement in the Progressive Era." *Social Service Review* 47 (September 1973): 397–415.

Lehrer, Susan. *Origins of Protective Labor Legislation for Women.* Albany, N.Y., 1987.

Lemons, Stanley. *The Woman Citizen: Social Feminism in the 1920s.* Urbana, Ill., 1973.

Levine, Daniel. *Poverty and Society: The Growth of the American Welfare State in International Comparison.* New Brunswick, N.J., 1988.

Love, Spencie. *One Blood: The Death and Resurrection of Charles R. Drew.* Chapel Hill, N.C., 1997.

Lubove, Roy. *The Struggle for Social Security.* Cambridge, Mass., 1968.

McBride, David. *From TB to AIDS: Epidemics among Urban Blacks since 1900.* Albany, N.Y., 1991.

————. *Integrating the City of Medicine: Blacks in Philadelphia Health Care, 1910–1965.* Philadelphia, 1989.

McCormick, Richard. *From Realignment to Reform: Political Change in New York State, 1893–1910.* Ithaca, N.Y., 1981.

————. "Prelude to Progressivism: The Transformation of New York State Politics, 1890–1910." *New York History* 54 (July 1978): 253–69.

May, Earl Chapin. *The Prudential: A Story of Human Security.* Garden City, N.Y., 1950.

Michel, Sonya, and Robyn Rosen. "The Paradox of Maternalism: Elizabeth Lowell Putnam and the American Welfare State." *Gender and History* 4 (Autumn 1992): 364–86.

Mink, Gwendolyn. *Old Labor and New Immigrants in American Political Development: Union, Party, and State, 1875–1920.* Ithaca, N.Y., 1986.

————. *The Wages of Motherhood: Inequality in the Welfare State.* Ithaca, N.Y., 1995.

Morantz-Sanchez, Regina. *Sympathy and Science.* New York, 1985.

Moscow, Warren. *Politics in the Empire State.* New York, 1948.

Moss, David. *Socializing Security: Progressive Era Economists and the Origins of American Social Policy.* Cambridge, Mass., 1996.

Muncy, Robyn. *Creating a Female Dominion in American Reform.* New York, 1990.

Munts, Raymond. *Bargaining for Health: Labor Unions, Health Insurance, and Medical Care.* Madison, Wisc., 1967.

Murray, Robert K. *Red Scare: A Study in National Hysteria, 1919–1920.* New York, 1955.

Nugent, Angela. "Fit for Work: The Introduction of Physical Examinations in Industry." *Bulletin of the History of Medicine* 57 (1983): 578–95.

Numbers, Ronald. *Almost Persuaded: American Physicians and Compulsory Health Insurance, 1912–1920.* Baltimore, 1978.

————, ed. *Compulsory Health Insurance: The Continuing American Debate.* Westport, Conn., 1982.

Opdycke, Sandra. *No One Was Turned Away: The Role of Public Hospitals in New York City since 1900.* New York, 1999.

Orleck, Annelise. *Common Sense and a Little Fire: Women and Working-Class Politics in the United States, 1900–1965.* Chapel Hill, N.C., 1995.

Orloff, Ann Shola. "Gender in Early U.S. Social Policy." *Journal of Policy History* 3 (1991): 249–81.

———. *The Politics of Pensions: A Comparative Analysis of Britain, Canada, and the United States, 1880–1940.* Madison, Wisc., 1993.

Oshofsky, Gilbert. *Harlem: The Making of a Ghetto.* New York, 1966.

Pedersen, Susan. "The Failure of Feminism in the Making of the British Welfare State." *Radical History Review* 43 (1989): 86–110.

———. "Gender, Welfare, and Citizenship in Britain during the Great War." *American Historical Review* 95 (October 1990): 983–1006.

Perry, Elizabeth Israels. *Belle Moskowitz: Feminine Politics and the Exercise of Power in the Age of Alfred E. Smith.* Oxford, 1987.

Poen, Monte M. *Harry S. Truman versus the Medical Lobby: The Genesis of Medicare.* Columbia, Mo., 1979.

Poole, Mary. "Securing Race and Ensuring Dependence: The Social Security Act of 1935." Ph.D. diss., Rutgers University, 2000.

Quadagno, Jill. *The Color of Welfare: How Racism Undermined the War on Poverty.* New York, 1994.

Quataert, Jean. "Social Insurance and the Family Work of Oberlausitz Home Weavers in the Late Nineteenth Century." In *German Women in the Nineteenth Century: A Social History,* edited by John C. Fout. New York and London, 1984.

Reitzes, Dietrich C. *Negroes and Medicine.* Cambridge, Mass., 1958.

Reverby, Susan. *Ordered to Care: The Dilemma of American Nursing, 1850–1945.* Cambridge, U.K., 1987.

Rimlinger, Gaston V. *Welfare Policy and Industrialization in Europe, America, and Russia.* New York, 1971.

Robertson, David Brion. "The Bias of American Federalism: The Limits of Welfare State Development in the Progressive Era." *Journal of Policy History* 1 (1989): 261–91.

Rodgers, Daniel T. *Atlantic Crossings: Social Politics in a Progressive Age.* Cambridge, Mass., 1998.

Rosen, George. *The Structure of American Medical Practice, 1875–1941.* Philadelphia, 1983.

Rosenberg, Charles E. "Social Class and Medical Care in Nineteenth-Century America: The Rise and Fall of the Dispensary." *Journal of the History of Medicine and Allied Sciences* 29 (1974): 32–54.

Rosner, David. *A Once Charitable Enterprise: Hospitals and Health Care in Brooklyn and New York, 1885–1915.* Cambridge, U.K., 1982.

———, ed. *Hives of Sickness: Public Health and Epidemics in New York City.* New Brunswick, N.J., 1995.

Rosner, David, and Gerald Markowitz, eds. *Deadly Dust: Silicosis and the Politics of Occupational Disease in Twentieth-Century America.* Princeton, N.J., 1991.

————. *Dying for Work: Workers' Safety and Health in Twentieth-Century America.* Bloomington and Indianapolis, 1987.

————. "Hospitals, Insurance, and the American Labor Movement: The Case of New York in the Postwar Decades." *Journal of Policy History* 9, no. 1 (1997): 74–95.

Rothman, Sheila. *Living in the Shadow of Death: Tuberculosis and the Social Experience of Illness in American History.* Baltimore, 1994.

Sauers, Evelyn L. "Thaddeus C. Sweet." *The Journal of the Oswego County Historical Society* (1976–77): 82–87.

Scharlach, Andrew E., and Blanche Grosswald. "The Family and Medical Leave Act of 1993." *Social Service Review* (September 1997): 335–59.

Sellers, Christopher. *Hazards of the Job: From Industrial Disease to Environmental Health Science.* Chapel Hill, N.C., 1997.

Sklar, Kathryn Kish. "A Call for Comparisons." *American Historical Review* 95 (October 1990): 1109–14.

————. *Florence Kelley and the Nation's Work: The Rise of Women's Political Culture, 1830–1916.* New Haven, 1995.

————. "Two Political Cultures in the Progressive Era: The National Consumers' League and the American Association for Labor Legislation." In *U.S. History as Women's History: New Feminist Essays,* edited by Linda K. Kerber, Alice Kessler-Harris, and Kathryn Kish Sklar. Chapel Hill, N.C., 1995.

Sklar, Martin. *The Corporate Reconstruction of American Capitalism: The Market, the Law, and Politics.* Cambridge, U.K., 1988.

Skocpol, Theda. *Boomerang: Clinton's Health Security Effort and the Turn against Government in U.S. Politics.* New York, 1996.

————. *Protecting Soldiers and Mothers: The Political Origins of Social Policy in the United States.* Cambridge, Mass., 1992.

————. "Soldiers, Workers, and Mothers: Gendered Identities in Early U.S. Social Policy." *Contention* 2 (Spring 1993): 157–83.

————. "Thinking Big: Can National Values or Class Factions Explain the Development of Social Provision in the United States? A Review Essay." *Journal of Policy History* 2 (1990): 425–37.

Skocpol, Theda, and Edwin Amenta. "States and Social Policies." *American Review of Sociology* 12 (1986): 131–57.

Skocpol, Theda, and Ann Orloff. "Why Not Equal Protection? Explaining the Politics of Public Social Spending in Britain and the United States." *American Sociological Review* 49 (December 1984): 726–50.

Skowronek, Stephen. *Building a New American State.* Cambridge, U.K., 1982.

Smith, Susan. *Sick and Tired of Being Sick and Tired: Black Women's Health Activism in America, 1890–1950.* Philadelphia, 1995.

Starr, Paul. *The Social Transformation of American Medicine: The Rise of a Sovereign Profession and the Making of a Vast Industry.* New York, 1982.

Stevens, Rosemary. *American Medicine and the Public Interest*. New Haven, 1971.

———. *In Sickness and in Wealth: American Hospitals in the Twentieth Century*. New York, 1989.

Stuart, M. S. *An Economic Detour: A History of Insurance in the Lives of American Negroes*. 1940. Reprint, College Park, Md., 1969.

Thane, Pat. *The Foundations of the Welfare State*. London and New York, 1982.

———. "The Working Class and State 'Welfare' in Britain, 1880–1914." *The Historical Journal* 27 (1984): 877–900.

Tishler, Hace Sorel. *Self-Reliance and Social Security, 1870–1917*. Port Washington, N.Y., 1971.

Tomlins, Christopher L. *The State and the Unions: Labor Relations, Law, and the Organized Labor Movement in America, 1880–1960*. Cambridge, U.K., 1985.

Tone, Andrea. *The Business of Benevolence: Industrial Paternalism in Progressive America*. Ithaca, N.Y., 1997.

U.S. Bureau of Labor Statistics. *Employee Benefits in Medium and Large Private Establishments, 1993*. Bulletin 2456 (1994).

———. *Employee Benefits in Small Private Establishments, 1992*. Bulletin 2441 (1994).

Viseltear, Arthur. "Compulsory Health Insurance in California, 1915–1918." *Journal of the History of Medicine and Allied Sciences* 24 (April 1969): 151–82.

Walker, Forrest A. "Compulsory Health Insurance: 'The Next Great Step in Social Legislation.'" *Journal of American History* 56 (September 1969): 290–304.

Watts, Sarah Lyons. *Order against Chaos: Business Culture and Labor Ideology in America, 1880–1915*. New York, 1991.

Weinstein, James. *The Corporate Ideal the Liberal State*. Boston, 1968.

Weir, Margaret, Theda Skocpol, and Ann Orloff, eds. *The Politics of Social Policy in the United States*. Princeton, N.J., 1988.

Weisser, Michael R. *A Brotherhood of Memory: Jewish Landsmanshaftn in the New World*. New York, 1985.

Wiebe, Robert. *Businessmen and Reform: A Study of the Progressive Movement*. Chicago, 1962.

Wikander, Ulla, Alice Kessler-Harris, and Jane Lewis, eds. *Protecting Women: Labor Legislation in Europe, the United States, and Australia, 1880–1920*. Urbana, Ill., 1995.

Wilsford, David. *Doctors and the State: The Politics of Health Care in France and the United States*. Durham, N.C., 1991.

Woloch, Nancy. *Muller v. Oregon: A Brief History with Documents*. New York, 1996.

Yellowitz, Irwin. *Labor and the Progressive Movement in New York State, 1897–1916*. Ithaca, N.Y., 1965.

Zahavi, Gerald. *Workers, Managers, and Welfare Capitalism: The Shoeworkers and Tanners of Endicott Johnson, 1890–1950*. Urbana, Ill., 1988.

INDEX

Studies in Social Medicine

Nancy M. P. King, Gail E. Henderon, and Jane Stein, eds., *Beyond Regulations: Ethics in Human Subjects Research* (1999).

Laurie Zoloth, *Health Care and the Ethics of Encounter: A Jewish Discussion of Social Justice* (1999).

Susan M. Reverby, ed. *Tuskegee's Truths: Rethinking the Tuskegee Syphilis Study* (2000).

Margarete Sandelowski, *Devices and Desires: Gender, Technology, and American Nursing* (2000).

Beatrix Hoffman, *The Wages of Sickness: The Politics of Health Insurance in Progressive America* (2000).